Divided
We Fall

The Secular vs. the Sacred

MarieAlena Castle

ARCHWAY
PUBLISHING

Archway Publishing books may be ordered through booksellers or by contacting:

Archway Publishing
1663 Liberty Drive
Bloomington, IN 47403
www.archwaypublishing.com
1 (888) 242-5904

ISBN: 978-1-4808-6132-9 (sc)
ISBN: 978-1-4808-6133-6 (e)

Library of Congress Control Number: 2018904357

Print information available on the last page.

Archway Publishing rev. date: 4/16/2018

Dedicated to the memory of
SUE ROCKNE,
religious liberal, political activist, friend and mentor,
and formidable lobbyist for reproductive rights
and separation of religion from government.
Her file folder on authoritarian religion's
assaults on our liberties was labeled,
"Tax the Bastards!"
She died too soon.
There are not enough like her.
We need so many.

. . . and to the unforgettable
ANNIE CHASE,
the shining light in the Chapter 6 Postscript

Contents

INTRODUCTION

If you are a believer—if you are committed to a theology—you should read this book. Yes, it is written by an atheist. But, no, it is not just about finding fault with theological doctrines, though it does that. What you read here is not so much against believers as against believers' religious beliefs forcibly impacting others through our laws and legal institutions. Even believers should not want that. Most believers will be surprised and disappointed at how supposedly well-meaning ideas are carried to absurd extremes to justify dreadful public policies with sometimes horrifying effects. This book explains how this has been happening routinely for many years, and how the situation has become worse with the political ascendency of religious extremists who helped elect Donald Trump.

If you are an unbeliever—if you once accepted one or more theologies before becoming disillusioned and leaving them behind, or never had one to begin with—you have much to learn from this book as well. Yes, it will explore the substance and absurdity of many theological doctrines, but unlike other books criticizing religion and its doctrines, the purpose here is different. This book is unique in not only showing how silly and wrong these things are, but in showing the how and why of their connection to our laws and legal institutions. Most importantly, this book shows how these entanglements corrupt our government and hurt all of us.

If you have simply not cared much about religion, you really, really need to read this book. For we stand now at the threshold of a global society ready to benefit from powerful new technologies and innovations for improving human life and happiness and diminishing human suffering and misery. Stem cell research, to name just one example, could reduce or eliminate many chronic degenerative diseases.

Even if you don't care much about other people's religious convictions, you can be assured that the most zealous and unreasonable of them will be making their best efforts to destroy that future: our future and your future. And those in political power seem willing (whether from ignorance or intention is hard to say) to support such efforts. Unlike other books critical of these trends, this book offers a strategy for countering these dangers that is based on the author's long history of political activism.

She has a been-there, done-that perspective that knows what works and what doesn't.

Of course, everyone knows we have religious liberty. Our Constitution—the First Amendment, specifically, backed up by the 14th Amendment after the Civil War—also means we have complete separation of state and church at all levels of government. Thomas Jefferson called it a "Wall of Separation" between the government and matters of religion. This guarantees that no one is subject through our laws or legal institutions to theological doctrines with which we disagree.

Marie Alena Castle shows that the reality is far from this ideal. She shows that what "everyone knows" about this subject is in some cases devastatingly wrong—that we are continually subjected to legal strictures and public policies that violate our religious liberties and state/church separation.

Thomas Jefferson ridiculed the idea that some people are "born with saddles on their backs" while others are naturally "booted and spurred, ready to ride them legitimately." Yet Jefferson himself owned slaves. It took a bloody Civil War to end the appalling institution of slavery and we still suffer from its legacy. What will it take, and how long will it take, for us to realize the First Amendment's guarantee of state-church separation and religious liberty? There is already a culture war underway, its outcome uncertain, that will answer such questions. This book outlines some aspects of this war that politically powerful religious groups and their leaders have declared and are waging against our liberties. At stake are not just principles of American freedom, due process and equal treatment under the law, but in some circumstances, our lives.

Religious leaders offer a multitude of excuses for why their religious doctrines should be part of our laws. "We are a Christian Nation!" is usually the first "explanation." But there is now generally a bit more skepticism about blatantly sectarian arguments, even in the courts. This is why creationists now call their doctrines "Intelligent Design Science" to get them taught to schoolchildren. This is also why all manner of false claims are repeated, over and over, such as that birth control pills and abortion cause cancer, gays are pedophiles and "legitimate rape" (as Missouri Congressman Todd Akin put it) cannot cause pregnancy.

Extremists also charge that defenders of state-church separation are anti-religious or mean to persecute believers. For example, a public policy requiring medical insurance to include contraceptive coverage was challenged successfully in court as "going against the religious convictions" of employers who happened to be Catholic.

This is like saying that someone religiously opposed to the Germ Theory of Disease (as "just a theory" after all) should be able to keep their employees' medical insurance from covering antibiotics!

You will enjoy this book. Even if you are a reasonably well-informed advocate of religious liberty and state-church separation, there are things here that will make you say: "What?! I didn't know that!" The author relates this in an engaging, entertaining way. Her warmth and depth of experience come through, especially when she relates personal experiences and events relating to those she knows or knew personally. This is not an exhaustive or scholarly treatment of a subject that deserves much attention, but it is an excellent introduction to a subject that has for too long been neglected. As Castle points out, there is an urgency about recognizing and addressing these problems before they become much worse.

—Dr. Tim Gorski, Pastor, North Texas Church of Freethought

PREFACE

*"Sometimes progress is made just by
not talking nonsense anymore."*— *RationalGal*

NOTE TO READERS: This is an updated edition of *Culture Wars: The Threat to Your Family and Your Freedom* (2013). That book described our social-political problems; this one shows how to resolve them. There have been a few negative comments. None have shown my arguments to be wrong, only that I am not polite, as if those who support inhumane laws have a point and I should respect it. This taboo against openly challenging the harm done in the name of religion is at the heart of our culture war.

To readers who want to keep that taboo in place, this book is not for you. You remind me of that part of Donald Trump's base that doesn't seem to care who gets hurt as long as the religious ideology or social fantasy that pushes some primal button in their psyche is validated. Apparently, I should kick the victim to the curb and placate the aggressor.

I can't do that.

Evil is as evil does and the evil in authoritarian religions is reflected in their doctrines, proclamations and especially their legislative agenda. The evil is expressed in their own arrogant words, and I quote them. It's a mindless kind of evil generated by an ideology that itself is empty of rational content. I have seen its destructive effects and I call it out for what it is. There is a quotation circulating on the Internet (most recently by writer/politician Cecil Bothwell, provenance unknown) that says: "We all place ourselves in danger to one extent or another when we stand up. But we place our children and grandchildren in even greater danger when we don't."

If some readers prefer not to stand up and prefer to believe that the religious right assaults on our freedom and civil liberties should be politely ignored, excused, respected or, worse yet, welcomed, there are books that support that view. This isn't one of them.

•••

"Eternal vigilance is the price of liberty." That inscription is on a statue in Washington D.C. at the National Archives. This book speaks to the need for that vigilance. But who threatens our liberty? As this book shows, it's the religious right interfering in our public life where religion does not belong. It's what allowed the rise of Donald Trump to the presidency. The effect is always harmful, sometimes disastrous, and potentially even lethal in matters of climate change denial and with nuclear warheads in the hands of fanatics and "stable geniuses." Yet no one on the liberal left in politics and the media warns us. They are liberals, and so they are eager to be open minded. The right wing elephant is in the room, but the left wing donkey steps around it carefully so as not to disturb it, even though it is crapping all over the floor.

Being a liberal myself, I sometimes find this niceness endearing. However, liberal though I am, I am not so open minded that my brain falls out. I live in the real world where there is real evil and I know it when I see it. I see that it does not care how much social damage it inflicts—it only wants obeisance, power and control.

This book not only describes that damage, but shows how to kick the elephant out of the room. It is easy to do but will take a critical mass of Anti-Trump Resisters and their progressive supporters to do it. I wrote this book because that critical mass, which did not exist before 2016, is available now.

We are in a struggle between the secular and the sacred worldviews for social and political dominance that has been going on in one way or another for centuries. At stake is whether we live under an authoritarian system ruled by rigid and irrational dogma or under a free democratic system where progressive policies protect our civil rights and liberties.

In 2016 Trump became president with campaign promises to "make America great again," but almost everything he proposed would undo the progressive social values that had come to define our nation—perhaps not entirely as it is but as many believe it can be.

Eternal vigilance was indeed necessary to protect those values but not enough of it was there among the voters. And so the upheaval came, orchestrated by a socially, morally and intellectually incoherent TV reality show hustler and real estate deal-maker who lives in an ideological vacuum, responds to charges that he is unstable by calling himself a "stable genius," brags about his crotch-groping assaults on women, and seems badly in need of adult supervision.

This book considers the social-political impact of the house of mirrors that is the Trump administration. As reported in the news media, we are in the hands of a man who has shown no interest in religion but found in the religious right an easily manipulated political base. Ironically, because of Trump's religious ignorance, the religious right has found him easily manipulated in return. He promised to give his "Christian nation" base their hearts' desire. He reaffirmed it in mid-October 2017 by addressing the annual religious right Values Voter Summit of the Family Research Council in Washington D.C. It was all about affirming the religious right agenda, although Trump has no idea what it actually is or how destructive it would be. Trump chose leaders from the religious right for his religious advisory committee. His healthcare committee consists of 16 men, all religious-right ideologues. He chose the devout Catholic Mike Pence for vice president—a man who describes himself as a Christian first, followed by Conservative and Republican. If Pence should become president he would be worse than Trump. He has political skills, discipline, and an extremist religious right worldview he would very likely try to impose on all of us by law. His history as a legislator and governor in Indiana makes that clear enough.

Trump exemplifies the statement attributed to the Roman philosopher Seneca (4 BCE – 65 CE) that, "Religion is what the common people see as true, the wise people see as false, and the rulers see as useful." It's the old dichotomy between the secular and the sacred—between reality and fantasy as a worldview. Almost all cultures throughout history have had the sacred option foisted on them by rulers who found it useful to invite that elephant into public life and speak for it. We've paid for that political blunder ever since.

As things stand, our social progress will remain hindered by the harmful and unnecessary religion-based laws embedded in our culture. Trump will only add to the problem, so the information in this book about those laws serves as a baseline for understanding what we are dealing with and how to fight back effectively.

As for fighting back, we have an endemic problem. Liberals are not exactly our social justice knights in shining armor. There are rust spots. Collectively, the liberal demographic has an adorable child-like tendency to shower everyone with love and kindness and sensitivity and understanding—even for the religious right, no matter how predatory they are. Liberals don't seem to mind accommodating their own repression, as this book will show.

Chapter 11 may be the most useful for overcoming this tendency. It takes us "To the Barricades," cheered by the millions of Resisters organizing, appalled at what the 2016 election has wrought. What I contribute to this movement is a specific strategy, proven effective, for how Anti-Trump Resisters can pull us out of the authoritarian rabbit hole into which Trump's reality-challenged voters dropped us.

Democracy by its nature can encourage either apathy or mob rule. Both were operating in the 2016 election. Now we need those with the passionate intensity to achieve a humane society to undo the damage. This book is here to help. You will not find the political information you need anywhere else, nor will you find any so useful and effective.

This book has a perspective no other political commentators I know of share. It comes from decades of hands-on grassroots political activism rather than from academic studies, journalistic reports and other views from the outside looking in. The view you get here is from the inside looking out, where I have stood face to face with predatory theocrats and seen the coldness in their eyes and experienced the hardness of their hearts. I have been to the funerals of their victims. I have watched human potential shredded in the service of barbaric medieval beliefs. I have fought to keep that sadistic worldview out of our laws. I am not done yet.

This is a been-there, done-that defense of our civil rights and liberties against the Nov. 8, 2016, pratfall into ideological delusions. Because I experienced much of what this book describes, the narrative is something of a memoir and I saw no need for footnotes or an index. Necessary sources are cited in the text; there is a Bibliography, and the detailed Contents helps in locating specific information.

Despite the liberal left opposition to religious claims that America was founded on Christian principles, our faith-based laws make this nation *de facto* Christian, although there has been progress. Some religion-based laws restricting women, sex and what we can do on Sundays have been mitigated or repealed. We now have same-sex marriage. Discrimination against ethnic minorities, the disabled and other disadvantaged groups is legally unacceptable. However, attempts to reverse progress remain strong, with no sign of letting up.

The liberal concept of social justice got no traction in Trump's campaign. Little did we know the extent to which that concept was rubbing raw the self-identity of a large segment of our population that included rural white males, traditional Christians and others fearful of losing a privileged (though marginal) status. The kindling of resentment was building, waiting for the match that would set it off. . . . and in walked Donald Trump.

Now we have reached the depths of our fantasy view of our nation as a welcoming melting pot. We have never been that. We are divided along religious/authoritarian and secular/progressive lines and always have been, perhaps as a function of our human nature that prefers homogeneity. Perhaps we are in another phase of a civil war that never ended. Perhaps we are not as conceived in liberty and equality as we thought. Perhaps President Abraham Lincoln's words in his Gettysburg Address still apply: ". . . Now we are engaged in a great civil war, testing whether that nation, or any nation so conceived and so dedicated, can long endure. . . ."

On Nov. 8, 2016, we were tested. And now we wonder what kind of people would elect a narcissistic, misogynistic, crotch-groping dirty old man as president—a man who bragged that he could shoot someone on Fifth Avenue in New York and not lose votes over it. It's unsettling to realize how true that is when we saw how Trump's jingoistic, misogynistic, incoherent, give-the-religious-right-their-hearts-desire ranting was greeted with cheers by his supporters—when, by general agreement, he was the most unqualified candidate for president in our history, and his female tradition-shattering opponent was—also by general agreement—the most qualified. Sexist chants of "Lock her up!" and an Electoral College fluke put Trump in office.

These are dire times. We can expect religious liberty to become primarily a liberty to impose religious beliefs on all of us. Despite Thomas Jefferson's opinion, belief in gods *does* pick our pockets and break our legs—not just metaphorically—with religion-supportive, socially harmful policies on taxes, health care, education, environmental protections, scientific and medical research, and civic rituals.

Even Trump's rejection of an international climate change treaty has a religious underpinning in a belief that God will not let Earth be destroyed. . . . And now he is destabilizing the Middle East by declaring Jerusalem the capital of Israel. The religious right applauds this. They believe it could bring on the biblical Armageddon and a nuclear warhead driven End Times. . . . "Ashes, ashes, we all fall down."

Given Trump's religiously illiterate background, he surely had no idea what he was doing when he did that! *No idea!* But the evangelicals understood. It satisfied their interpretation of the *Book of Revelation* and their longing for the Rapture. The sacred by its nature brings contention and harm into public life. . . . Divided we fall.

As religious beliefs, these mystical musings are culturally off-limits for questioning, and that is our problem. This taboo is like the magician's shield against discovery of how the trick works: never look behind the curtain. But this book does just that. If you don't like what you see behind that curtain, the last two chapters show what you can do about it. It's a four-step strategy. 1: walk in; 2: sit down; 3: raise your hand and 4: . . . (read it and see how easily success slips into place when the simple desire is there to do i

1

THE FANTASY OF STATE-CHURCH SEPARATION

"The legitimate powers of government extend to such acts
only as are injurious to others. But it does me no injury for
my neighbor to say there are twenty gods, or no god.
It neither picks my pocket nor breaks my leg."
—Thomas Jefferson, Notes on Virginia, 1782

Much is made of the supposed success of state-church separation exemplified by John F. Kennedy's 1960 speech in Texas as he campaigned for the presidency. He talked to the Greater Houston Ministerial Association about the importance of secular issues, such as poverty, hunger, education and health care, and the irrelevance of religious belief in dealing with them.

But how secular was our nation with so many laws based on religious doctrines? Why didn't secularists see this? Some of those laws are gone but many remain—and still secularists don't see this and insist that we have a secular government. We didn't then; we don't now. We blundered into state-church entanglement, too close to it historically to see it. The United States Constitution was the first in history to separate religion from government, so it was a simple and blunt "Congress shall make no law . . . "

No attention was paid to the ancient laws embedded in our legal system, inherited from a time when state and church were united and mutually supportive. That common law was accepted as-is without awareness of the religious basis of some of it.

At the time Kennedy spoke, that common law allowed religious institutions to have it all, as they do now. Their views on social morality were part of our legal system, enforced on everyone as an unquestioned cultural legacy.

Despite this, the Catholic Church unabashedly claimed support for freedom of conscience, as expressed in a 1938 book, *The Faith of Millions,* by the Rev. John A. O'Brien Ph.D. Regarding Protestant fears of papal control that defeated the Catholic Al Smith's campaign for the presidency in 1928, O'Brien wrote:

> . . . [I]n the century and a half of our national existence there has never been a single instance of a Catholic proving false to his civic duties because of any pull exerted upon him by his religious faith. No matter how much men may speculate about a theoretical conflict of civil and spiritual loyalties on the part of Catholics, the stark fact remains that no Catholic incumbent has ever yet discovered any obligation arising from his Catholic faith at variance with that which presses inexorably upon his conscience to discharge to the full the duties of his civil office.

It was a claim easy enough to make because the laws supported the dominant religious beliefs of the time, however much they violated the freedom of conscience of those who believed differently. Most were state laws, sometimes inconsistently enforced, making them appear to be only a reflection of local cultural habits and prejudices. Given the scattered nature of their effect, their violation of the religion clauses of the First Amendment was not generally noticed.

The first sign of change toward separating religion from government appeared only as recently as 1947 with the Supreme Court's ruling in *Everson v. Board of Education.* This landmark decision made the religion clauses of the First Amendment binding on the states. In *Everson,* the issue was New Jersey's reimbursement to parents for the transportation costs of sending their children to private schools, 96% of which were Catholic parochial schools. Justice Hugo Black's ruling is worth noting:

> The 'establishment of religion' clause of the First Amendment means at least this: Neither a state nor the Federal Government can set up a church. Neither can pass laws which aid one religion, aid all religions, or prefer one religion over another. Neither can force nor influence a person to go to or to remain away from church against his will or force him to profess a belief

or disbelief in any religion. No person can be punished for entertaining or professing religious beliefs or disbeliefs, for church attendance or non-attendance. No tax in any amount, large or small, can be levied to support any religious activities or institutions, whatever they may be called, or whatever form they may adopt to teach or practice religion. Neither a state nor the Federal government can, openly or secretly, participate in the affairs of any religious organizations or groups and vice versa. In the words of Jefferson, the clause against establishment of religion by law was intended to erect 'a wall of separation' between church and state.

The civil strife of the 1960s ameliorated some of the historically repressive laws. However, that awakened authoritarian religions to the danger such rebellion posed for their control of society. The clash between the secular and the sacred grew fierce. Authoritarian religions set up resistance at all levels through political and social action and public relations campaigns. To make matters worse, they attracted allies who, although disinterested in the religious agenda, passively adopted it to increase support for their goal of less government control over profit enhancing economic and fiscal policies.

Corporate funding sources did much to put religious right candidates in office as they rode in on the backs of "values voters." As this religious/economic movement developed over the turn of the millennium, accompanied by global economic distress, a political take-no-prisoners climate was created where compromise has become almost impossible. With the election of Donald Trump, the dysfunction not only continues but appears to be getting worse.

The Reagan Revolution Opens the Door to Religion

As the culture war escalated, almost everything Kennedy said he would not allow was achieved through religious pressure and accommodative Supreme Court rulings. Presidents began seeking advice from the likes of Billy Graham and the Catholic hierarchy. Religious schools and activities got taxpayer support (though indirectly, to appear to circumvent state-church separation issues), and religious institutions began to impose their beliefs through electoral politics.

For example, Ronald Reagan, as Governor of California in 1967, said his administration would be based on the teachings of Jesus. In this connection, he had Billy Graham address the state legislature twice and then asked him to discuss the Second Coming of Christ with his cabinet. When Graham held one of his religious crusade events in Anaheim, California, Reagan supported it, saying, "I'm sure there will be those who question my participation here tonight. People have become so concerned with church-state separation that we have interpreted freedom of religion into freedom from religion. (See *The Prince of War: Billy Graham's Crusade for a Wholly Christian Empire*, by Cecil Bothwell, for an in-depth look at the role Graham played in U.S. Politics.)

As president, Reagan maintained this view by appointing a U.S. ambassador to the Vatican. His ignorance was stunning. For example, consider this statement he made: "We establish no religion in this country. We command no worship. We mandate no belief, nor will we ever. Church and state are and must remain separate."

Sounds good, doesn't it? Secularist organizations quote it as supporting their position even when told it does just the opposite. That supposedly pro-separation statement was made on October 21, 1984, at Temple Hillel in Valley Stream, New York. Reagan was referring to a Connecticut Supreme Court ruling that denied religious employees the right to impose their beliefs on both their employer and their co-workers. The religious employees had demanded a strict workplace-wide adherence to their Sabbath religious practices at much inconvenience to everyone.

Reagan (as he said in his speech) was actually urging the Supreme Court to overturn the Connecticut decision and allow the religious imposition. "This is what I mean by freedom of religion," he said, "and that's what we feel the Constitution intends." The Supreme Court thought differently and upheld the Connecticut Court's ruling. (http://open.salon. com/blog/douglas_berger/2012/04/03/putting_reagans_church_state_ quote_in_context._shows_a_hypocrisy.) The ruling (we should have more like this) said:

> The Connecticut statute, by providing Sabbath observers with an absolute and unqualified right not to work on their chosen

Sabbath, violates the Establishment Clause. To meet constitutional requirements under that Clause, a statute must not only have a secular purpose and not foster entanglement of government with religion, its primary effect must not advance or inhibit religion. Lemon v. Kurtzman, 403 U.S. 602. The Connecticut statute imposes on employers and employees an absolute duty to conform their business practices to the particular religious practices of an employee by enforcing observance of the Sabbath that the latter unilaterally designate. The State thus commands that Sabbath religious concerns automatically control over all secular interests at the workplace; the statute takes no account of the convenience or interests of the employer or those of other employees who do not observe a Sabbath. In granting unyielding weighting in favor of Sabbath observers over all other interests, the statute has a [p704] primary effect that impermissibly advances a particular religious practice. Pp. 708-711."

In opposition to this and reflecting the skewed view of state-church separation Reagan favored, political agitation by the Catholic hierarchy and Jerry Falwell's newly formed Moral Majority had already begun an attempt to return society to the 1950s, triggered by the 1973 *Roe v. Wade* decision on abortion. This religious political campaign has been extensively documented by Stephen Mumford in *The Life and Death of NSSM 200: How the Destruction of Political Will Doomed a U.S. Population Policy* and is discussed in this book. Mumford exposes the Catholic Church's efforts to force its beliefs on non-Catholics as well as Catholics, nationally and globally, by exerting political power. Papal infallibility, a dogma, and therefore forever beyond retraction, had to be protected at all costs.

We are in a religious war that pits secular worldviews against the sacred—reality against myth and delusion. It is an attempt to "make America great again" as in the 1950s when white male Christians were in control of society. The Trump administration has been in full support of the "religious liberty" of Trump's evangelical base to impose those 1950s "values" on all of us.

In 2011, as reported in the New York Times on Nov. 11, the war took an astonishing turn when the United States Conference of Catholic Bishops

(USCCB) suddenly shifted its tactics. Instead of continuing to oppose abortion rights, gay rights, stem cell research and other "moral values" issues that victimized the objects of restrictive laws, the bishops began to claim the Church was the victim. Their "Religious Liberty Drive" redefined the secular vs. sacred conflict into a governmental assault on the Catholic Church's religious freedom. Archbishop (now a cardinal) Timothy M. Dolan of New York said, "We see in our culture a drive to neuter religion," and a move "to push religion back into the sacristy."

Dolan was promoting a politicized religion that overrides the civil rights and civil liberties of everyone who thinks differently. This is divisive and arrogant, so, yes, such a religion should be politically neutered and pushed back into the sacristy where it belongs. It does not belong in public life.

What set Dolan off was the federal government's decision to stop funding social programs operated by the Catholic Church on the government's behalf if the Church insisted on imposing its doctrinal beliefs on its non-Catholic employees and recipients of its services. These impositions meant no contraceptives or morning after pill for women trying to avoid a coerced pregnancy due to rape, incest, psychological abuse or for victims of sex trafficking. No abortion if a pregnancy resulted from that coercion. No abortion and no referral to another source even if the woman's life was in danger. No adoption or foster-care services for same-sex couples.

This is sheer brutality but, in the view of the Catholic bishops, they have religious freedom to brutalize people in this way, and to stop them is to discriminate against them because of their beliefs. They claim the government is taking away their liberty, but what kind of liberty is it that takes away the legitimate right to liberty of others? If religious facilities choose to limit their social services to what conforms to their doctrines, they should reject all government funding and support the services themselves.

This book exposes the fraudulent arguments for laws that validate religious doctrines. Those of us in the community of decency know the value of democratic freedoms. We recognize the self-serving evil that threatens them when we see it . . . and we are seeing it now.

2

THE CONSTITUTION:
MAKING POLITICS SACRED

"I tell you naught for your comfort, Yea, naught for your desire,
Save that the sky grows darker yet, And the sea rises higher."
(G. K. Chesterton, The Ballad of the White Horse, Book I, 1911)

There is no good news here. The First Amendment's religion clauses begin: "Congress shall make no law . . ." But Congress does make religion-based laws and we pay for them with our money, our health, our freedom and sometimes our life. The courts consider these laws when they are challenged and decide if they are constitutional.

That has not been going well for state-church separation lately, and with the 2016 election putting all three branches of government—the executive, the legislative, and the judicial—in the hands of the religious right, it is getting worse. The sky indeed grows darker and the sea rises higher. (Perhaps literally with Trump's withdrawal of the U.S. from the international climate change treaty.)

The social and political chaos generated by reality vs. mythology world-views would not exist if laws that serve only to support religion's unverifiable theology were declared unconstitutional as a violation of state-church separation. One Supreme Court Justice, Antonin Scalia (he died February 13, 2016), openly rejected the concept of state-church separation, while the Court as a whole, judging by its rulings under the direction of Chief Justice John Roberts, appeared to be leaning toward favoring religious beliefs.

That leaning is now a firm stance with Donald Trump's appointment of Neil Gorsuch to take Scalia's place. Gorsuch has an unsettling record of being hostile to state-church separation. As an appellate court judge he ruled in favor of Hobby Lobby, agreeing that business owners could use their religious beliefs to justify denying their employees legally mandated contraceptive coverage in their insurance plans. In the case of *Little Sisters of the Aged v. Burwell*, Gorsuch argued that religious nonprofits should not even have to fill out a form requesting an exemption from the mandate because doing so would violate their religious freedom. In another case, Gorsuch argued that placing the Ten Commandments on a courthouse lawn in Oklahoma was constitutional because it was not necessarily a religious symbol. At the same time he also said the Ten Commandments played a part in shaping our laws and so did not violate the Establishment clause. (Gorsuch's stunning ignorance of legal history, U.S. history and even the Commandments should have disqualified him right there for any judicial position.) And then there is the book Gorsuch wrote—*The Future of Assisted Suicide and Euthanasia*—in which he argued for a total ban on death with dignity laws, even though such laws have been in effect in several states for years with no sign of their being abused.

Gorsuch is just the first court appointee to begin fulfilling Trump's campaign promise to his evangelical Christian followers to give them their heart's desire. Not only are there likely to be other Supreme Court openings for Trump to fill, but there are many lower appellate court vacancies, which Trump has been filling with religious-right supporters. These courts are steppingstones to Supreme Court rulings and religion-favoring decisions can push them along.

Social Progress As Contemptible and Excessive

Jeffrey Toobin in his 2012 book, *The Oath: The Obama White House and the Supreme Court,* writes that Chief Justice Roberts has expressed contempt for what he called the "fluid and wide-ranging jurisprudence" of the Court that brought about so much progress in civil rights under Chief Justices Earl Warren and then Warren Burger during the 1960s and into the 80s. This progress included improvements in protection for minorities, state-church separation, the ability of citizens to challenge governmental as well as business practices, and the establishment of women's right to abortion. All of these rights and liberties (called "excesses" by Roberts) were weakened when William Rehnquist became Chief Justice in 1986. Now, as Toobin documents, it has become "Roberts' mission to lead the counterrevolution" to finish the job," (page 39).

There is great danger in this. It has long been assumed that our freedoms are protected by the Constitution, but this is not true. The Constitution does absolutely nothing to protect us until and unless a Supreme Court ruling spells out that protection—or, in some cases, denies it, as in the notorious 1857 *Dred Scott* decision that affirmed the status of slaves as property and fueled a controversy ultimately resolved by a civil war.

We are actually governed not by the Constitution but by constitutional law, which is based on the Supreme Court's interpretation of the Constitution. However, there can be no interpretation unless a law is challenged. This is required by the Constitution itself. Article III, Sec. 2, limits federal judicial power to cases of controversies arising under the laws and Constitution of the United States. Unless someone brings a legal challenge to a particular law or practice there is no controversy over which the Court has any legal autonomy. Without that, freedoms can exist in some states while being denied in others. Although state-church violations have been rampant throughout our history (and are today), no significant challenges were brought until the 1940s because it takes considerable personal courage and financial resources to challenge them.

A Free Country If You Can Afford to Pay For It

Before the founding of the American Civil Liberties Union (ACLU) in 1920, individuals who wanted to litigate a state-church violation had to bear the legal costs themselves, so no one did. The ACLU changed that by supplying plaintiffs with the attorneys and funds needed for cases it deemed important to take on. Since then other state-church separation groups have supplied funding, as has the federal government. In 1976, Congress passed the Civil Right's Attorneys Fee Award Act. It provides that any governmental unit that enacts an unconstitutional law must pay the attorneys' fees and costs for a party that successfully challenges that law.

For example, as reported on the Patheos web site on Oct. 26, 2017, the State of Kentucky had to pay plaintiffs $224,703 in legal fees when the state lost its case in which Rowan County clerk Kim Davis claimed the religious right to not grant marriage licenses to same-sex couples.

In another case, in Minnesota, in 2015, it was a bit different. My organization, Atheists For Human Rights, was the plaintiff when Washington County refused to register one of our members as a marriage officiant because we are an atheist organization, not a church. I humorously offered to change our name to the Church of Smoke and Mirrors and the county said that would be OK. (Apparently, it's all about making religion look important at any ridiculous cost. It's why the Church of the Flying Spaghetti Monster and the Church of the Latter Day Dude can and do have marriage officiants.)

Our attorney, Randall Tigue, argued our case on constitutional grounds. That meant the county would have to argue that it is constitutional to require a religious test to officiate at a civil marriage bound by secular laws—a little hard to do, even for the religious right. The very conservative Washington County realized that, so they dropped the case and said we could authorize marriage officiants as an atheist organization. Since that made the case moot, Washington County did not have to pay our legal fees (fortunately reasonable). In effect, the court ruling made the statutory requirement that only clergy and court personnel could perform civil marriages meaningless. The statute stays on the books but cannot *and will not* be enforced out of religionist fear of it being ruled unconstitutional and they lose that bit of superficial top-dog validation.

Truth be told, the marriage statutes in most states that specify clergy as officiants are not preferential, as is generally assumed. They actually put a leash on that top dog. They require religions to conform to civil marriage laws—no multiple wives, no child brides, no coerced marriages, no male ownership of wives. That takes all the pervert-attracting fun out of biblical marriages, as Roy Moore found out in 2017 when his sexual interest in 13-year-old girls (once the legal age for marriage in Bible-soaked Alabama) became public knowledge and derailed his campaign for U.S. Senator.

So our clergy statute can be ignored, which it is—we authorize marriage officiants regularly. I discussed the matter of politically uncomfortable laws being simply ignored with one of my elected officials. She said, "We have a lot of laws like that." The establishment clause probably tops the list of ignored laws. Several state laws, for example, forbid atheists to hold public office. They can't be enforced because they have been ruled unconstitutional and they can't be removed because the religious right throws a fit. They simply stay there, like Confederate Civil War statues, as silent monuments to bigotry and ignorance. (The Catholic Church does the same thing when an "infallible" dogma becomes too ludicrous to even mention any more. That's why we no longer hear that witches exist—or limbo, so recently tossed out. In time, we may stop hearing the "infallible" dogma that using contraceptives is a sin worthy of hellfire.) Sometimes progress is made just by not talking nonsense any more.

So much for that. But even with legal fees covered, plaintiffs have often faced daunting perils. Challenges frequently bring death threats, social ostracism and job or business losses due to the hostility of those who want religious beliefs and practices enshrined in law. They often have to file a challenge anonymously, go into hiding or move far out of the hostile area to ensure their safety.

Even if these problems are dealt with, and with the best legal skills, there remains the potential for rulings that favor state-church entanglement rather than removing it, thus setting a legal precedent that makes the success of subsequent challenges almost impossible.

Here is an example of how legal cases can be withheld—and justice denied—when the Supreme Court is unreliable regarding the First Amendment: On June 7, 2001, the ACLU of Ohio announced that it would not appeal the ruling of the full 6th Circuit Court that said Ohio's motto, "With God All Things Are Possible" was constitutional. The ruling overturned a previous three-judge panel ruling that the motto infringed on the First Amendment of the Constitution.

The reason the ACLU did this was that the conservative bloc on the court had hacked away at the wall of separation of church and state in previous rulings. According to an article in the *Columbus Dispatch* at that time, Raymond Vasvari, legal director for the ACLU of Ohio said: "It's no secret that there's a conservative bloc on the Supreme Court that takes a skeptical view of church and state separation. For now, this will be the last word."

In 2007, in *Hein v. Freedom From Religion Foundation* (FFRF), the Supreme Court ruled that taxpayers do not have standing to challenge the constitutionality of expenditures by the Executive branch of government. FFRF had argued that the use of money appropriated by Congress to support faith-based social programs was unconstitutional. The Court ruled, however, that the funds involved had been appropriated for use by the Executive branch for unspecified purposes and the president was therefore free to use those funds as he wished. This, of course, means that money can be appropriated for religious activities as long as it is laundered through an appropriation designated for *carte blanche* use by the president.

Taxpayer money laundering seems to be the up-and-coming preferred strategy in circumventing the First Amendment—as well as state constitutions, which tend to be more specific and therefore stronger in prohibiting taxpayer support for religious schools.

In 2011, in the *Arizona Christian School Tuition Organization v. Winn* case, the Supreme Court ruled that taxpayers do not have standing in federal court to challenge state tax credits for contributions to school tuition organizations that then provide scholarships to students at private schools, including religious schools. (In 2010, in Arizona, this amounted to $60 million, 92% of which went to religious schools.) The effect of this is that, instead of giving money directly and unconstitutionally to religious schools, the state can launder it through a tuition organization that takes a parental donation and turns it over to the school of the parent's choice. The parent is then reimbursed by the state in the form of a dollar-for-dollar tax credit in the amount of the tuition donation.

The Roberts Court based its ruling on the plaintiff not having claimed a personal financial injury. This effectively negated the 1968 Warren Court's ruling in *Flast v Cohen* that taxpayers could sue to stop government expenditures that violated the Establishment Clause. Chief Justice Warren had argued that, without this right, the courts would have no controversy brought to them that would allow any examination of constitutional violations. So now one must show a personal financial injury.

But is it not injurious to be forced indirectly to help support a religious school not of one's choosing? Those tax credits come from taxes paid by citizens who did not expect their contributions to the common good to end up in a money laundering scheme to circumvent the First Amendment. One would think that challenging such a constitutional run-around would be an essential right—even a duty—of a citizen in a constitutional democracy. But the U.S. Supreme Court thinks otherwise. So now we must show that a state-church violation does tangible harm to us personally.

Destroying the civil liberties the Constitution was created to protect is not harmful enough.

Even when there is personal injury, religious institutional prerogatives often outweigh the rights of victims and trump our secular laws that would otherwise protect them. For example, in 2012 the Supreme Court ruled in favor of a religious school in *Hosanna-Tabor Evangelical Lutheran Church and School v. Equal Employment Opportunity Commission*. The case concerned the church's claim that it had an unrestricted right to discriminate on the basis of race, sex, disability and other characteristics regardless of secular laws prohibiting such action; therefore, its firing of a teacher because of a medical condition should be allowed.

Several civil liberties and religious organizations asked the Court to rule for the plaintiff, saying that the right of religions to discriminate in their personnel practices should not apply in situations not related directly to the institution's religious mission. They argued that religion-specific justifications for discrimination should not be extended into—as an amicus filed by Americans United for Separation of Church & State said—"a shield for all forms of discrimination and retaliation, regardless of motivation." The Court, by its ruling, evidently thought such a shield was perfectly acceptable. Because the Supreme Court's interpretation can be, and inevitably is, influenced by the ideological mindset of the Justices, constitutional law can just as easily destroy our freedoms as protect them. The current makeup of the Court is such that there is reason to fear a destructive phase is at hand and it will uphold at least some, if not all, of our theology based laws if they are challenged. But those who love freedom and the civil rights and liberties promised by our Constitution must accept the danger. There may be some hills worth dying on, and so—although care must be taken—challenges must be made. Religious beliefs must be removed from government involvement and privatized if we are to be a nation dedicated to liberty and justice for all.

The Problem With Challenging Religion-Based Laws

Challenges to theology based laws have been attempted, but are seldom, if ever, presented as a violation of the First Amendment's establishment clause. Instead, non-religious arguments are used, although they require a much more complex and sophisticated legal argument to be persuasive, generally based on a right to privacy or equal treatment under the law or some other non-religious aspect that can be interpreted as enshrined in the Bill of Rights.

It is important to note how subjective these interpretations can be. For example: Robert Bork—President Ronald Reagan's unsuccessful nominee for the U.S. Supreme Court in 1987—was defeated because of strong opposition to his belief that the Constitution conferred no right to privacy relating to women's reproductive decisions, that the civil rights decisions of the Warren and Burger courts were made in error, and that the Federal government had no right to impose standards of voting fairness on the states. In an October 24, 1987, article in the *New York Times* about the Senate debate on the confirmation, the following was reported. It shows the philosophical differences that underlie so many Court decisions and the impact they can have on our rights:

> Later, in closing the debate, the Judiciary Committee chairman [Senator Joe Biden] said: "This has been a great debate, a debate about fundamental principle, about how one interprets the Constitution." Senator Biden repeated the statement with which he opened Judge Bork's confirmation hearings last month, and which he has made a theme for the entire proceeding. "I believe I have rights because I exist, in spite of my government, not because of my government," he said. "Judge Bork believes that rights flow from the majority, through the Constitution to individuals, a notion I reject."

Justice Antonin Scalia echoed Bork's views of the limited scope of the Constitution and the unlimited power of whatever constitutes the majority of voters at any time. He found no protection in our founding document. His words are instructive as to the value of the Constitution in protecting our civil rights. This is what he said during a Q&A interview, "The Originalists," published by *The Daily Journal Corporation* as part of "Legally Speaking," a series of interviews with legal specialists (see: http://www.callawyer.com/common/print.cfm).

> **Q.** In 1868, when the 39th Congress was debating and ultimately proposing the 14th Amendment, I don't think anybody would have thought that equal protection applied to sex discrimination, or

certainly not to sexual orientation. So does that mean that we've gone off in error by applying the 14th Amendment to both?

A. Yes, yes. Sorry, to tell you that. . . . But, you know, if indeed the current society has come to different views, that's fine. You do not need the Constitution to reflect the wishes of the current society. Certainly the Constitution does not require discrimination on the basis of sex. The only issue is whether it prohibits it. It doesn't. Nobody ever thought that that's what it meant. Nobody ever voted for that. If the current society wants to outlaw discrimination by sex, hey, we have things called legislatures, and they enact things called laws. You don't need a Constitution to keep things up-to-date. All you need is a legislature and a ballot box. You don't like the death penalty anymore, that's fine. You want a right to abortion? There's nothing in the Constitution about that. But that doesn't mean you cannot prohibit it. Persuade your fellow citizens it's a good idea and pass a law. That's what democracy is all about. It's not about nine superannuated judges who have been there too long, imposing these demands on society.

Chief Justice John Roberts expressed a similar sentiment in July, 2012, in explaining the sometimes ideologically inconsistent way he voted. "It is not our job to protect the people from the consequences of their political choices," he said. Really? But does not the Constitution exist precisely to protect a minority from the harmful consequences of the majority's political choices when its civil rights and civil liberties are at stake? And is it not the job of the Supreme Court to see that the Constitution does just that?

It is true that you don't need a Constitution if you think the majority should rule at all times. But we do have a Constitution, whose very purpose is to protect the rights of the minority against the tyranny of the majority. It's also true that when Thomas Jefferson wrote, "All men are created equal," he meant, literally, only men, not women, and only white men, not blacks, and only white men who owned property. Women were, at that time, considered men's property (and in some respects, still are). Slavery was also condoned at that time.

So were many other religion-based laws and policies (some still operating—the motivation for this book). But, countering that, the Constitution and its amended Bill of Rights provided for a government that could adjust to changing times. It's all there in the Preamble: "We the people of the United States, in Order to form a more perfect Union, establish Justice, insure domestic Tranquility, provide for the common defense, promote the general Welfare, and secure the Blessings of Liberty to ourselves and our Posterity, do ordain and establish this Constitution for the United States of America."

No exceptions were listed for gender, creed or color. All references to religion were exclusionary—religion and government were not to be involved with each other. How would Bork and Scalia establish justice consistently if that was left to majority rule? How could the blessings of liberty be secured (and for whom) if we had liberty in some states but not in others, as the whims of a state's current majority allowed it? How could we be equal citizens under the law or have the basic right to privacy in our personal lives if it depended on what the shifting sands of the majority preferred at any time and place? What would it mean to be the land of the free if our freedom depended, election by election, on the whims of whatever group had at least 50% plus 1 of the votes at that time?

The rights Bork and Scalia could not find in the Constitution, and that Roberts considers "excesses," have tended to be rights that run counter to archaic religious beliefs embedded in our laws, such as those related to sexuality and reproduction. Their basis in religion shows they do not belong in our laws. They are an establishment of religion in the most harmful way possible. Of course, the current religious right activists who agree with Bork and Scalia don't accept the concept of state-church separation any more than they accept the concept of liberty and justice for all in any meaningful way.

If theology-based laws were challenged forthrightly on First Amendment grounds as an establishment of religion, the courts would be faced with a clear issue: Is this law based on a religious belief and, if so, does it still have a *valid* secular purpose that justifies supporting it? (*Valid* is important. After all, one can—and society once did—find a secular economic purpose for slavery, but let's hope our civilization has advanced enough to consider that unacceptable.)

A religious basis and a valid secular purpose either exist or they do not. The following chapters will take on the task of resolving this question for at least the most destructive theology-based laws. An establishment of religion is not just about government god-talk, pledges of allegiance and slogans on money. It is also about the far more harmful establishment of religious doctrine through laws that affect our life, liberty and pursuit of happiness.

Attorneys Must Argue For the Establishment Clause

So why is the establishment clause used so little in challenging laws that essentially force everyone to live by some particular religious belief? The answer is straightforward. The clause was adopted as a response to the centuries of religious wars in Europe. This nation's founders, a mix of Christians and Deists, were determined to keep America free of such bloody strife. They assumed the religion clauses of the First Amendment would be effective in disentangling government from religion. However, the consequence was that they also effectively disentangled religion from public discourse lest hostilities break out. As a further consequence, it has become politically incorrect to criticize religious beliefs publicly, with harmful religious behavior euphemized as "socially conservative." Thus, religious beliefs are seldom if ever used to argue that a law is unconstitutional.

This is a mistake. If democracy means anything, it should enable us to engage religious institutions in debates about the beliefs they want us to live by, just as we question political parties' socio-economic positions. We should hear their theological arguments, not just their specious "secular" arguments. If they fear exposing their antiquated and unverifiable dogma to public scrutiny, that is all the more reason to scrutinize it. Yet that is not done.

Here is an example of the problem: My organization, Atheists For Human Rights, has been assisting Final Exit Network (FEN) in various ways in its defense against charges that it "assisted a suicide." (See the chapter on Theology Based Healthcare, under "End of Life Decision Making" for details.) All FEN does is provide information that is already in the public domain about self deliverance to members who are hopelessly ill and want to end their suffering in a dignified way on their own terms.

FEN, which has argued its case as a free speech issue, lost its latest appeal because the appellate court accepted the prosecution's argument that providing information was essentially the same as physically assisting a suicide.

Our attorney, Randall Tigue, filed an amicus brief that got to the theological heart of the matter. In addition to supporting FEN's free speech argument, here is what it said, in part (citations deleted), and why this could not be used in legal arguments:

> . . . Therefore, it is clear that the state's interest in preventing Appellant's speech is not in preventing suicide or loss of life generally, but rather in mandatory or compelled suffering by the mentally competent terminally ill whose condition causes them to suffer intolerably. To date, no party and no court has advanced any secular government interest that is served by compulsory suffering, against his or her will, on the part of a terminally ill patient. Indeed the only interest that has been advanced in support of such compulsory suffering is entirely religious in nature. For example, the U.S. Catholic Bishops' "Ethical and Religious Directives for Catholic Health Care," states, in pertinent part:

> "The truth that life is a precious gift from God has profound implications for the question of stewardship over human life. We are not owners of our lives and, hence, do not have absolute power over life. We have a duty to preserve our life and use it for the glory of God, but the duty to preserve life is not absolute, for we may reject life-prolonging procedures that are insufficiently beneficial or excessively burdensome. Suicide and euthanasia are never morally acceptable options."

What if a terminal condition causes intractable pain and suffering? The U.S. Catholic Bishops answer as follows:

> "Since a person has the right to prepare for his or her death, while fully conscious, he or she should not be deprived of consciousness without a compelling reason. Medicines capable of alleviating or suppressing pain may be given to a dying person, even if this therapy may indirectly shorten the person's life so

long as the intent is not to hasten death. Patients experiencing suffering that cannot be alleviated should be helped to appreciate the Christian understanding of redemptive suffering."

This religious concept of "redemptive suffering" was discussed by Pope John Paul II in Kaczor, "A Pope's Answer to the Problem of Pain," Catholic Answers Magazine 1:

"A source of joy is found in the overcoming of the sense of the uselessness of suffering, a feeling that is sometimes very strongly rooted in human suffering. This feeling not only consumes the person interiorly but seems to make him a burden to others. The person feels condemned to receive help and assistance from others and at the same time feels useless to himself. The discovery of the salvific meaning of suffering in union with Christ transforms this depressing feeling. Faith in sharing in the suffering of Christ brings with it the interior certainty that the suffering person 'completes what is lacking in Christ's afflictions'; the certainty that in the spiritual dimension of the work of redemption he is serving, like Christ, the salvation of his brothers and sisters. Therefore, he is carrying out an irreplaceable service."

Clearly, the notions that each person is not the owner of his or her own life, exists only to live for the glory of God, and that each person must experience "redemptive suffering" are anything but secular concepts. They are religious principles that cannot be the basis of public policy. Yet these principles appear to be the only basis for pursuing a policy of compulsory suffering for the terminally ill. They cannot provide a compelling state interest for First Amendment purposes.

That is a solid constitutional argument, if ever there was one. based on a violation of the Establishment clause. Was it persuasive? Only if one or more of the judges took time to read it, saw the constitutional logic, and allowed it to influence their decision in favor of FEN. (Sometimes it works, so is worth the effort.) It could not be used at the appellate court level because all arguments on appeal have to be based on the arguments made when the case was first filed. No new ones are allowed.

This was a new one. But it could not easily have been part of the initial lawsuit because religion based arguments are considered socially and politically problematic. (It's one of the reasons why fighting faith healing laws is so difficult.)

Regardless, progressives need to challenge that taboo and bring up the religious basis for every law where it is relevant right from the start so it can be carried through in the appeals process. If this creates a problem for religions in trying to justify their beliefs, so be it.

3

The Rabbit Hole Theology of Sex

" I learned two things growing up in Texas.
1: God loves you, and you're going to burn in hell forever.
2: Sex is the dirtiest and most dangerous thing you can possibly do,
so save it for someone you love." —Molly Ivins

If you are thumbing through this book and thinking that having some laws based on religious beliefs is no big deal, read this chapter and think again. You are about to take a trip down a theological rabbit hole curiouser and curiouser than any Alice ever went down.

This chapter is about sex and the medieval views of it supported by the Catholic Church's papal-infallibility-based theology and the Protestant fundamentalists' inerrant-Bible-based beliefs. I am not going to give these views any respect because they are ludicrous at best and barbaric at worst.

I am not alone. According to numerous surveys, most Catholics don't care much for their Church's archaic views, and the liberal Protestant religions have given them up entirely. However, because of the political influence exerted by religious institutions, these medieval views are affecting all of us in harmful ways through our laws, many described throughout this book.

Because so many of our religion-based laws reflect an obsession with sex, an introduction to the supporting theology is needed. Regardless of the appeal this theology may have for its proponents, no social value can be found. Ironically, that harm does not come only to society but often enough to its facilitators—those celibate priests who preach the avoidance of religiously non-conforming sex.

These men were recruited into the priesthood around age 13, innocent and eager to become servants of God. But they are human, and that includes having innate yearnings that can be severely at odds with their vow of chaste celibacy. They fight against them, and I believe most of them succeed well enough and find satisfaction in their vocation, but others do not. The yearnings are acted upon in sometimes destructive, tragically newsworthy ways, but perhaps more commonly in a wistful loneliness.

Here is what one Catholic priest, John A. O'Brien, wrote in his 1938 book, *The Faith of Millions,* in a chapter on the joy and fulfillment marriage brings to men. (He doesn't say much about what it brings to women other than economic support.)

> Among the worst miseries of life is that of unrelieved loneliness. To go to one's dwelling at evening, only to find it empty of any person interested in your struggles, rejoicing in your achievements, softening the sting of defeat with the balm of sympathy and understanding, is to live in a darkened chamber whither the sunshine of human comradeship and love scarcely penetrates. As other forms of life, when deprived of the sun's rays, wither and die, so human life, robbed of the sunshine of love and sympathy, loses its zest, its enthusiasm and its vigor. Love is the radiance that brightens the world of human life with the sunshine of happiness.

It's easy to sense here the unrelieved loneliness of a dedicated priest who got into the ministry too soon to know what he would be sacrificing of his humanity. Where do these men go if the loneliness becomes unbearable? To prostitutes? To vulnerable altar boys? There is no "sunshine of love and sympathy" there, only the "sloppy fusion of genitalia" (as I once heard it rather graphically described). This is so sad, and those frustrated yearnings are so devoid of real meaning or worthwhile purpose.

But back to the theology. If we're going to discuss the theological underpinnings of our laws, the underpinnings of the theology itself can use some explaining. As a start, get a copy of the 60-page *A Pastoral Letter of the United States Conference of Catholic Bishops* titled "Marriage: Love and Life in the Divine Plan," then pause to wonder what planet they are from. (To order a copy, visit www.usccbpublishing.org and click on "New Titles.")

The real world is nowhere to be seen, only mystical musings that glorify an existence focused on an imaginary and unverifiable realm ruled by directives no one with any real life experience would recognize as even sane.

In such a world, sex is only for procreation by one man and one woman—and limited to the missionary position—united until death in a monogamous marriage. Sex in any other context, for any other purpose, is immoral, evil and depraved. Any problems arising from adhering to this limited view of sex can be resolved by prayer and reliance on the grace of God through receiving the sacraments.

The Pastoral Letter's entire premise is based on accepting—as an historical, literal, reality—the biblical creation story of Adam and Eve in the Garden of Eden. As it says, "Conflicts, quarrels, and misunderstandings can be found in all marriages. They reflect the impact of Original Sin, which (quoting the *United States Catholic Catechism for Adults*) 'disrupted the original communion of man and woman'."

Fine for those who can believe it, but the Catholic bishops, along with their Protestant fundamentalist counterparts, campaign endlessly to keep existing laws and pass new ones based on this mythical worldview. The following chapters will discuss those laws. This one will focus on the underlying theology the advocates for those laws evidently prefer you didn't know about, since they carefully ignore them in their public arguments.

Sex As the Transmitter of Sin and Death

Of all bodily processes, sex seems to always have been especially unsettling in some way to the religious mind, at least in the Abrahamic religions. Belief systems based on nature worship or multiple gods are less inhibited (Hinduism's ancient sex instruction book, the *Kama Sutra*, even includes graphic examples). Some cultures, for non-religious reasons, have tended to worry that sexual activity could make one physically vulnerable.

The view of sex as harmful—but in a sinful rather than physical sense—was embraced most energetically by Christianity and turned into an astonishing number of ways to control it, turn it into the very definition of morality, and make people miserable. All for a natural function that, of itself, has no moral implications. Only the irresponsible use of sex has moral aspects, as when it is careless of consequences, exploitive, deliberately or thoughtlessly hurtful—or just plain stupid. Given the power of the sex drive, unwise sexual encounters are extremely common. After all, who hasn't been there?

In Christian theology, this is all our fault. All the troubles humans endure have been caused by "the fall" in the Garden of Eden. Eve was deceived by the serpent and seduced Adam into eating the forbidden fruit, said to be a metaphor for sex. That mythical unwise sexual encounter was the Original Sin that doomed humanity to pain, suffering, disease and death.

Or maybe not. As myths go, this one has interesting competition. The creation story in the Bible was not the only one making the rounds when the Bible was created. The Bible we have has only a few of the many gospels, epistles, legends, historical fictions, and spiritual commentaries that were circulating at the time. Of the creation stories, the best one, the intriguing tale of Adam's first wife, was left out. (See *The Other Bible: Ancient Alternative Scriptures*, Willis Barnstone, ed., Part 1, Creation Myths, "The Creation of the World.")

Absolutely fascinating, it tells of how the Most High God first created Lileth to be Adam's wife. Both were created equally out of dirt. Because of that equal creation, Lileth insisted on having full equality with her husband. That being denied her, she left him. Adam complained to God so God made him another wife, Eve. This time, God used one of Adam's ribs so Eve could not claim to be his equal. How desperate the fear of equality or the need for control must have been that the storytellers felt compelled to reverse the natural process by having Eve "born" of man. The Bible's version of the story has Adam almost gloating when he says (in Genesis 2:23): "This one, at last, is bone of my bones and flesh of my flesh; This one shall be called 'woman' for out of her man this one has been taken."

Ancient writings are full of fables that make man the original child bearer in some magical way, thus denying women that status. A lot of misogyny is reflected in these stories while showing that some progressive views of male-female relationships were present too. Also, in the non-biblical creation story, the serpent's role changes the sex picture significantly:

Among the animals, the serpent was notable. Of all of them he had the most excellent qualities. Like man, he stood upright and in height was equal to the camel. His superior mental gifts caused him to become an infidel. It likewise explains his envy of man, especially of his conjugal relations. Envy made him meditate ways and means of bringing about the death of Adam. Knowing that Adam, in his zeal to keep Eve from eating of the Tree of Knowledge, had told her to not even touch it, he formed a plan.

You have to admire the writing—humans have always been great story-tellers. Here we learn that eating the forbidden fruit was not a euphemism for having sex. Adam and Lileth and Eve had been going at it all along, which seems to have bothered the serpent. The serpent's plan was to talk Eve into just touching the tree so that when nothing happened she could be persuaded to eat the fruit, then get Adam to eat it. The plan worked beautifully. . . . By the way, the fruit was a fig, not an apple. That's why Adam and Eve covered themselves with fig leaves to hide their newly discovered "shame." The fig tree was the only one that allowed its leaves to be taken, due to its role in the downfall of humanity. (Would make a great movie!)

Although the cause of Original Sin differs in the biblical and non-biblical versions (disobeying an order vs. having sex), and both are ridiculous, the Bible's compilers went with the one that blames sex. Why, you ask. Well, it created a handy explanation for how Original Sin could be passed on through succeeding generations by attaching itself to the soul of each fertilized egg through sex at conception. It also provided an explanation for the strength of the sex drive, which makes controlling it so difficult. Original Sin gave the sex drive that power! (Actually, it was evolution through natural selection that did it. The stronger one's sex drive, the higher one's reproductive rate, resulting in a preponderance of individuals in the gene pool with strong sex drives.)

There are a couple of problems with these theological inventions beyond the fanciful nature of the creation stories.

1. Souls are said to be created by God at the moment of conception, so the only way they can acquire Original Sin is for God to put it there.

Sex alone couldn't do that because it only creates the body. This whole thing looks like a punishment for engaging in sex, although God had ordered humans, in Genesis 1:28, to "be fruitful and multiply." Theology has an amazing ability to put humans between a rock and a hard place. Interestingly, science can now remove both the rock and the hard place with fertility technology, explained later.

2. The soul cannot enter the fertilized egg at the moment of conception because it needs a reasonably operational body to function. This is evident from the Catholic Church's instruction for the baptism of infants that was in place for 700 years, until 1917, in its *Codex Juris Canonici*. Canon Law 748 said severely defective babies ("monstrosities") must be baptized conditionally just in case they are ensouled persons.

Current canon law leaves this out, although it is still a necessary consideration. What, after all, is a priest to do when he is called to baptize conjoined twins, one of which consists of only part of a body? Years ago, when carnival "freak shows" were still allowed, I saw a fully formed woman being exhibited who had most of another body growing out of her side—torso, arms, one leg, no head. I suppose that would qualify as a "monstrosity" in canon law. Were there two souls there or one? How much of an attached body has to be there to be considered a separate baptizable person? Would two heads with one body do it? How about two bodies with one head? If a soul is present, where would it reside? Anywhere in the body? In every cell? Only in the brain, since that is where thinking occurs? If in the brain, there is no possibility of ensoulment at the moment of conception. If anywhere or everywhere in the body, wouldn't any partially formed conjoined twin be eligible for baptism? Not long ago, the media reported on a girl in India who was born with two sets of arms and legs—obviously a twinning that did not go well. Would the extra set of limbs qualify for baptism?

This is an example of the problems the advocates for the preservation of archaic theology face, given their locked-in belief in Original Sin as an historical fact. This theological rigidity also exposes a more basic problem. If the Original Sin story is taken as a metaphor (the only way it can make sense), the end result—the Bible's crucifixion and redemption story—must also be taken as a metaphor (also the only way it can make sense). But there goes the historicity—the very foundation on which

Christianity is based! The stories stand together as either all (easily dis-provable) history or all (interestingly creative) metaphor. We'll leave it to the theologians to work that out.

The Original Sin story is a fable to explain why life is hard, bad things happen, childbearing is difficult and to justify male ownership of women. Creative writers have always speculated about how things in nature came to be. *Aesop's Fables*, Rudyard Kipling's *Just So Stories*, and others, are replete with these tales. The Garden of Eden story is of the same genre as "How the Leopard Got its Spots." For believers who accept it as fact, it serves as the ultimate guilt trip to compel them to seek solace and salvation in religion. Consider this Catholic priest's answer to a questioner's objection to the severity of the punishment for Original Sin. (This is from one of my Catholic books from the 1940s, *Radio Replies*, Vol 2, by Rev. Dr. Leslie Rumble and Rev. Charles Mortimer Carty. The Church doesn't talk this honestly about its beliefs any more—doesn't sell well):

> . . . I do deny that God has treated the human race unjustly. It has deserved far more suffering than it has received, and has not deserved the great blessings God has deigned to bestow on it.

How comforting. Fortunately, the human condition is far more easily explained, and without the punitive bullying, by the scientifically verifi-able evolutionary process. The reliance on Original Sin to explain life's hardships creates a theological version of "Alice in Wonderland" where one disappears down a metaphysical rabbit hole and things get curiouser and curiouser. The absurdity starts with a talking snake . . . goes to a man made of clay and a woman made of his rib . . . has them tricked into eating a forbidden fruit that gives them the knowledge of good and evil (which they didn't have before, so why were they wrong in eating it?) . . . goes on to justify patriarchal misogynistic views of women and that any sex act done in any but the missionary position is immoral . . . winds down with doctrinal fiats opposing fertility technology . . . and hits rock bottom with the current insanity that there are such things as microscopic single-celled persons who must be saved at all costs, with dozens of laws proposed and enacted to ensure that.

Thanks to theology's endless mystical pratfalls over hundreds of years, much of our society has been dragged down that rabbit hole. Below are examples of what it's like in that theological Wonderland.

The Varieties of Theological Sex Absurdities

This is a summary of the more noteworthy theological absurdities that have caused people so much misery and frustration for engaging in harmless sexual behaviors. The beliefs come from the Catholic Church because its views tend to dominate the culture. Its strength and influence derive from being the only institution that has been in existence continuously for 2,000 years and having the global monolithic structure that can ensure a consistent doctrinal discipline. No other religious institution comes close to its theological depth and breadth, however much that distances it from reality.

More importantly, it has always insisted that the laws of society support its views on moral issues. Every election year brings dogma-directed voters' guides along with threats of excommunication for Catholic politicians who refuse to establish the religion of the Catholic Church in laws related to sex, marriage and reproduction. Fundamentalist Protestants agree with the Catholic Church on moral issues generally (with some exceptions regarding divorce and contraception), while basing their position on Bible verses alone. Together, these authoritarian institutions are a formidable threat to our secular democracy and freedom of conscience.

The theology of sex covers about two millennia of obsessing over one idea—that sex is a necessary evil to be used only for procreation, always open to the transmission of life, and not to be thought about lustfully or acted upon in any circumstances other than within a monogamous marriage between one man and one woman united for life in the sacrament of matrimony. Here is an excerpt from a Catholic pamphlet titled "How to Conquer the Most Common Sin of Impurity." It follows a list of four actions (all innocuous thoughts, mostly sex-related) that lead to the dreaded mortal sin described, inexplicably, as "self-abuse":

> These principles apply equally to married and single persons, and equally to men and to women. They flow directly from the established premise that sex actions and sex pleasure must never be deliberately separated from the sublime primary purpose for

which God designed them, a purpose that even in marriage must never be destroyed or frustrated.

The problem here is with the claim that there is an "established premise" supporting these tightly constrained, irrational conclusions regarding sex and marriage. The pamphlet states:

> It is from these basic concepts and principles that we draw a knowledge of the natural law forbidding any deliberate indulgence in sex pleasure outside of marriage, whether alone or with others, and any deliberate frustration or destruction of the purpose of sex in marriage.

Aha! So it is from unverifiable religion-based assumptions that we derive the "natural law" that all sex is sinful except when tightly constrained as specified. The actual verifiable fact is that natural law is only a description of how nature works. It's not something deliberated about somewhere and enacted into a "law." It just describes what is. Where sex is concerned, from what we can observe, it does not conform to religious notions of "basic concepts and principles."

But the belief is there, and so down the rabbit hole we go, where the following are acts said to be so evil that they deserve eternal hellfire—or at least a few laws and public policies based on the theology to complicate the lives of those who aren't buying any of this.

Masturbation. We have here the ultimate safe sex—effective, harmless, free and readily available. In the great scheme of things, it is no more significant than scratching an itch. Yet sex-phobic religions have elevated it to cosmic importance. From the pamphlet:

> . . . [O]ne addicted to solitary acts of impurity is corrupt and depraved . . . . The only way to protect the higher interests of all human beings, both individually and socially, is to cling to or return to Christian standards. Sex has duties as well as privileges. It is an opportunity for self-sacrifice, and the serving of God as well as the best interests of the human race. The procreation of children is the explanation and justification of sex indulgences. That is lawful only in the married state. Outside marriage, therefore,

all indulgences in sex pleasure deliberately sought is a perversion, immoral, and sinful before God.

To put this foolishness in context, keep in mind that it is brought to you by the same people who see leftover frozen embryos in fertility clinics as "snowflake children" to be adopted by a willing uterus, and who seek a "personhood amendment" to the Constitution that declares fertilized eggs to be persons with all the attendant rights to life, liberty and the pursuit of happiness. . . . Well, at least until birth. They never show much (if any) concern for the life, liberty and pursuit of happiness of born persons.

The idea that sex might be enjoyed without any adverse consequences is apparently too horrible for some religious people to contemplate. Two examples:

1. In 1995, President Bill Clinton was pressured to remove Dr. Joycelyn Elders as U.S. Surgeon General by the huge controversy that erupted when Dr. Elders suggested that masturbation could usefully be included in high school sex education classes. She was accused of wanting it taught (although it hardly requires teaching). As Dr. Elders said, "God taught us how," and the only thing students need to learn is that "masturbation never got anybody pregnant, does not make anybody go crazy, and what we're about is preventing HIV in our bright young people."

Notice theology's shifting sands at work here as Dr. Elders, a religious liberal, redefines the reproductive-purpose-only theology of the religiously conservative to move it closer to reality. And she's right. If one believes in God, it makes sense to say, "God taught us how," because humans come equipped knowing how to enjoy sex in many ways. If the transmission of life were the only purpose of sex, one would expect that to be the only way it could be enjoyed. Obviously it's not. Religious speculation about lessons from God aside, it is far more likely that solo sex is a harmless consequence of the variety-loving evolutionary process. No doubt it is beneficial when other types of sexual outlets are unavailable or unwise.

2. Then, in 2010, Christine O'Donnell, a Tea Party candidate for the U.S. Senate in Delaware, won the Republican primary. She became notoriously newsworthy with her announcement that masturbation should be outlawed because she considered it adultery, which is based on lust,

which the Bible opposes. Although outlawing masturbation is impossible, its underlying theocratic assumptions about sex are reflected in other restrictive laws and social policies.

Interestingly, there appears to be little theological attention paid to female masturbation beyond a generalized opposition to sex being enjoyed free of reproductive consequences. All attention is on the male experience. Perhaps it's due to the theological concern for men "wasting their seed," even though they have zillions of sperm always available and the supply never seems to run out. Several planets could be populated with a few ejaculations. Women have no "seed" they are physically able to waste, other than by avoiding sex during an ovulatory period . . . but wait! *Isn't that what they do when they follow the Vatican-approved rhythm method of birth control!?*

Contraception. This is a problem foisted on us in various legal ways by those who have no workable understanding of sex. Ranking in first place in all-time, world class, dumb-as-a-rock ignorance is the Vatican. The Protestant fundamentalists, whose position is a bit more nuanced, are mostly horrified by teens enjoying sex; the Vatican is horrified by anyone enjoying it except in the most carefully controlled and approved libido-deadening situations.

Reinforcing this ignorance is the papal view of evolution as having a God-given purpose. Since sex so often leads to procreation, that must be its purpose. It's not. Nothing evolves for a purpose. Evolution is a mindless process that has no purpose, only consequences, some we interpret as bad, some as good, depending on their effect on us. People deal with these consequences, accepting some and rejecting others according to their needs. The consequences of consensual sex include physical pleasure, the transmission of microbial life (disease) and the transmission of human life. So what purpose do we humans derive from these consequences? Simple observation shows the primary purpose is almost always pleasure. The transmission of disease and life are side effects, with disease fought off relentlessly and life often welcomed, but sometimes not.

The Catholic theological view of contraception has no understanding of this and so is overrun with contradictions and absurdities. The following is from the Pastoral Letter "Marriage, Love and Life in the Divine Plan" cited earlier. Does any of it look like a reflection of reality? Quoting from an earlier pastoral letter, the bishops say:

"By using contraception," married couples "may think that they are avoiding problems or easing tensions, that they are exerting control over their lives." At the same time, they may think they are doing nothing harmful to their marriages. In reality, the deliberate separation of the procreative and unitive meanings of marriage has the potential to damage or destroy the marriage. Also, it results in many other negative consequences, both personal and social.

> Conjugal love is diminished whenever the union of a husband and wife is reduced to a means of self-gratification. The procreative capacity of male and female is dehumanized, reduced to a kind of internal biological technology that one masters and controls just like any other technology.

> . . . The procreative capacity of man and woman should not be treated as just another means of technology, as also happens with *in vitro* fertilization (IVF) or cloning. When that happens, human life itself is degraded because it becomes, more and more, something produced or manufactured in various ways, ways that will only multiply as science advances. Children begin to be seen less as gifts received in a personal communion of mutual self-giving, and increasingly as a lifestyle choice, a commodity to which all consumers are entitled. There is a true issue of the dignity of human life at stake here.

It would be helpful if examples of this supposed damage—this destruction and negative consequences, this diminished conjugal love, this treating of children as a commodity—were provided. I know of none, neither in my personal experience and among my relatives and friends, nor in stories from others—not even in literary fiction. (I suppose somewhere in time and space there may be exceptions, but they only prove the rule.) On the other hand, don't all of us know many examples of the harm done by lack of contraception from the same personal experiences and associations, as well as from observing the effects of poverty and overpopulation throughout the larger society?

Contraception is closely related to masturbation in the medieval theological view. It is actually defined as mutual masturbation ("reciprocal vice"). Here's the infallible doctrine, taken verbatim from another of my old Catholic books, Vol. 3 of *Radio Replies* by Rumble and Carty (Vol. 2 referenced earlier), officially authorized with the imprimatur of John Gregory Murray, archbishop of St. Paul, with a Preface by the renowned Msgr. Fulton J. Sheen, famous for having his own prime time TV show in the '60s. It answers the question, "Where is birth control forbidden in Scripture?"

It is rather grimly hinted at in the case of Onan as recorded in Genesis 38:10, for Onan was struck dead by God. [Onan was supposed to impregnate his brother's widow, as was the custom, but he did not want to do that, so when he had sex with her, he "spilled his seed on the ground."] And Scripture describes his contraceptive practice as a detestable thing. However, it would not matter in the least if there were no concrete reference to birth control in Scripture. Scripture gives the general principles of morality, and lays down clearly the obligations of marriage. Birth control by contraception is immoral of its very nature, being but reciprocal vice; and violates the Christian obligation of marriage. No sane person would deny the immorality of one's becoming a cocaine fiend. Yet that is not mentioned in Scripture. The natural moral law existed before a line of Scripture was written, and still exists, being in no way abolished by Scripture.

OK, let's see how this works. Contraception is immoral because it is mutual masturbation, which is immoral, just as using cocaine is immoral. This argument falls apart because harm is assumed, not demonstrated, based on an assumed immorality based on unverifiable religious beliefs. Only the use of cocaine (which is not immoral, just stupid) can be demonstrated to harm one's health and ability to function. The theology holds that great spiritual and temporal harm is caused by masturbation and contraception, although no examples are given. What we get are endless repetitions of this "rabbit hole" thinking, like the following (again from Rumble and Carty), which is useful to show definitively the nonsense we are up against:

. . . Man's intelligence must rule blind passion by self-control, not abdicate in favor of the irresponsible beast. Like the conductor of an orchestra, the mind of man must coordinate perfectly all the impulses of that marvelous instrument called the body of man. Introduce into this temple of art an unclean brute beast, and what becomes of reason? Contraceptive birth control weakens the flesh, poisons the blood, tangles the nerves with disorderly destructive and spasmodic violence, and renders those guilty of it less and less fit to be parents at all. . . .

Now let's take a more realistic look at this vacuous claptrap. I will quote from the best and most comprehensive book I have come across on the theology of sex, *Eunuchs for the Kingdom of Heaven: Women, Sexuality and the Catholic Church*, by Uta Ranke-Heinemann. She is a German Catholic theologian who has taken it upon herself to investigate the Catholic Church's theological absurdities and give them the boot they deserve. Here she observes the Vatican's "fruits of theological imbecility" as it has struggled to maintain doctrinal consistency since the advent of the pill forced it up and out of the rabbit hole, giving Pope Pius X11 a unique problem.

> Since his predecessor Pius XI had condemned any kind of ster-ilization for the purpose of preventing conception, the pill had to be banned as well. No surprise there; we cannot expect a pope to deviate from the opinions of his predecessor. Papal infallibility serves as a brake on independent thinking. But Pius XI was unable to provide Pius XII with a special justification for rejecting the pill, because there was no pill in 1930. Here Pius XII had to be creative. . . . The pope means that nature's intention, procreation, may under no circumstances be thwarted, even when nature cannot bear the procreation, and the woman will die on account of the pregnancy. The pope, then, is defending a morality that marches over corpses.

Well said, but more has to be said about sterilization. It gets mentioned frequently as a contraceptive method, but that's not the whole story. Sterilization runs up against the Catholic Church's prohibition against mutilating the body for non-therapeutic reasons because the body is said to be the temple of the Holy Spirit and belongs to God. The 1994 Catechism of the Catholic Church, #2297, states. "Except when performed for strictly therapeutic medical reasons, directly intended amputations, mutilations, and sterilizations are against the moral law." When done to avoid pregnancy or to have a more "uninhibited and guilt-free sex life," as the Secretary General of the Bishops' Conference of Bogota, Colombia, said in 2010, it is immoral.

If so, why didn't the Church see anything immoral about it during the Middle Ages (from 1600 to 1750) when it approved the castration of young male singers to preserve their soprano voices for the church choirs? This was deemed necessary because high voices were needed and women were not allowed to participate in church services. Not exactly a "strictly therapeutic medical reason."

The effects on these boys (called the *Castrati*—"the castrated ones") as they grew older included personality disorders and an inability to lead a normal sex life. Most of them had poorly developed sex organs and the growth of their limbs was distorted. Apparently, it was better to mutilate those temples of the Holy Spirit and destroy those boys' lives than to allow women to sing in church choirs.

The Missionary Position. This is something theology no longer dwells on any more (at least not directly), but it deserves some attention to highlight the appalling lack of intellectual competence at work these past 2,000 years. It's not a pretty sight. Here is Ranke-Heinemann again, quoting St. Thomas Aquinas (1225?-74), called "the Angelic Doctor," the Church's preeminent theologian whose writings are widely quoted by church authorities and form the basis for much of Catholic doctrine.

> . . . Deviation from the missionary position, [Thomas Aquinas] believes, is one of a series of unnatural vices that were classified, in a system going back to Augustine, as worse than intercourse with one's own mother. This ban on other sexual positions does not quite fit into Thomas's schema, because the other unnatural vices he catalogues have the common feature of excluding generation. In exceptional cases he does allow other positions, when couples cannot have sex any other way for medical reasons. . . . Thomas holds that the other most seriously sinful— because they are unnatural—vices, worse than incest, rape and adultery, are masturbation, bestiality, homosexuality, anal and oral intercourse, and coitus interruptus (*Summa Theologiae* II/

II q. 154 a. II). Thomas appears to put deviation from the missionary position on the list of the most serious sins because he thought that, like the other acts on this list that prevented conception, this one made conception more difficult.

What is difficult here is to see anything that makes sense. However, the Catholic Church does seem to have at least qualified the sinfulness of non-missionary-position sex since then. This is hearsay, but according to what I've been told about the advice given by at least one Catholic priest, all sex positions are now OK "as long as you end up in the right place."

Perhaps we can consider that as some kind of progress. But maybe not. There still remains the theological position on the missionary position regarding its effect on people whose disabilities make that unworkable. Canon law does not consider a marriage valid if the couple is sexually incapacitated, although procreation is possible for them in some circumstances. Once again, Ranke-Heinemann separates the real-world from what is going on down in that rabbit hole:

> . . . [F]or some paraplegics . . . Catholic marriage law is as unbearable now as it ever was. . . . The Church dictates the precise form of the conjugal act to everybody and does this in a way that demotes a paraplegic and his partner to the level of infants, because according to Catholic sexual morality intimacies are allowed only in marriage and only in connection with the standardized intercourse conceded by the Church. This sort of interference in everyone's right to marriage is intolerable and shows once more that the celibates running the Church would be better advised not to get mixed up in such matters.

Then there's the matter of condoms. There's no need to go into the well-known theological hostility toward them as contraceptives. But when the AIDS virus entered the human population, the hostility reached a level of depravity almost unimaginable. Quoting Ranke-Heinemann:

> With the International Congress of moral theologians held in Rome in November 1988, the papal campaign against contraception reached new heights. If the pope weren't the pope, his position might put him at odds with the state penal code.

According to John Paul II and his spokesman, Carlo Caffarra, head of the Pontifical Institute for Marriage and Family Matters, a hemophiliac with AIDS may not have intercourse with his wife, *ever*, not even after her menopause, because God has forbidden condoms. And if the hemophiliac husband can't manage to abstain, it's better for him to infect his wife than to use a condom. Catholic sexual morality has turned into a morality of horror."

But can the woman refuse to have sex under such conditions? Possibly, if it is *certain*—not just highly probable—that her life is in danger. However, public outrage over this twisted view of morality may be having some effect. In 2009, when Pope Benedict, on a visit to Africa, said condoms could not be used to combat AIDS because they might make the epidemic worse, outrage followed. And so, in 2010, the pope cautiously made it public that condoms may be a lesser evil to prevent the spread of AIDS in homosexual relationships. Janet Smith, a Vatican advisor who teaches ethics at Sacred Heart Major Seminary in Detroit, spun the about-face this way:

The Holy Father is simply observing that for some homosexual prostitutes, the use of a condom may indicate an awakening of a moral sense, an awakening that sexual pleasure is not the highest value.

Or is it that, since there can be no transmission of life in homosexual sex, and the participants are probably bound for hell anyway, why not at least try to keep AIDS from spreading? Regardless, the door is now open to possibly protecting the wives of AIDS infected men—at least those who are past menopause. It's a start.

However, refusing to have sex just to prevent a pregnancy is also forbidden, and always has been. Spouses are obliged to fulfill their "marital duty" to each other to prevent the other person from "stumbling into fornication." OK, so we can see that a husband can demand his marital rights and his wife could comply, willing or not, because she just has to lie there. Regardless of any harmful consequences to the wife, at least she saved her husband from committing a sin. On the other hand, if the wife demands her marital rights, she is out of luck if her husband can't "get it up." Her demands are useless and any sinful stumbling on her part is all her fault, not her husband's. Medieval theology considers the woman's circumstances as of no importance. (Of course, now that men have Viagra . . .)

Better Dead than Raped. On the other hand, refusing to have sex is not only allowed but demanded when a woman is attacked by a rapist. It's about protecting one's chastity. The Catholic Church has the saints to show for this. It has something of a tradition of conferring sainthood on women who resist a rapist at the cost of their lives. The first step to sainthood is beatification and earns the recipient the title of Blessed. The most recent of these ultimate recognitions of holiness was in 1987 when Pope John Paul II beatified two Italian women who had allowed themselves to be killed rather than submit to rape. One of the women was murdered in 1957 at the age of 26. The other was murdered in 1935 at the age of 16.

In 1950, another Italian girl, Maria Goretti, was elevated from Blessed to Sainthood. She had died in 1902 at age 12 at the hands of a rapist— Alexander, an 18-year-old neighbor. Pope Pius XII canonized her as a model of sexual purity, declaring her the patroness of youth, young women, purity, and victims of rape. Maria's story was the preeminent morality tale for girls when I was going to Catholic school as Maria's canonization approached. The last time I checked (in 2013) she was still being promoted as a role model for chastity (www.catholic.org/saints/saint.php?saint_id=78). As the web site says, "She is called a martyr because she fought against Alexander's attempts at sexual assault."

I well remember the nuns telling us the inspiring story of that assault: how Maria had been stabbed to death while resisting rape, how she cried out that she would not submit because to do so would be a mortal sin, how Alexander was sent to prison, where in due time he piously repented and spent his last years praying for forgiveness to the saint he had such an important role in creating.

Of course, every woman who is killed resisting rape does not get honored by the Catholic Church. The facts of the woman's life—and death— must show that: 1) She was an intensely devout and dutiful servant of the Church throughout her life. 2) She had made it clear in words and deeds that she would rather die than commit a sin. 3) Her death was a direct result of her refusal to submit to rape. In other words, she knew she could save herself by submitting, but chose death rather than offend God by sinning.

What is a rational person to make of this? What can we say of a theology that puts forth the belief that a woman, when she is threatened by a rapist, must not even consider submitting when the knife is at her throat? What kind of moral teaching is this that says a woman who submits to rape, rather than be killed, commits a sin of any kind? How many women have died at the hands of rapists because their Catholic indoctrination so confused them when they were under attack that they could not save themselves?

This raises another question: Why is submitting to rape when one's life is in danger a sin? Is it that Catholic theologians assume that any time a woman engages in sex, regardless of circumstances, she enjoys it? Is it that their theology compels them to regard any sexual activity outside of monogamous marriage for the purpose or procreation as sinful? One has to wonder at the workings of the celibate priestly mind, that these men would think a terrified woman, desperately trying to save her life, would enjoy such an encounter.

But perhaps there is another rationale underlying the Church's better-dead-than-raped theology. It is patriarchal religious beliefs, after all, that have promoted the idea that women have no value in their own right, but only as they serve men's purposes, as men's property. Female virginity is mandated by patriarchal religions as a way of ensuring male sexual control over women—of keeping women "unspoiled" until they become a man's property through marriage. If Catholic theologians have so little respect for a woman's humanity, if they consider her men's property, why wouldn't they encourage her to die rather than have that property "spoiled"?

Fertility Technology. Here we are dealing with couples who want to have children, not avoid having them. One would think the Church would be supportive. But no, it's just another descent into immorality. Why? Because fertility testing requires a man to ejaculate into a Petri dish, usually while looking at a pornographic magazine to help the process along. This is how fertility clinics get the sperm needed for testing. But the theological pinheads see only lustful thoughts and sex that is not open to the transmission of life, with no wife involved and not even in the missionary position. All they see is that dreaded masturbation. I read about a woman teacher in a Catholic school in Indiana being fired for using fertility treatments to get pregnant with her husband. Normal people would think that admirable, but the woman's parish priest called her a "grave, immoral sinner."

However, all is not lost, for a way has been found to provide sperm for testing while still having sexual intercourse in the theologically correct way. All you need is a leaky condom. Ridiculous religious beliefs are satisfied because the perforations allow for the possibility of conception while enough semen remains in the condom for fertility testing. The standard masturbation way of collecting semen would be much better because it is less complicated. However, since religious nonsense requires nonsense workarounds, for those hooked on that nonsense, this is one way to deal with it.

Then there's *in vitro* fertilization (for which no leaky loopholes have been found) that might allow the couple to have a child. The sperm get mixed in the Petri dish with the woman's eggs so embryos can develop and be implanted in the woman's uterus. Several embryos have to be created to ensure that at least one takes hold. The rest are destroyed or frozen for possible later use.

This brings us up against the theology of abortion, where a fertilized egg is proclaimed to be a person. *Yes!* . . . a microscopic single-celled person the size of the period at the end of this sentence. This is human imagination run amok—a clear case of insanity! But the "pro-life" fanatics are sticking with it.

The religious mind is nothing if not inventive. Because abortion is sometimes necessary to save a woman's life, the theologians have been forced to find a way to avoid the public outrage if these maternal deaths get out of hand. One of the causes of these deaths is an ectopic pregnancy (when the fertilized egg attaches itself to something outside the uterus, sometimes the woman's intestines, but usually within one of the two fallopian tubes. It cannot get very big in there—maybe only to seven or eight weeks gestation—and has to be removed or the woman will die. And, of course, it will die too.

It is a case of an abnormal pregnancy in an abnormal place—but that's nature's "intelligent design" for you. Yet the Catholic Church decrees that no abortion can be performed. What to do? This is where the theology of secondary effects comes in. To deliberately remove the fetus would be considered murder. *But* to remove a fallopian tube that is causing trouble by entrapping the fetus is OK. If the fetus dies, that is considered an unintended secondary effect.

Sounds like a way out? Not quite. If the fetus is removed from the tube the woman's ability to bear children is preserved. If the tube (which just happens to contain a fetus) is removed, her childbearing ability is severely compromised if not ended. But that doesn't matter to those who put dogma before people as long as the anti-abortion political position can be salvaged.

Finally, there's yet another problem, and it's a theological biggie. If Original Sin is transmitted through sexual intercourse, but there is no intercourse—only sperm ejaculated into a Petri dish and mixed with some eggs retrieved from the woman's ovaries—how would Original Sin be transmitted?

Maybe the Church hopes to avoid that conundrum by getting laws passed that outlaw this form of fertility technology, but the problem remains. Lots of babies are out there that have been created this way without intercourse. Lots of fertilized eggs and embryos created the same way are stored in clinic freezers. Do any of them have souls? If not, how can they be considered real persons? If so, did God implant the soul but not the Original Sin because sexual intercourse wasn't involved? Would such persons be immaculate conceptions, incapable of sinning?

The theologians have their work cut out for them. For those of us not living down that rabbit hole, our work is cut out for us too, and it consists of keeping these theological absurdities from infesting our laws.

Religion vs. Theology

Time to come up out of the rabbit hole. These are purely religious views that have no place in our public life. Some directly affect only believers but may produce indirect social costs that affect the larger community. Regardless, the underlying theology clouds our entire legal and social-policy approach to sex-related issues.

Laws criminalizing birth control services were ruled unconstitutional only as recently as 1965 in *Griswold v. Connecticut.* Laws criminalizing anal and oral sex were declared unconstitutional in 2002 in *Lawrence v. Texas.* Laws against same-sex marriage are the latest to be repealed. Given the embedded nature of our theology-based laws, these cases should have been argued as a violation of the Establishment Clause, rather than on the right to privacy. That right is only implied, leaving it open to being compromised—which is happening.

The Establishment Clause might have produced clearer rulings. Laws against contraception and homosexuality either have a religious basis or they do not. They either have a *valid* secular purpose or they do not. (Contrived "secular" purposes don't count.) The same either-or argument applies to all restrictive theology-based laws. To mean anything, the Establishment Clause has to be concerned with more than religious mottoes and patriotic pledges. It has to extend to laws that do real harm to people.

The *Griswold* and *Lawrence* right to privacy rulings get compromised as religious-right legislative opposition tries to redefine almost all contraceptives as abortifacients, restricts sex education and invents dire warnings about homosexual relationships' effect on society. There is a major legislative effort to further restrict abortion rights, defund Planned Parenthood, reverse same-sex marriage rights, and generally undo the social progress made in the last half-century or more. What is the secular justification for any of this?

4

NATURE'S SEXUAL DIVERSITY: MUGGED BY MYTHOLOGY

"If writing the demands of the Book of Leviticus into the Constitution is not a state-church separation issue, then I don't know what is."
—Randall Tigue, constitutional law attorney

Never discount the tenacity of sex-obsessed religious authoritarians. They go down fighting when their punitive legislative demands are rejected but pop up again as soon as a new aspect of sexuality surfaces that can be greeted with horror and restrictive legislation. In June of 2015, the U.S. Supreme Court ruled that same-sex marriage is allowed by the Constitution. It's a done deal, the sky hasn't fallen, and one more religion-based law has gone into the legal trash bin. But the battle goes on as we continue to be mugged by mythology.

Now it's all about the "religious liberty" established by the U.S. Supreme Court's *Burwell v Hobby Lobby* decision that granted employers the religion-based right to impose their beliefs on employees through employer-provided healthcare insurance.

Of course, "employer-provided" does not mean it is a gratuitous benefit. It is part of a wage package strategy developed years ago when President Nixon imposed wage and price controls to help stabilize the economy. With labor unions unable to negotiate wage increases, employer-paid healthcare insurance was negotiated as a substitute and soon became a standard part of most wage packages. Therefore, reducing employees' insurance coverage for any reason is a cut in pay.

To reduce insurance coverage for economic reasons is a matter for negotiation, but to do it to impose the employer's religious beliefs on the employees is religious tyranny. In the *Hobby Lobby* case, the religious right-dominated Court ruled that the employer's religious liberty superseded the employees' First Amendment right to be free of such tyranny.

The *Hobby Lobby* ruling was all about protecting believers in a politically favored religion from being complicit—even at an absurdly marginal level—with a behavior they believe is immoral. That includes, of course, same-sex marriage, contraception, abortion, and the whole range of religious views covered in this book. Are there more? Of course. Now we have religious right bakers and photographers refusing to provide wedding cakes and photography. Other forms of discrimination are beginning to follow as opportunities arise. As of this writing, it looks like "religious liberty" is heading for the Supreme Court where it is likely to get a majority for approval.

We have a president who promised to nominate Supreme Court justices who will do the religious right's bidding. Neil Gorsuch is the first, filling the vacancy left by the death of Antonin Scalia. Gorsuch is on record for (as a judge in the 10th Circuit Court) having concurred with that lower Court's decision in favor of Hobby Lobby.

The Court is now back to a 5-4 conservative majority. Within the next few years there will probably be an opening on the Court among the always left-leaning justices and the sometimes left-leaning Anthony Kennedy. Meanwhile, Trump has started filling the many openings in lower level district appellate courts that have long been vacant because the Republicans refused to confirm President Obama's nominees or even give them a hearing.

Recently a new aspect of sexuality surfaced that almost no one saw coming. Welcome to the newly discovered fluid world of gender identity and the ridiculous bathroom battles it has set off. More on that later, but first we need to review the same-sex marriage controversy and the nature of sexuality so we can put gender identity in context.

Theology vs. Sexual Common Sense

For several years now the religion-based culture war against homosexuality has been facing defeat. Sodomy laws were declared unconstitutional and same-sex marriage was heading that way. Granting civil rights to lesbians, gays, bisexuals and transgenders (LGBT), which had long horrified authoritarian religions, was a done deal in legal terms, despite ongoing threats of punitive legislation and individual exercises in bigotry and harassment.

But the festering homophobia was still out there. The culture war between the religious right and the liberal left had been too long and too hard to end easily with gay rights-supportive court rulings. For centuries, armed with papal pronouncements and a Bible that calls homosexuality an abomination deserving of capital punishment, the religious authoritarians had established laws that marginalized and persecuted sexual minorities and criminalized their sexual behavior. But there was progress.

Since the 1970s in the United States, a gay rights rebellion against religion-based restrictive laws has achieved repeal of most of them. In 2003, the U.S. Supreme Court ended the worst of the discriminatory laws: the criminalization of homosexual sex (sodomy) in its *Lawrence v. Texas* ruling. The decision reversed the *Bowers v. Hardwick* lower court ruling that upheld Georgia's statute prohibiting oral and anal sex by both homosexuals and heterosexuals. The statute had used a "community consensus" on morality to deny a right to privacy. *Lawrence* rejected the idea that majority perceptions can justify the denial of rights for a minority.

In *Lawrence*, Justice Anthony Kennedy, supporting reversal, noted that centuries of majority hatred of homosexuality *based on religious views* had driven discrimination against homosexuals. Justice Sandra Day O'Connor, also supporting reversal and noting the element of hatred, said, "We have consistently held, however, that some objectives, such as a bare desire to harm a politically unpopular group, are not legitimate state interests . . . [and] have applied a more searching form of rational basis review to strike down such laws under the equal protection clause."

Despite the *Lawrence* ruling, discrimination persisted and has been covered substantially in the mainstream media. In 29 states gays and lesbians could be fired because of their sexual orientation, and in 35 states they could be fired for being transgender. Because of this, LGBT people often hid who they were. In many school districts, LGBT students could be bullied and harassed with little recourse to prevent it. Since then, many anti-bullying statutes have been passed. However, because Trump has expressed such an eagerness to satisfy his Christian evangelical base, he may be willing to support Republican efforts to undo much of this progress.

One of the worst forms of abuse was and continues to be the bullying in high school of gay teens, driving some of them to suicide. Here's an example of the religious right's barbaric manner of dealing with this form of persecution as described in a *Huffington Post* report: In 2011 the Republican controlled Michigan senate passed "Matt's Safe School Law." It was an anti-bullying law, but it exempted religion-motivated bullying from prosecution.

Ironically, the bill as originally proposed was a response to the 2002 suicide of a gay teen who had been bullied by his classmates for being gay. Although the intent of the bill was to penalize such behavior, the Republicans modified it to exempt religion-based bullying. The Republican-passed version of the law "allows harassment by teachers and students as long as they can claim their actions are rooted in a 'sincerely held religious belief or moral conviction.' Therefore, those who truly believed homosexuality was wrong were free to torment classmates consequence-free."

Strong opposition to this bill from Democrats caused its sponsor, Republican senator Rick Jones, to reconsider it. He allowed that it "may not be perfect," but believed it to be "a step in the right direction." In 2012 in Minnesota, the same barbarism was exhibited when an anti-bullying school policy was deemed by religious right opponents as "unfair to students with conservative values."

In many states when same-sex marriage was still illegal, opponents of homosexuality attempted to deny lesbian and gay couples the right to adopt children or become foster parents. In Minnesota (and probably other states), a gay couple with children was treated differently under the law with regard to obligations, rights, taxes, benefits, etc., from an identically situated straight couple with children. Until same-sex marriage was ruled constitutional, Minnesota actually had 515 statutes that discriminate against committed domestic partners, including same-sex couples.

LGBT and Same-Sex Marriage Skirmishes

Of course, the religion-based views of one religion are not the same as those of another, though all are based on the Bible. Liberal religions aim for a humane approach, choosing the Bible's "love" verses, while conservative religions tend to prefer the equally mandatory "kill" verses.

Some have tried the middle road of loving the sinner while hating the sin by being at least socially accepting. Others have decided that God loves everyone and have gone the whole nine yards, ordaining gay clergy and marrying same-sex couples.

With laws against sodomy declared unconstitutional, same-sex marriage moved to the political front lines in the secular vs. sacred controversy. By 2013, only seven states had legalized it—Connecticut, Iowa, Massachusetts, New Hampshire, New York, Vermont, and the District of Columbia.

In 2000, in California, voters passed Proposition 22, which banned same-sex marriages. This was challenged and went to the state Supreme Court, which, in 2008, ruled that same-sex marriages were constitutional based on 1) the state constitution's equal protection clause, 2) marriage being a civil right, and 3) the state having no compelling interest in prohibiting same-sex marriages. As a result, about 18,000 same-sex couples got married.

This set off a campaign to prohibit same-sex marriage by constitutional amendment, so Proposition 8 went on the ballot and passed. This was challenged and this time the state Supreme Court ruled Proposition 8 constitutional because 1) being a constitutional amendment, its provisions were automatically constitutional, 2) the equal protection didn't apply because only the word "marriage" was relevant and domestic partnerships were not affected, and 3) not being retroactive, existing same-sex marriages were not affected.

The state of California refused to defend the constitutionality of Proposition 8 and left the defense to the religious zealots who started the petition drive. This placed the religious motive front and center and supporters of same-sex marriage filed a separate lawsuit on federal constitutional grounds.

Their case went before federal district court Judge Vaughn Walker, who ruled in 2010 that Proposition 8 was unconstitutional, with the Ninth Circuit Court affirming the decision in 2012. Judge Walker's reasons (as well as those of the Ninth Circuit Court) demolished the supposedly secular arguments against same sex marriage, finding "no rational basis" to oppose it. Walker noted how weak the arguments were. He cited all of them and concluded:

> The court provided proponents with an opportunity to identify a harm they would face "if an injunction against Proposition 8 is issued." Proponents replied that they have an interest in defending Proposition 8 but failed to articulate even one specific harm they may suffer as a consequence of the injunction. . . . Proponents had a full opportunity to provide evidence in support of their position and nevertheless failed to present even one credible witness on the government interest in Proposition 8.

With these controversial state and federal rulings, the only place left to go was the U.S. Supreme Court. The makeup of the Court did not inspire confidence in a secular-based ruling. However, one thing working for advocates of same-sex marriage was that the opponents found it impossible to come up with arguments that made sense that didn't include "Because God says so."

The Supreme Court turned out to be unwilling to blatantly repudiate the First Amendment's establishment clause and in 2015, in *Obergefell v. Hodges*, it held, in a 5-4 decision, that the right to marry is guaranteed to same-sex couples by the Due Process clause and the Equal Protection clause of the 14th Amendment to the U.S. Constitution. (See https://en.wikipedia.org/wiki/Obergefell v. Hodges.)

Sexuality and the Natural Law: It Is What It Is

Arguments for denying sexual minorities the same rights the heterosexual majority takes for granted are based on Bible-based religious doctrine along with a religious interpretation of natural law. It is taken as a given that this "law" has produced males and females for reproductive purposes. Therefore, all sexual activity must be limited to male-female copulation and anything else is unnatural. The Protestant fundamentalists and the U.S. Catholic bishops mounted a ferocious campaign to outlaw same-sex marriage based on this religious view of natural law. Here is the rationale, from the United States Conference of Catholic Bishops' 2009 Pastoral Letter:

. . . Marriage is a unique union, a relationship different from all others. It is the permanent bond between one man and one woman whose two-in-one-flesh communion of persons is an indispensable good at the heart of every family and every society. Same-sex unions are incapable of realizing this specific communion of persons. Therefore, attempting to redefine marriage to include such relationships empties the term of its meaning, for it excludes the essential complementarity between man and woman, treating sexual differences as if it were irrelevant to what marriage is.

Male-female complementarity is intrinsic to marriage. It is naturally ordered toward authentic union and the generation of new life. Children are meant to be the gift of the permanent and exclusive union of a husband and wife. A child is meant to have a mother and a father. The true nature of marriage, lived in openness to life, is a witness to the precious gift of the child and to the unique roles of a mother and father. Same-sex unions are incapable of such a witness. Consequently, making them equivalent to marriage disregards the very nature of marriage.

Jesus teaches that marriage is between a man and a woman. "Have you not read that from the beginning the Creator 'made them male and female' . . . For this reason a man shall leave his father and mother and be joined to his wife, and the two shall become one flesh" (Mt 19:4-6).

. . . Today, advocacy for the legal recognition of various same-sex relationships is often equated with non-discrimina-tion, fairness, equality, and civil rights. However, it is not unjust to oppose legal recognition of same-sex unions, because marriage and same-sex unions are essentially different realities. "The denial of the social and legal status of marriage to forms of cohabitation that are not and cannot be marital is not opposed to justice; on the contrary, justice requires it" [quoting from the Catholic Church's 2003 Congregation for the Doctrine of the Faith publication No. 8, "Considerations Regarding Proposals to Give Legal Recognition to Unions Between Homosexual Persons"].

To promote and protect marriage as the union of one man and one woman is itself a matter of justice. In fact, it would be a grave injustice if the state ignored the unique and proper place of husbands and wives, the place of mothers and fathers, and especially the rights of children, who deserve from society clear guidance as they grow to sexual maturity. Indeed, without this protection the state would, in effect, *intentionally* deprive children of the right to a mother and father.

. . . [T]he Church teaches that homosexual acts "are contrary to the natural law. They close the sexual act to the gift of life. They do not proceed from a genuine affective and sexual complementarity. Under no circumstances can they be approved" [quoting from the Catechism of the Catholic Church, No. 2357].

. . . The legal recognition of same-sex unions poses a multifaceted threat to the very fabric of society, striking at the source from which society and culture come and which they are meant to serve. Such recognition affects all people, married and non-married, not only at the fundamental levels of the good of the spouses, the good of children, the intrinsic dignity of every human person, and the common good, but also at the levels of education, cultural imagination and influence, and religious freedom.

Lots of fearful claims there, but not one example from real life of the supposed harm caused by same-sex marriage. Not even a hypothetical example. So now that we have read these dire predictions that the workings of natural law, civilization as we know it, and religious freedom would be destroyed in some mysterious way by same-sex marriage, let's visit reality, something on which the bishops seem never to have had much of a grip.

The Varieties of Sexual Orientation

The case for equal rights (including same-sex marriage) for sexual minorities stands on much firmer ground than Bible verses and papal pronouncements. The basic problem is the religion-based misunderstanding of what is meant by "natural law." A toxic stream of wrongheaded ideas has spewed forth from that, causing needless suffering, hateful actions, and punitive laws to be inflicted on society.

Natural law is not something handed down by a creator god, as the religious right assumes. There is no "lawgiver" involved. Natural law is simply a description of how nature works, as best we can understand it from observation, experimentation and testing at this time. And what does all this observation, experimentation and testing tell us? Nothing at all that is even close to religious assumptions. It tells us that homosexuality is just one of the more harmless ways nature works. It is not contrary to natural law, but part of it. Religion has no relevance here.

Further deepening the religious confusion is an assumption that the way nature works reflects a purpose. Therefore, since heterosexual sex usually produces offspring, that is nature's purpose. This idea prevails because so many people are scientifically illiterate, thanks to fundamentalists' efforts to dumb down any science that contradicts the Bible. They attack evolution, denying its massive factual support, and try to replace it with intelligent design, which has no facts at all to support it.

Nature is prolific and varied. This creates constant change, called evolution. The process has produced an assortment of sexual and gender variations and orientations. In humans (and maybe other species), both sexes have observable physical parts of the other sex, although usually only the parts for one sex are developed.

But physical manifestations of sex are not the only options nature has come up with. Often enough, there are psychological variations too. The body may be configured for one sex while the brain is configured for the other. The result is that some people are transgender.

Transgenders can be any orientation because gender identity and sexual orientation are not the same. Some transgenders are simply cross-dressers. Some are transsexual, meaning their brain configuration tells them they are one sex, even though their bodies are of the opposite sex. Some transsexuals feel so strongly about this that they have sexual reassignment surgery.

And then there are those with Klinefelter's Syndrome. It is said to affect about 1 in 1,000 boys. These boys have three sex chromosomes (XXY). Since girls are XX and boys are XY, someone who is XXY is physically a male but infertile while genetically being both male and female. Such boys can and do have girlfriends but be psychologically drawn to female behaviors. Since they are in two sexes in one, if such boys want to marry, which sex should they be able to claim or to partner with?

Some states try to deny the right to change one's sexual configuration to conform to one's self identity on the grounds that the genitalia one is born with one has to keep. But what if a baby is born with male and female genitalia, and both are about equally developed? It happens. Doctors used to ask the parents which gender they preferred and remove the unwanted parts. However, as these babies grew, it was discovered that sometimes the selected sex did not match a psychological orientation toward the other sex. So now the doctors wait a few years until the child's gender-expressive behavior tells them which parts to remove.

Every form of sexual attraction is out there. It may even be that pedophilia is a natural variation. However, that involves a coercive power relationship that harms children, so, natural or not, our laws prohibit it, just as rape—apparently another natural inclination—is prohibited. We simply have to resist and prohibit some harmful behaviors to which nature mindlessly inclines us. Homosexuality is not one of them. It is because heterosexuality produces offspring that it predominates in the gene pool. Until humans figured out where babies came from, sex was naturally directed by sexual orientation solely because it was enjoyable.

As for marriage, history shows many forms and rationales, including same-sex marriage. I read of a primitive tribe that settled all marriage/paternity questions by lining up the boys and girls at age 5 and assigning each boy to a girl. That boy was thereafter legally the father of any children the girl had, regardless of who either of them had sex or children with. Seems to have worked for them.

In our less creative world, an overriding reason for institutionalizing marriage was male interest in controlling women to ensure a prolific, no-guesswork paternity and, therefore, inheritance, economic aggrandizement, and ruling authority. Women became men's property, as noted in the Ten Commandments and enforced until recently by all religions, and even today by some religions. The Bible says Solomon (the wisest of all kings, according to 1 Kings 10:23) had 700 wives and 300 concubines (meaning sex slaves). Where was the one-man, one-woman tradition then? With such exploitation of women now illegal, marriage essentially legalizes a sexuality-based interdependent social/economic bond without regard for procreation.

The Varieties of Anatomical Complementarity

Religious arguments against same-sex marriage tend to center on anatomy. Since male and female genitalia fit together and fitting them together often results in offspring, that must be nature's purpose—its sole purpose. And because there are offspring, there must necessarily be marriage. Because there is marriage, government has the duty to oversee and protect that arrangement, limiting it to one man and one woman. (Lots of *non sequiturs* there.) Here's what the former Archbishop John C. Nienstedt of the Archdiocese of St. Paul and Minneapolis wrote in 2011 in a letter to the editor of the *Minneapolis Star Tribune*. (He claimed he was defending reality, not his religious position.) The Catholic Church, he said,

. . . does not seek to impose its own beliefs on others . . . . The reality we are defending predates any religion or government. It finds its logic in the complementarity of the human anatomy, as well as the male/female psyche and in the propagation of the human species.

What he meant by the male/female psyche in this context is anyone's guess. As for anatomical complementarity, people of all sexual orientations have found more than one route to complementarity. If nature was purposeful and wanted sex to be limited to one form of male-female complementarity, there wouldn't be other options available—some even useful for preventing unwanted propagation.

And speaking of sexual purposes, I don't recall ever reading any Vatican pronouncement about the female clitoris. Unlike the male penis, which has three distinct and useful purposes, the clitoris has only one—pleasure. It has no complementarity function. Yet there it is, conforming fully to natural law, doing nothing but providing the one thing that has historically made the Vatican nervous—sex-related pleasure. No wonder there is silence on this.

Now, from the Protestant fundamentalist side, we offer another theological opinion, also expressed in a letter to the *Star Tribune*, by Rev. Elden

Nelson, a Lutheran minister. It was in reference to a proposed amendment to the Minnesota constitution that defined marriage as between
one man and one woman.

> There is nothing discriminatory about the Minnesota Marriage
> Amendment, nor is it a political matter. Neither is it intended as
> an offense against any individual or group. Rather, it is a moral
> and ethical matter that finds its basis and answer in the infallible,
> inerrant and inspired word of God.

How that word of God squares with the Catholic Church's claim that it
is the pope who is infallible, inerrant and inspired, not the Bible, or with
the First Amendment's "Congress shall make no law concerning an establishment of religion" clause, he did not say. These views assume that
the paramount cultural authority lies in religion; therefore, religions must
be allowed to interfere with and control public life.

Desperate For a New Cause,
Homophobia Finds Gender Identity

This is the latest catalyst for sky-is-falling action by legislators with a
religious agenda (or with aggressively religious constituents). Only in the
last few years has gender identity become a matter for public discussion.
The gay rights movement brought everything to the surface and no one
wants to hide their "different" sexual identity any more. They are what
they are and so what?

Actually, until recent decades *everyone* hid their sexual identity because
no one talked openly about sex. It was private and your orientation or
identity became known only if you did something to make it known. Of
course, only heterosexuals did things to make it known; everyone else
just kept quiet about it. Now, those who are gay or lesbian or biologically
of one sex but see themselves as the opposite sex now admit it. They
are fed up with being bullied when they allow their LGBT status to be
noticeable.

Some of this gender identity thing, being so newly recognized, is hard to
understand. I don't understand it, but I'm giving it deep rational thought.
Here's what I have so far, which may qualify more as shallow sludge than
deep rational thought, but I'm trying:

I go back to evolution and its ever-varying variations and I notice this: Our brains are evolved to control our behavior in ways that drive us to survive and to reproduce with maximum efficiency. Male brains tend toward muscular, aggressive and controlling behavior, the better to ensure access to females, while female brains tend toward self-protective, nurturing, and sexually reticent behavior, the better to improve the chances of their own survival and that of the children they bear. But human brains are pretty much the same otherwise, with both male and female aspects, one of which predominates more or less according to the biology within which it operates.

Because we are all partly male and partly female, it's no wonder we get sexual variations that now seem to require almost the entire alphabet to express concisely. LGBT—for lesbian, gay, bi-sexual, transgender—is just the start. The default identity is cisgender—what most people are. I saw one list that had at least a dozen alphabetical designations, and I read of another that had the list up to 40. As for those who are gender-fluid or multi-gender or whatever and their gender identity keeps changing—sometimes from day to day—I don't know what to say. Maybe some transgenders just have dysphoria and can never be satisfied with their body as it is.

I've read of parents deciding to let their 5-year-old son live as a girl because that's what he seems to want. All I can say, as the mother of two boys and three girls, 5-year-olds live as 5-year-olds as far as I could tell. The behaviors were pretty much the same within a common passive-assertive spectrum. It's when puberty hits that gender differences show up plainly. That can be a problem when the gender of the brain does not match the gender of the body. We need to recognize this and deal with it in some reasonably simple way—like shrugging it off as just another no-big-deal sexual variant.

This issue needs more study, especially since Trump issued a presidential order that transgenders could no longer be allowed to serve in the military. Right after that the Department of Justice (DOJ) submitted an amicus brief in a New York civil rights case arguing that sexual orientation is not covered under the Civil rights Act; therefore, employers are free to discriminate against them.

On the other hand, the military leadership vehemently opposed Trump's order. They said there are about 15,000 transgenders in the service and there have been absolutely no problems with them. Maybe we should be asking the military how they worked out whatever needed to be worked out with transgenders instead of mucking around trying to solve a problem that may not even exist.

Where this ends is anyone's guess, but it's not likely to be supportive of civil rights and liberties given an administration filled with religious ideologues. What do Trump or the DOJ or any of their followers know about sexual orientation or transgender issues (beyond doctrinal mandates or pressure from their ignorant political base) that qualifies them to make any decision?

Let's see what we are talking about before we jump to stupid and no doubt harmful conclusions. For starters, I'm waiting to see how this gender identity thing works out in the Democratic party where there are hard and fast rules requiring female/male gender balance in the election of delegates and for party positions. The party already allows candidates for party positions to choose the pronoun by which they want to be addressed, using some variation of his/her and he/she that creates new gender-identity words. And then there is the proposal to allow drivers license applicants to put an X in the M/F gender identity box. This would appear on the license. How the traffic cop who pulls the driver over would deal with that, I have no idea. We live in interesting times.

However, for the religious right, there is a lot here for them to pursue their goal of establishing more of their religious doctrines into law. They found their new cause for moral alarm in public restrooms and high school gym showers and locker rooms. They heard that transgender people wanted to use the wrong facilities! The sky was falling! Legislation was needed to force people to use the restroom that matched the biology they were born with! The Battle of the Biffies was on.

This is a classic example of a solution in search of a problem. Usually people whose gender identity is at odds with their biological identity try to look like the gender with which they identify. Sometimes they get sex reassignment surgery but that is a major project and expensive. More often they settle for cosmetic changes. If their gender identity is female, they take female hormones to control beard growth, wear makeup and female clothing, and pitch their voices higher. They use public restrooms marked "Women" and use one of the stalls. Women who identify as male take testosterone to encourage beard growth, wear male clothing, and pitch their voices lower. They use public restrooms marked "Men" and use one of the stalls. This works because people using public restrooms aren't interested in gender details. They just want to get in and get out.

But I wonder how people who feel a gender identity that is the opposite of their biological identity can know what it feels like to be the opposite sex. Female and male brains are not much different except in the evolutionary drive for reproductive success. That has produced males with muscular strength, an attraction to combative activities and risky behavior and, as one man said, "a primal desire to fuck anything that moves." Males have enough sperm in one ejaculation to populate a galaxy and a very limited supply of females to accommodate that potential. So they fight each other for access to females and seek multiple sex partners through plural marriage or concubines or prostitutes or rape or all of the above. Civilization controls this by shunting it off into sports and football stadiums and wars but it is still an identifying element in what it means to be male.

Evolution has produced females with far less muscular strength, making them physically vulnerable and with a full-on biological makeup that enables them to bear and nurture children. That requires a brain that—compared to males—produces behavior that is more cautious, cooperative, self-protective and sexually reticent—also perhaps better able to "read" people and therefore well suited for political maneuvering, diplomacy and peacekeeping. Since women seem to be good at this, perhaps they should be encouraged to dominate the field. It might save the human species from the testosterone-driven "race to the precipice" that Noam Chomsky fears.

Now let's consider the sex drive, which works in the brain. Put those brains in the bodies of the opposite sex and you can expect more noticeably assertive girls and more noticeably passive boys. But I wonder how a male brain in a female body deals with menstrual periods and if it still produces that Darwinian "primal desire" and if so, how that works out.

Then there's the female brain in a male body. Does a male-bodied female-brained transgender put on makeup and seductive clothing to attract a mate and sashay up to a cisgender male? How would that work out? Probably not well. Regardless, the only response society should have to this is, "So what?" There is no reason why this difference should matter. But the religious right doesn't see it that way and so we have legislative attempts to require people to present birth certificates to show their gender at birth before being allowed to use a public restroom.

But what are people doing that would make proof of gender useful? Why would transgenders who just need to pee call attention to themselves? Why are restrooms a problem at all? The sign on the door simply identifies the facility as arranged to accommodate either a male or female biology. The user's gender identity is irrelevant.

However, putting nonsense aside, there are biological realities that need to be respected. This becomes a matter of public concern when it expands to whether biological boys who feel they are female can shower naked with naked girls after a high school gym class. The media have reported on one or two instances of this, which the religious right uses to define the whole issue. There may be supporters of gender identity rights who think public showers, restrooms and locker rooms should be gender-neutral, but that is not going to work. The girls freaking out (female brains might do that) will almost certainly cancel any demands for the boys' gender identity civil rights. Besides, how can a biological boy who feels like a girl not be aware of how girls feel if he comes into the gym shower room naked? You'd think his female brain would be horrified.

More interesting, perhaps, might be a naked girl who feels she is really male coming into a high school gym shower full of naked boys. The boys might not freak out, but I'd expect that some male biology would be standing at attention (male brains might do that). There again, the situation would not do much for a gender identity argument based on civil rights.

Despite religious right claims that we need laws to protect us from gender-identity public restrooms and high school co-ed gym showers, biology-oblivious facilities are not likely to happen. It's all about common sense in meeting physical needs in privacy. We should just accept this. Use the facilities that match what you physically look like to the public and use a stall. It's not your gender identity that has to pee or shower; it's your biology. But as I said, I don't have a very good understanding of this. Any help will be appreciated.

But we may be discussing the wrong problem. If it's about different brain configurations we should look at which one is causing trouble. And that is the religious right's cognitive mess. That has caused more misery throughout history than any other single idea with its racist/sexist/ho-mophobic god-groveling prejudices and mean-spirited punitive irrational beliefs.

We are plagued with people who are so gullible, delusional and addicted to absurd supernatural beliefs that they will kill and die for them. They cannot mind their own business and now it's gender identity! They are a threat to public safety. Brains this unhinged from reality need the full attention of psychologists, psychiatrists and social science professionals. The mismatched but harmless gender identity brains might seem a bit odd because we're not used to this yet, but they aren't a problem.

Why Laws Supporting the Sacred Must Be Nullified

Laws that support unverifiable religious views of sex and marriage and gender identity have no place in a secular government. They should be nullified as unconstitutional. Some have been, but progress is slow. It does seem, however, that laws discriminating against sexual minori-ties are on their way out, due to the tenacious political organizing of LGBT people and their supporters. Public opinion is increasingly on their side.

Same-sex marriage was the latest battle won in the sexual orientation phase of the culture war. Arguments raised by the Catholic Church and religious right fundamentalists for defining marriage as only between one man and one woman were ludicrous. All were based on religious dogma tied to an intractable ignorance of human sexuality. If the religious right zealots had any understanding of how evolution works, they would know it could be no other way. Nature can neither know nor care what humans do with their genitalia. If what they do results in reproduction, then reproductive behavior is passed on.

As for legislative efforts to control who can use which public restroom or locker room based on gender identity, this is a silly solution in search of a manufactured problem.

5

WOMEN AND RELIGION: THE PUBLIC UTILITY SYNDROME

"[Mother Teresa] was not a friend of the poor. She was a friend of poverty. She said suffering was a gift from God. She spent her life opposing the only known cure for poverty, which is the empowerment of women and the emancipation of them from a livestock version of compulsory reproduction." — Christopher Hitchens in The Missionary Position: Mother Teresa in Theory and Practice

What is it about women that we need a chapter like this? Reports of assaults on women's bodily autonomy just keep coming and the nuttier they are the more likely they are to be true. From a crotch-groping president to the recent sudden outpouring of news about similar behavior by male authority figures spanning decades, to the obsessively hysterical outrage over abortion, there is no end. Women do seem to be viewed at some basic Darwinian level as the community's breeding stock—essentially, a public utility.

After months of Trump ranting about jobs going overseas, gun rights, immigration, taxes, and jailing Hillary—with crowds cheering every word—the first thing the Republicans did after taking over the White House, Congress and the Judiciary was to introduce bills defunding Planned Parenthood.

In November, 2017, there were news reports that Trump may nominate Penny Young Nance as Ambassador at Large for Global Women's Issues, but since then she has withdrawn her name from consideration. The position was created by Pres. Obama to support women's rights but Nance was expected to do just the opposite as a leader of Concerned Women for America and a supporter of its anti-abortion, anti-LGBT, anti-feminist agenda. We can assume that new nominees will be just as regressive.

There are state bills that would not allow private insurance companies to cover abortion, or would require women to inform their families—and even a rapist—that they would be getting an abortion. Regulations piled on regulations in the anti-abortion red states have forced most abortion clinics to close. Women are driving across state lines and to Mexico for abortions. They are going to the Internet to buy abortifacient drugs. All of this, except the crotch groping, is driven by religious beliefs that a fertilized egg—a cluster of microscopic undifferentiated cells—is a person entitled to all the rights of a real born person. (To put this in perspective, look at the period at the end of this sentence. *That is the size of a fertilized egg.* If you can see a person there, you are badly in need of psychiatric help.)

Even the groping is driven by a religious assumption that women are men's property. Actually, so is the anti-abortion legislation, since its proponents never show interest in the welfare of actual born children. I haven't seen any bills from these sources that would help the woman or the child after the enforced birth, just cutbacks in welfare assistance. And why are some women in these states holding still for this? Religious beliefs? Of course. Self-centered "abortion is not an issue for me" disdain for the suffering of others? Yeah, that too. Maybe it's the Stockholm Syndrome: women feeling too weak-willed to free themselves absorbing the views of their masters.

Maybe it's not misogyny as much as it is a fundamentally deep concern for survival. After all, the most basic thing standing between human survival and extinction is women's ability and willingness to produce the next generation. That depends entirely on them doing it in adequate numbers. Now, with 7 billion people overpopulating the planet, we hardly need more, but the Darwinian drive is still there.

It has taken all kinds of economic, social, religious and political pressure to make sure the women produce. They have, therefore, been treated worldwide as a public utility for childbearing. Saving "women and children first" in a disaster is not chivalry—it is a DNA-level instinct for species survival.

Roe v. Wade actually reinforced women's public utility function by making them subject to government regulation. As a result, their access to safe, legal abortion has been regulated almost out of existence by court rulings. Centuries of pressure on women to reproduce is why we have a problem with climate change. There are too many people. We have exceeded Earth's carrying capacity. And what do we do about it? Defund Planned Parenthood? We may cause our own extinction because of centuries of mistreatment of women.

A Primal Urge to Control Reinforced by Religion

It is impossible to talk about religion-based laws without discussing the people most severely victimized by them—women . . . half the world's population. They are society's child bearers so you'd think that would count for something in terms of decent treatment, but it doesn't. Largely if not entirely because of that primal function, no other demographic group has been more the object of male dominance, abuse and social control throughout history and across all cultures. With some rare exceptions at various times and places, women have existed as men's property ever since people figured out where babies came from.

Women traditionally have been culturally limited to bearing children and not allowed to do much else. The social reforms of the '60s did begin to remove that limitation to some extent. Although "women's lib" was ridiculed, increased higher educational opportunities for women got some support by attaching it to motherhood. I heard the argument made in those days that an educated woman would be better able to raise children to be productive citizens. That always reminded me of the story of Moses, who was allowed to lead his people to the Promised Land, but for some arbitrary reason was condemned to see it only from afar and never go there himself.

With all their macho tendencies, are men (well, at least some of them) more emotionally dependent on women than they will admit? Is that the real source of the urge to control women? Or maybe it's a deep fear of watching women's opportunities increase, not wanting to accept that change and not knowing how to deal with it. Consider this statement in an op-ed piece titled "Social-Issue Politics a New Battleground" by Charles Lane (reprinted from the *Washington Post*) in the June 12, 2017 *Minneapolis Star Tribune* that noted the growing consensus in favor of progressive issues:

"One interpretation of the overwhelming support of the country's most religious, tradition-minded voters for a thrice-married, hedonistic tycoon is that it demonstrates their desperation to stop the progressive cultural wave. . . . The main exceptions to this consensus are abortion and gun control, about which a relatively even and highly partisan divide persists—and which candidate Trump exploited to win over red-state voters who might otherwise have distrusted him. That suggests our partisan battles over abortion and guns are far from over."

So something is going on here for which abortion and guns are the battle flags but not what the fight is about. These anti-abortion, pro-gun fanatics don't give a rat's patoot about "unborn babies" and they have no real personal defense need for guns. It's the primitive lizard-level survival instinct operating—all action and reaction—giving them a feeling of power and control. I leave it at that for now.

Politics and Dogma As Ideological Gang Rape

When sex discrimination was included in the Civil Rights Act of 1964 as a last-minute amendment, it was greeted with laughter. It was proposed by Sen. Howard K. Smith, a Virginia Democrat, an opponent of the Civil Rights Act. His motives were unclear. There was speculation that he thought his amendment would kill the bill; however, he had always been a strong supporter of the Equal Rights Amendment, so perhaps (as others speculated) he only wanted to embarrass fellow Democrats from northern states who opposed women's rights in deference to male-dominated, sexist, labor unions. But the Civil Rights Act was passed and additional protections for women's rights followed. Whether they hold is uncertain.

Religions seem always to have played on and reinforced these anti-woman prejudices, assuming the right to control women's childbearing function with no consideration given to what women themselves might want or need. Their irrational—even punitive—views have become so embedded in their theology *and in our laws* that one could argue that controlling women's sexuality and childbearing role has been the primary purpose of most religions. The justification for this is the Bible, justified further in the interpretations by its followers:

Be fruitful and multiply. (Genesis 1:28)

To the woman he said, I will greatly multiply your sorrow and your conception; in pain you shall bring forth children; your desire shall be to your husband, and he shall rule over you. (Genesis 3:16—God's punishment of Eve for seducing Adam into eating the forbidden fruit)

You shall not covet your neighbor's house; you shall not covet your neighbor's wife, nor his male servant, nor his female servant, nor his ox, nor his donkey, nor anything that is your neighbor's. (Exodus 20:17)

[Women] will be saved in childbearing. (1 Timothy 2:15)

No gown worse becomes a woman than the desire to be wise. Men have broad and large chests, and small narrow hips, and are more understanding than women, who have but small and narrow chests, and broad hips, to the end they should remain at home, sit still, keep house, and bear and bring up children. (Martin Luther, in *Table Talk*)

Married life presupposes the power of the husband over the wife and children, and subjection and obedience of the wife to the husband. (Pope Pius XI, in *Casti Connubii*)

Much of this claim of male power is laid to Eve having been created for Adam, assuming that relegated her to an inferior status. The Bible even speaks of Eve's creation as a form of male birthing, thus usurping the female role and making women even more inferior. But since it was Adam who needed Eve, wouldn't he, as the needy person, be the inferior one? There is nothing in the creation stories to indicate Eve needed Adam.

This is mythical nonsense, of course, but the restrictive and demeaning attitudes toward women reflected in these stories remain much the same today around the world. Only since the 1960s have patriarchal cultures and the religions that support them been forced in some places to loosen their control of women significantly. These pockets of enlightenment, where women are free to make their own social, educational, economic and childbearing decisions, have been the secular democracies.

The Last Stand and NSSM 200

But not all of them. In the United States the fight to maintain control continues, carried on by the Catholic hierarchy and Protestant fundamentalists. It has become increasingly ferocious, although concentrated primarily in one area only. Control of women is no longer about opposing women's right to vote or get an education or pursue a high-level career or (to some extent) practice birth control—those battles have been lost.

What is left now is the last stand—women's right to abortion, to have ultimate control over their own bodies. The Catholic-Fundamentalist coalition will not concede that right. It is the point at which retreat is unthinkable. In 1973, the U.S. Supreme Court marked that point with its *Roe v. Wade* decision and the line was drawn.

It was drawn on November 20, 1975, by the United States Catholic bishops, acting in defense of papal authority, when they issued their "Pastoral Plan for Pro-Life Activities." It signaled the start of the culture war and drew in Protestant fundamentalist allies acting in defense of biblical authority.

The Pastoral Plan was not a reflection of either group's desire to "save innocent pre-born babies"—as the hysterical anti-abortion rhetoric would have everyone believe. According to the Guttmacher Institute, which tracks reproductive issues, Catholic-dominated countries in Latin America (where abortion is illegal) have abortion rates much higher than in the United States, yet there is no campaign to stop them. Before *Roe v. Wade*, there were clandestine abortion clinics all over the United States, and doctors willing to do abortions in their offices. I knew about them and knew how to find them, as did most savvy women who were willing to ask around, yet there were no Catholic or Protestant campaigns to stop them (other than an occasional dustup somewhere by a vote-pandering politician). The reason is that *they were illegal*. And *that* is all the anti-abortion movement cares about.

The following quotations expose the fundamental, governing rationale for the bishops' Pastoral Plan: the protection of the Catholic Church as an institution and the credibility of the pope as the infallible representative of God on Earth. They are from *The Life and Death of NSSM 200: How the Destruction of Political Will Doomed a U.S. Population Policy* by Stephen D. Mumford. This 579-page highly readable book, published in 1996, spells out in great detail the plans and strategies the United States Catholic bishops implemented to bring about the culture war that has fragmented society.

The book's focus expands outward from the failed efforts of the Nixon and Ford administrations to implement the recommendations of National Security Study Memorandum 200 (NSSM 200) for controlling population growth. NSSM 200 detailed the security threat to the United States of uncontrolled global population growth. It urged efforts to free up women economically and socially through education, and to make family planning options available to them. It emphasized that population growth could not be controlled if abortion was not among those options.

Mumford carefully documents the Catholic bishops' efforts to derail the Study. They were successful and the Study was shelved permanently by the Reagan administration. Because of Mumford's thorough documentation—including reproduction of original texts—his book is arguably the most important ever written on the cause of the culture war and the social-economic-political dysfunction that has ensued. Consider the following from page 124:

> In his book, *Persistent Prejudice: Anti-Catholicism in America*, published by *Our Sunday Visitor* [the leading Catholic newspaper at the time] in 1984, Michael Schwantz summarized the position of Catholic conservatives on the abortion issue: "The abortion issue is the great crisis of Catholicism in the United States, of far greater import than the election of a Catholic president or the winning of tax support for Catholic education. In the unlikely event that the Church's resistance to abortion collapses and the Catholic community decides to seek an accommodation with the institutionalized killing of innocent human beings, that would signal the utter failure of Catholicism in America. It would mean that U.S. Catholicism will have been defeated and denatured by the anti-Catholic host culture."

In April 1992, in a rare public admission of this threat, Cardinal John O'Connor of New York, delivering a major address to the Franciscan University of Steubenville, Ohio, said, "The fact is that attacks on the Catholic Church's stance on abortion—unless they are rebuffed—effectively erode Church authority on all matters, indeed on the authority of God himself." It is important to note that, as Mumford says, laws outlawing abortion

> ". . . need not be enforced to meet the needs of the Vatican. The Vatican requires only that the civil law not conflict with canon law. Then papal authority and civil authority are not pitted against one another. It is only legal abortion that threatens papal authority." (pp. 310-311)

I encountered this view myself several years ago when I was organizing for abortion rights. The anti-abortion man who was leading the opposition against me told me that if abortions were outlawed the Church would have no interest in enforcing the law because all they cared about was having the law validate Catholic doctrine.

And so for *that* we have been dragged through decades of social and political chaos with no end in sight. Even birth control, long considered a basic, settled right, again became a major controversy in 2012 with the presidential candidacy of Rick Santorum, staunch Catholic, father of eight, and a member of Opus Dei, the highly secretive society of the Catholic Church.

Mumford describes how the problem of papal infallibility and institutional authority had surfaced in 1964 when Pope Paul VI authorized the Papal Commission on Population and Birth Control to see if there was a way to approve contraceptive use. (p. 126) The Commission met until 1966 without finding a way to do this consistent with Catholic doctrine.

Of the 15 cardinals and bishops and 64 lay members of the Commission, the lay members voted 60 to 4 in favor of approving contraceptive birth control, and the clerical members voted 9 to 6 in favor. Even though it undermined papal infallibility, the commission's majority voted that way "because it was the right thing to do." (p. 124) However, the minority (which included Karol Wojtyla, who became Pope John Paul II) prevailed to such an extent that Pope Paul VI, in his 1968 encyclical, *Humanae Vitae*, re-enforced the condemnation of abortion and contraceptive birth control as well as his claim to infallibility. Here is an excerpt from the minority report (p. 126):

> If it should be declared that contraception is not evil in itself, then we should have to concede frankly that the Holy Spirit had been on the side of the Protestant churches in 1930 (when the encyclical *Casti Connubii* was promulgated), in 1951 (Pius XII's address to the midwives), and in 1958 (the address delivered before the Society of Hematologists in the year the pope died).

> It should likewise have to be admitted that for a half a century the Spirit failed to protect Pius XI, Pius XII, and a large part of the Catholic hierarchy from a very serious error. This would mean that the leaders of the Church, acting with extreme imprudence, had condemned thousands of innocent human acts, forbidding, under pain of eternal damnation, a practice which would now be sanctioned. The fact can neither be denied nor ignored that these same acts would now be declared licit on the grounds of principles cited by the Protestants, which popes and bishops have either condemned or at least not approved.

In other words, the Vatican found that it had dug itself into a hole and decided the only way out was to keep on digging. This would not be a matter of concern—or even noteworthy—if *Humanae Vitae* applied only to Catholics (most of whom have ignored it). However, in the Vatican's worldview, *Humanae Vitae* applies to everyone, and governments have the duty to enforce its view of morality, as in this excerpt from Mumford's book (p. 114), quoting Msgr. John A. Ryan in a 1940 book, *Catholic Principles of Politics*:

> If there is only one true religion, and if its possession is the most important good in life for States as well as individuals, then the public profession, protection, and promotion of this religion and the legal prohibition of all direct assaults upon it, becomes one of the most obvious and fundamental duties of the State. For it is the business of the State to safeguard and promote human welfare in all departments of life.

The Power of a Living Fossil

Any rational, thoughtful person would want to dismiss such an absurd, arrogant claim out of hand, but that would be unwise. As Mumford's book explains in detail, the Catholic bishops in the U.S. have shown they have such a high level of organizational expertise, political shrewdness, public relations skills, and talent for negotiating alliances with religious-right fundamentalists that they have now brought those "state duties" alarmingly close to realization.

Even with little enthusiastic support from rank and file Catholics, one is led to assume there must be something there in Catholicism. But it's just an anomaly, a living fossil, an institution still mired in the Middle Ages and still insisting that governments bow to its demands as in that "golden age of faith" of fond ecclesiastical memory. This living fossil has us caught up in a culture war to protect its dogma that the pope is infallible, motivated by the fear that his credibility will be lost if governments don't legislate his infallible views into law.

Yet all the evidence from surveys and church attendance shows that most Catholics have little or no interest in papal restrictions on sexual matters and they dismiss his pronouncements. (Mumford's book documents this too.) Almost every Catholic I know fits this description. They remain Catholic out of habit or because they think of the Church as a social welfare service that feeds the hungry and shelters the homeless (but see the chapter on welfare recipients for what is really going on) or because they love the pageantry or for other personal reasons. They will turn out in massive numbers to see the pope, listen to him rant about abortion and birth control, then go home and guiltlessly engage in all kinds of non-doctrinal, essentially harmless, sexual and reproductive behavior.

So what explains the political power of the Catholic Church? Single-minded dedication and organizing ability, which can outweigh almost any majority opinion. Mumford explains it in describing the Church's initial failure to get a Human Life Amendment passed (page 172):

> . . . In September 1991, Catholic activist William Bennett, former Secretary of Education, and other Catholic "conservatives" announced the formation of Catholic Campaign for America.

Creation of this organization even 20 years ago would have been unthinkable. For nearly 200 years, Protestants have warned that the Vatican plans to create such organizations in the U.S. and that American democracy was threatened.

One needs only listen to what these Catholics are saying now to understand that the strategy Stephen Settle described in the *National Catholic Register* is being implemented—and to recognize that this minority, with its "stamina, smarts and perseverance" intends to impose papal law using any means necessary and to "co-opt" our democratic institutions.

Although Catholics are no longer a reliable voting bloc, politicians seem to tremble at the thought of opposing the bishops' imperious anti-abortion demands. None of them have the courage to stand up for the victims of such tyranny. Oh, some of them speak legalistically, and almost apologetically, of defending *Roe v. Wade* as the law of the land. But none of them, as far as I know, defend the women it protects. I've listened to this stuff many times and am always appalled at the obtuseness of it. It is too *pro forma* to inspire confidence.

What might be the impact on how women (and the men who love them) vote if a candidate said something like this in response to a question about abortion: "Of course I support *Roe v. Wade.* I support it because I respect women. They're our child bearers but that shouldn't make them a public utility for us to regulate. I respect their intelligence and their ability to know what's best for themselves and their families. I do not think they are airheads who need me or any legislative body to make their personal decisions for them. As legislators we have the responsibility to provide whatever help they need, for whatever decision they make, not stigmatize them, not demonize them, not punish them for being female, and certainly not insult their intelligence, but to stand by them. And that is what I intend to do if elected." Sounds like a vote-getting speech to me.

The Problem With Roe v. Wade

Roe v. Wade started it all. It was a bad ruling because it regulated the timing and circumstances under which abortion was permitted. It thus assumed what societies have always and everywhere assumed—that women, as society's child bearers, are something of a community resource, a public utility to be controlled and regulated.

Granted, *Roe v. Wade* did end the criminalization of abortion that existed in almost all states, thus saving the lives of several hundred women a year who otherwise would have died of botched illegal abortions. Its three-trimester regulatory system was hardly restrictive. It was nothing more than what women had always worked out on their own by common sense and need.

The Supreme Court should have dismissed *Roe v. Wade* on the basis that abortion is not the government's business; it is a medical matter involving a woman's bodily functions to be resolved between the woman and her doctor. Instead, by creating an unnecessary regulatory structure, the Court opened the door to all the modifications, restrictions and bureaucratic hoops to jump through that regulations invite, and that we have today, with more on the way.

The Court's ruling that the Constitution implied a right to privacy consistent with the right to abortion was weak, since governments invade one's privacy all the time. A better ruling—along with upholding a woman's right to bodily autonomy in medical matters—would have invoked the First Amendment's prohibition of an establishment of religion, since the history of opposition to abortion centers around theological notions about ensoulment as defining when life begins. Unfortunately, the Court's ruling implied that women's autonomy stops where their childbearing function begins; therefore they are—yes—a public utility in need of government regulation.

The Equal Rights Amendment failed in 1985 precisely because opponents hammered away that it would give women autonomy and therefore the right to be in control of their own bodies and therefore the right to abortion. The practical effect of *Roe v. Wade* and the defeat of the ERA has been to make women slaves of the state where an unwanted or disastrous pregnancy is concerned.

The Pastoral Plan for Pro-Life Activities

Mumford's book provides the complete text of the bishops' plan. It describes strategies for manipulating government processes at all levels, for creating political action units at all levels, for recruiting members of Catholic professional, business and civic associations, for forming "pro-life" organizations in every parish in the nation, and for recruiting Catholic writers and intellectuals to promote the "pro-life" agenda. The Plan has been largely successful as can be seen from the mounting restrictions on obtaining an abortion.

The 1976 Hyde Amendment started the legislative brutality by ensuring there would be no federal funding for abortion for poor women on Medicaid. Further legislation ensured that poor women in rural areas have virtually no access to abortion even if they could afford it. Servicewomen serving on a military base are denied the right to abortion even in cases of rape or incest and even if they pay for it themselves. There are waiting periods (supposedly to forestall a hasty decision—though any woman facing a traumatic pregnancy doesn't think of anything else after a missed period). There are parental notification requirements (never mind that some parents get physically violent when their teenage daughter informs them she is pregnant).

There are informed consent requirements (including, in Texas, a rape-like requirement that doctors insert a probe in the woman's vagina to provide a video of the fetus—in case she is too dumb to know what pregnancy is). Abortion clinics have been forced to close because they can't afford the unnecessary, hospital-like remodeling mandated by anti-abortion legislative "regulations." In 2009, because of the bishops' interference, Pres. Obama was forced to remove abortion coverage from his health care reform plan. It goes on and on. These and other busybody hoops for women to jump through are far more than can be kept track of or covered in this book.

Where the Religious Right Came From

The bishops' plans for ecumenical activities with conservative Protestant organizations were calculated and effective. The strategy was guided by Virgil Blum, a Jesuit priest and founder and first president of the Catholic League for Religious and Civil Rights. Mumford writes:

> [Blum offered the bishops] a set of well thought out guidelines which capitalized on centuries of experience of Jesuit manipulation of governments. (p. 155)

... Blum recognized early on that "ecumenism" would be an essential weapon to counter the criticism certain to come with the blatant involvement of the bishops in making public policy. He saw that constant defense of the Catholic bishops by Protestant leaders, in the name of "ecumenism" was critical. In hindsight, he was obviously correct. Protestant leaders have served as tools of the Catholic bishops to blunt criticism by branding such criticism as anti-Catholic or anti-freedom of religion and thus un-American. Protestants with good intentions were used like pawns to advance papal security interests at the expense of our country's. (p.160)

Almost everyone assumes the Moral Majority and later the Christian Coalition were founded by Protestant fundamentalists. They weren't. They—and numerous "grassroots" religious right organizations such as Heritage Foundation, Free Congress Foundation, Eagle Forum, and many others—were created at the direction of the bishops with Catholics as key players. Jerry Falwell, Pat Buchanan, Paul Weyrich, Richard Viguerie, Phyllis Schlafly, and many others were all recruited to provide the organizational expertise to get the religious right up and running (Mumford, chapters 9 & 10). Mumford shows, as an incontrovertible fact, that without the Catholic bishops and their Pastoral Plan for Pro-Life Activities there would be no anti-abortion movement and no culture war.

TRAP and ALEC: "Miracle of Life" To "Sniveling Welfare Cheat"

After the religious right's political takeover of Congress and most state legislatures in the 2010 mid-term elections, the push for control moved into what can only be called a "shock and awe" phase in its sudden intensity. The Guttmacher Institute created a chart giving an historical perspective on the number of abortion restrictions enacted from 1985 to 2011. It's a J-curve like the one for population growth! The horizontal line, although quite jagged, is fairly constrained until 2011, then it shoots straight up from around 200 to 300 restrictions to nearly 1,000 in one year! Yes, about 1,000 bills were introduced in 2011 at the state and federal levels that would further restrict or deny women's right to abortion and to contraceptives that would prevent the need for abortion.

One-thousand! That was out of about 40,000 bills of all types and does not include the many bills that give increased preferential treatment for religion. Every possible restriction, criminalization and humiliation was in those bills. One even required miscarriages to be criminally investigated. (In Iowa a pregnant woman was arrested for falling down a flight of stairs—she had called 911 for help—on suspicion that she might have been trying to induce a miscarriage.) Another bill protected murderers of abortion doctors from prosecution.

Another defined rape as such only if the woman was physically beaten and had the wounds to prove it—thereby putting statutory rape, rapes at knife-point, date-rapes, etc. in the "get out of jail free" category. There was one that denied federal funding for training doctors in how to perform abortions, even though this medical knowledge is necessary when a pregnancy threatens a woman's life. There were several state-federal fetal "personhood" amendments (part of a nationally organized campaign).

There were TRAP bills (Targeted Regulation of Abortion Providers) that shut down several abortion clinics that couldn't afford the hospital-level modifications. The National Organization for Women (NOW) newsletter for September 2011 reported that, "During the healthcare reform debate, Senator Jon Kyl of Arizona objected to including prenatal and maternity care in the basic benefits package by saying, 'I don't need maternity care. So requiring that in my insurance policy is something that I don't need and will make the policy more expensive.'" Well, yes, since women get pregnant all by themselves, why should men share the costs? All of the above is the from-another-planet mindset that created our dysfunctional political system.

Why so many bills hostile to women's welfare and so similar from state to state? It is not a coincidence. It is organized. It's called "blueprint legislation." For some time there have been national organizations that craft bills to be used by supportive legislators around the country. It works for both the left and right political interests. Only one has recently come to light enough to generate public interest—ALEC, the American Legislative Exchange Council. It has provided legal language for many bills, most notably for voter ID laws (called voter restriction laws by opponents) and "stand your ground" gun rights legislation (characterized as "shoot first and ask questions later" by opponents).

Similar to ALEC in strategy, but unknown to the general public is AUL—Americans United for Life. That is where all those anti-woman bills are coming from—and the fingerprints of the Catholic bishops' Pastoral Plan for Pro-Life Activities are all over it. AUL was founded in 1971 (before *Roe v. Wade*) by a Unitarian minister, but its purpose then was only to hold intellectual discussions on the pros and cons of abortion. After *Roe v. Wade*, in 1975, it was completely reorganized as a legal entity to find ways to overturn *Roe v. Wade*. As with so much anti-abortion activity, Catholics hold leadership positions in it and the Pastoral Plan informs its activities. Some of the most visible Catholic leaders of AUL have been Charmaine Yoest and Abby Johnson, heading up the attacks on Planned Parenthood and the Obama health care plan.

The extent of the legislative brutality towards women is difficult to keep up with; it is punishment for "Eve" all the way down. There is no "personhood" for her; she is only a vessel for childbearing purposes, and a disposable one at that. Of course, the most absurdly abusive bills go nowhere, but many others get passed, though some face legal challenges.

Examples: A bill was passed in Arizona and upheld by a federal judge that makes it a crime for doctors to perform an abortion after 20 weeks counting from the start of the last menstrual period (realistically, that's 18 weeks or four months into pregnancy). The judge bought the argument that the fetus can feel pain by then and ignored medical testimony to the contrary. There just isn't enough cognitive development by then to feel anything.

In July, 2012, a federal district judge in Colorado, John Kane, ruled that a Catholic business owner did not have to comply with the Obama healthcare mandate to provide his employees with insurance coverage for birth control. The judge noted that numerous religious organizations had been granted exemptions, so why not commercial businesses with religious owners? (See the chapter on taxes for how this domino effect works once religions are exempt, then consider who will be left to cover the costs of civilization if this keeps up.)

On July 24, 2012, in Missouri, the Eighth Circuit Court in St. Louis ruled that a South Dakota law allowing doctors to lie to patients about the risks of suicide following an abortion is constitutional. Seems the Court thought the law didn't unduly burden a woman's abortion decision, that it supported the free speech rights of doctors, and the intent of the law was informative. This despite testimony that no such risk existed, and the clear legislative evidence that the law was passed precisely to hinder a woman from having an abortion. (Read the chapter on the Constitution again about the difference between the Constitution and constitutional law.)

Then there is Plan B, the so-called "morning after" pill that prevents pregnancy if taken within 72 hours after unprotected intercourse. After years of conflict between knowledgeable scientists who presented abundant evidence for the pill's safety for over-the-counter (OTC) distribution, and religious right opponents who insisted with no factual knowledge whatsoever that 1) the scientists were wrong and 2) the pill was an abortifacient, it was approved for OTC for girls and women 17 and older. Only girls 16 and younger still needed a prescription. In 2011, when further studies had shown the pill was safe for all females of childbearing age, the Food and Drug Administration (FDA) approved it for OTC across the board for anyone.

Normally, when the FDA approves a medication that is the end of it. However, contrary to all past practice, Health and Human Services Secretary Kathleen Sebelius stepped in and overruled the FDA. By all accounts, this was suspected to be a political decision to avoid a controversy with the religious right in the run-up to the 2012 presidential election.

Part of the stated opposition to the full OTC approval was that there might be harmful side effects for girls as young as 11, an age group that had not been studied for Plan B. Yet, many common OTC medications—such as aspirin, Tylenol and cough syrups—have side effects, sometimes fatal (read their labels), but can be bought OTC by pre-teen children (who have not been studied for those side effects).

For vulnerable young girls, who can be so easily seduced into an unwise sexual encounter or are the victims of incest, how does the potential side effect of, say, a headache from taking Plan B compare with the potential side effect of a pregnancy from not taking it? Yet, in the religious right's view, nothing can be allowed to interfere with a potential fetus's "right to life" or (as some claim) to provide such an easy inducement to be promiscuous.

Really? Contraception is not exactly cheap when used regularly. Although it can be free at some clinics, Plan B costs between $25 and $60 at pharmacies. As one sexual health activist said, "The cost is one reason why it *is* plan B, not plan A." Regarding promiscuity, here is what an ob/gyn doctor friend told me, "Even a $9 pill costs $108 a year, which is $540 for five years, getting into the range of what an IUD costs. Besides, a lot of OTC contraceptives are prescribed for non-contraceptive reasons, at times even for a woman without a uterus. All contraceptives should be OTC. No prescription is needed for getting pregnant, after all, and *any* OTC is less dangerous than pregnancy."

With so much hostility to abortion, one would think there would be strong legislative support for family planning programs and widely available and cheap contraceptives. What better way to greatly reduce the need for abortions? Pro-choice organizations have repeatedly tried to introduce legislation to do just that, but have been opposed every time by the anti-abortion lobbyists. For them, birth control is all of an evil piece with abortion. Obama's Affordable Care Act recognized the importance of free and available contraceptives in reducing unwanted pregnancies and abortions, but the Republican effort to "repeal and replace" the ACA in some way is unlikely to include accessible and affordable contraceptives.

With this relentless campaign to restrict contraception, and then save the resulting fetuses at all costs, it's not like there has been a compensating legislative push to do anything for children who have been born. On the contrary, the same legislative agendas that seek to bring every pregnancy to term also include tax and spending cuts that reduce or eliminate programs that provide born children with the social support needed to turn them into productive adults.

The overall legislative theme seems to be "reproduce and abandon" as that precious little "pre-born baby," a "miracle of life" while *in utero*, gets transformed by birth into a "sniveling little welfare cheat" (as one particularly apt political cartoon put it). Completely forgotten, evidently, was the "jobs, jobs, jobs" theme they campaigned on. . . . Oh, wait! The U.S. House of Representatives did spend a lot of time developing and passing legislation to engrave "In God We Trust" on every federal building in the country. Maybe that was their jobs bill.

What It Means to Be a Politically Generated Person

Since 2010, a campaign for a "personhood" amendment to state and federal constitutions has developed. Generally, the wording is some variation of this: "The life of each human being begins with fertilization, cloning or its functional equivalent, at which time every human being shall have all the legal and constitutional attributes and privileges of personhood." That would outlaw legal abortions forever. (Illegal ones with their lethal potential would take their place.)

Well! Whoever first said there's nothing new under the sun didn't reckon with the imaginations of religious ideologues. No society has ever defined fertilized eggs as people. They all have sense enough to wait and see if a person actually develops. Usually this is at birth because a lot of personhood-obstructing mishaps can occur during nine months of gestation. Not even the Bible treats fetuses as persons. Not even the Catholic Church did until recently. For centuries it held a variety of views about abortion related to when ensoulment (the Church's criterion for personhood) supposedly took place. The only consistent position taken by the Church over the centuries was that abortion was wrong if it was a cover-up for sin. (See Jane Hurst, "Abortion in Good Faith: The History of Abortion in the Catholic Church." Catholics for A Free Choice, Washington D.C. 1981.)

The discovery of DNA gave the anti-abortionists a new argument: Since a fertilized egg has DNA it must be a person! Of course, every cell in one's body has DNA. This means that when we shed skin cells we are sending zillions of "pre-born babies" to their deaths. St. Augustine (5th century Church father), despite the flat-Earth level of his thinking, was smarter than the Church's dimwits today. He said:

> The law does not provide that the act (abortion) pertains to homicide, for there cannot yet be said to be a live soul in a body that lacks sensation when it is not formed in flesh and so is not endowed with sense.

A few facts about biology would be helpful. Let's see what theology's politically generated person looks like. Fertilization begins the process of cell division. What we have is a cluster of undifferentiated cells no bigger than the period at the end of this sentence. Yet the Church sees a person there. That is delusion of a high order indeed or, more likely, politically motivated institution-saving desperation. But what about that heartbeat so endearingly called to our attention on "pro-life" billboards? Yes, a heartbeat can be detected at about two-months gestation, but it is a two-chambered heart—the lizard level of development. A real person's heart has four chambers. But what about brainwaves, suggesting some cognitive development? Yes, they can be detected very early, but they don't suggest anything. As a medical doctor friend informed me: "All 'brainwaves' means is 'living tissue,' not thoughts. The anti's are ignoramuses."

Abortion before the third trimester never kills a baby—it only keeps a baby from forming. The "ingredients" haven't come together sufficiently to form anything viable. It takes time and that doesn't happen until the third trimester. By then we are dealing almost always with a truly wanted baby, so if something goes wrong it is heartbreaking. If the fetus has to be removed, delivery can be induced or a Caesarian performed. There is no need for an abortion except in rare medical situations. Religion-based laws forbidding "partial birth" abortions force doctors to use procedures that could endanger the woman's life or health or future childbearing ability for no useful purpose.

Personhood defined as "from the moment of fertilization" could limit fertility treatments. There could be criminal charges if the embryo doesn't survive. Couples would be going to other states for fertility treatments to avoid the religiously restrictive states. All pregnancies would be forced to be carried to term regardless of rape, incest, maternal health problems or severe birth defects. There are annually in the U.S. thousands of pregnancies started by rape (5% of rapes start a pregnancy). For example, a 1996 estimate in "PubMed" (at www.ncbi.nlm.nih.gov/pmc in August 2010) was 32,101. This is out of hundreds of thousands of rapes.

Many contraceptives would be outlawed, including the morning-after pill and the IUD, because anti-abortionists ignorantly insist that they are abortifacients. Miscarriages would be criminally investigated and would require both birth and death certificates. What about inheritance laws? Think about that—and a whole host of other laws based on real personhood—and then try to fit a politically generated person into them. You would have a legal mess to end all legal messes.

No rational person believes a cluster of undifferentiated cells is a person. The typical question posed is: "If a building was on fire and you could save either a year-old baby or a container of frozen embryos, but not both, which would you save?" The expected answer, and the one always given, is that the baby would be saved.

But maybe not if Catholic theology ruled the day. A story the nuns told me in Catholic school to emphasize the sacredness of the Eucharist was about a priest who, when his church was on fire, rushed in to save the Blessed Sacrament being displayed on the altar for adoration. He saved the Eucharist but died as a result. The nuns held him up as a hero for giving his life to save the consecrated Host. Really? It occurs to me now that the Blessed Sacrament was encased in a gold receptacle designed for the purpose. Very valuable. Maybe that is what the priest was really trying to save.

At any rate, throughout this trip through politically generated personhood land, what did it mean to that fetal "person"? Nothing. Cognitive development sufficient to support some level of sentience does not occur until the third trimester. If problems arise then, it is a medical case that only medical professionals are qualified to deal with, and they do what they can to save what they can.

Meanwhile, all through this fetal development process there has been only one claimant to real personhood—the woman, fully cognitive, fully sentient, and aware of everything. What does personhood mean for her?

What It Means to Be a Real Person

Frances was a real person, a pretty 22-year-old blonde. She lived next door when I was 10 years old. One weekend she went out of town and came back dead. It was the first funeral I went to. They said she died of obstruction of the bowels from eating peanuts on the train. I later learned Frances actually died of a botched abortion and that, in those days, doctors would give the cause of death as obstruction of the bowels to save the family from embarrassment.

Vera was a real person too. She was my best friend when she and I were devout Catholics trying, with little success, to make the rhythm system ("Vatican roulette") work. It didn't. Vera had a blood condition that caused cerebral palsy or death in a fetus unless it could be delivered early in the third trimester. Vera's first child had severe cerebral palsy. Every pregnancy after that, a Caesarian was done to try to save the fetus in time but they all died. Vera went through six uterine surgeries. During the seventh pregnancy, her uterus ruptured, blood got into her lungs, and she drowned in her own blood, in the ambulance, on the way to the hospital.

That was the second funeral I went to. Vera thought if she practiced birth control she would go to hell. But it was her heartbroken husband and a child in need of constant care who were put in hell—the real one created on Earth by inhumane doctrines that good, trusting people—real persons—are conned into believing and no one is allowed to question publicly because that would be disrespectful. In no other business can an organization get away with brutalizing people and yet be treated with unquestioning respect and given government grants, subsidies, contracts, and tax exemptions besides.

Not to be left out of the gullible "good, trusting people" category, I—also a real person—will mention one of my real-person experiences as a devout—therefore often pregnant—Catholic. (This story was intensely boring to anti-abortion people when I told it a couple of times, thinking it might call up some level of humanity. It did not.) One of my pregnancies went very wrong (as opposed to only partially wrong in others) when, at the fifth month I started filling with fluid. Doctor's diagnosis: It was a sign of defective fetal development. What kind or how bad he couldn't say. I was carrying 40 pounds of fluid plus a large twisting tumor that caused tremendous pain. No abortion, since I was still a devout Catholic and obviously a slow learner, having learned nothing from those funerals I'd attended.

Long story short: At the eighth month of this horrendous mentally and physically traumatic pregnancy, the doctor decided there was no point in continuing the misery for what would most likely be nothing, so he induced labor. The baby was a girl, a sweet little thing with red hair, looking good despite weighing only four pounds. Well, that was on the surface. Her intestines were mostly a fibrous mass and her esophagus was solid instead of hollow. She couldn't eat. It took her a few days to starve to death. But, hey, she did get baptized, and isn't that the most—the only—important thing here? Certainly the anti-abortion religious zealots would say so. Sadism may be abhorred generally, but it seems that, in the world of dogma-driven religion, it is elevated to a place of honor.

Trying to avoid getting pregnant has always been difficult for women, made even more difficult by archaic theology-based laws that deny their autonomy. As recently as the 1970s, a woman who wanted a tubal ligation had to get her husband to sign off on it. If he wouldn't sign, too bad. Here's what it was like: The *Minneapolis Star Tribune* on Oct. 9, 2011, had an article titled "Minnesotans look back on 1968." Among the women it profiled was a peace activist. It said:

> [She] was also busy raising her six kids. "I tried using the rhythm method," she said. "It didn't work." A few years later, after giving birth to an eighth child who died, she wanted to get a tubal ligation, "but in those days the husband had to sign off on that." John [her husband], a staunch Catholic, was initially reluctant, but eventually agreed after consulting with medical professionals.

That's what we had to put up with. I had one friend who wanted a tubal but the doctors refused because (as my friend said) they assumed they knew better than she did what she wanted. She finally got her tubal by threatening a lawsuit. My frequently pregnant friends and I had doctors refusing to do a tubal unless we were at least 35 years old and/or had five children. (Now you know where the baby boom came from.) One friend faced and survived a life-threatening pregnancy her doctor had warned against, but he would not do a tubal until that 5 and/or 35 "rule" kicked in. Doctors seemed to think that, because we were women, we surely must want lots of kids. No, we didn't, as should be obvious by the way the birth rate dropped like a rock when the pill became available. We had a saying: "Before they're born you wouldn't give two cents for them; after they're born you wouldn't take a million bucks for them."

In those days of large families, Vatican roulette and unreliable contraceptives, miscarriages were welcomed, even hoped for, definitely envied, and never regretted—at least in my post World War II blue collar working class environment. (Hysterectomies too. We regarded them as trading in a baby carriage for a playpen.)

The abortion providers have stories to tell about real persons too. They are not like the ones just described where there was no way out. They are stories of finally being able to take control of one's life. They are stories of the clinic staffs who help them despite the murder of abortion doctors, the vandalism, the onerous regulations, the death threats, the need for excessive security procedures, including wearing bulletproof vests to work and taking random routes to get there. This is terrorism, yet it is accepted as just the way life is for women. But why should it be this way?

Informed Consent: Fiction vs. Reality

Anti-abortion laws always include a requirement for "informed consent." A woman seeking an abortion must listen to a script stating rare and sometimes untrue possible complications of an abortion, listen to the fetus's (lizard-level) heartbeat, watch a sonogram showing (non-volitional) fetal movements, and hear details of a fetus's development. These are exaggerated descriptions of what happens, designed to dissuade the woman from aborting the pregnancy.

But if informed consent is so important for an abortion, why is it not even more important for pregnancy and childbirth? After all, those are inherently life threatening conditions and doctors routinely approach the onset of labor as a disaster waiting to happen. Yet, the anti-abortion zealots never show any interest in informing a woman about the problems she could face during a pregnancy. None are trivial. They are prevented or managed to the extent possible only with good medical care. They are the reason for that care and why, without it, throughout history, death in childbirth was (and in some countries still is) common. They are the reason obstetrics is a medical specialty and why its malpractice insurance premiums are the highest in the medical field.

There are so many things that can go wrong: anemia, major birth defects, blockage of the birth canal, breech birth, eclampsia, ectopic pregnancy, fistulas, hemorrhage, high blood pressure, late-miscarriage hemorrhaging, pernicious vomiting, placenta previa, post-partum depression, post-partum fatal blood clots, toxemia, and many more. All are serious, many are life-threatening. None are of such a nature that treatment should be subject to legislative or religious control.

In addition, economic and social problems can be disastrous for a woman's ability to control her destiny. Nothing has a greater impact on her than childbearing. No one else can take on her physical, emotional, economic and social burdens (certainly not the self-righteous busybodies who promise a year's supply of diapers to women who decide against abortion). And because no one else can do this, no one else has a right to decide for a woman whether she should terminate a pregnancy. It's no one else's business.

Reverence for Life: Paving the Road to Hell

But what about the "reverence for life" mantra that marks anti-abortion rhetoric? Let's visit this particularly vacuous theological landscape and see what meaning that term might have.

Here is the experience of Cecil Bothwell, author of 10 books including *The Prince of War: Billy Graham's Crusade for a Wholly Christian Empire*, and *Whale Falls: An Exploration of Belief and its Consequences*.

For eight years Bothwell was one of a very few out-atheist elected officials, serving on the Asheville, NC, City Council from 2009-2017. He has addressed audiences in 25 cities in a dozen states on matters of ethics, governance and the environment. This is from *Whale Falls*. The story—and the truth it exposes—speaks for itself:

It was 1981 and I and my then-partner Susan were working in Arizona as house parents for a program to help mainstream developmentally disabled/mentally retarded kids. The house was brand new, having been constructed by a wealthy doctor for the benefit of two of his children who were among our seven charges.

One truly memorable client was "Donna" (not her real name). She was 19 years old with language skills at about a three-year-old level. She was angry and violent. Left alone with "Lynn" (another child) she would invariably dump her out of her wheelchair and laugh at the younger girl's inability to regain her seat. She repeatedly tore the heads off of Lynn's dolls and once grabbed me from behind as I drove the crew to school in nearby Prescott in our household passenger van. Donna was very strong and was choking me as I wrestled the vehicle to the apron.

She was given to disrobing in the boys' restrooms at the high school where she was being "mainstreamed," and by multiple accounts she was very sexually active in that situation, attracting a willing crowd of young partners. So we "progressed," to the extent that progress was possible, going through the motions of teaching language and life skills to a household full of young adults with no prayer of learning language or life skills.

The crowning irony of that period involved Donna. Thanks to her sexual activity her parents had authorized a birth control pill prescription and she'd been taking them for four years (when she didn't spit them out). But she reacted violently to medical examination and didn't ever experience menstruation during the months that we were her caretakers.

Based on the advice of her doctor, who suspected tumors, and with her parents' consent, we scheduled Donna for a hysterectomy. Wrong. Her caseworker intervened, insisting that Donna was an adult, had a right to parent, and that we were interfering with that basic human right. Oh, indeed. She would be a great parent. Maybe tear the head off her baby? But we were legally outgunned at the requisite hearing. Donna was granted continued fertility.

In the decades since I have occasionally pondered how the parents of young men in that high school would have felt about their sons lining up to have at it with Donna, perhaps gracing them with a grandchild or, for that matter, how those now middle aged men might feel about their first sexual encounters with a too-compliant mentally deficient woman. In those pre-AIDS days they probably didn't pass around anything terminal, but there's little doubt that "safe sex" didn't figure in her picture.

I still wonder from time to time whether Donna ever enjoyed the great satisfaction of parenting and whether any resultant baby survived. I fully understand the legal and ethical arguments concerning forced sterilization and the idea that we are all endowed with inalienable rights, but it seems clear that there have to be rational exceptions to any rule. Good intentions really do sometimes only pave the road to hell.

My take-home lesson from that home-parenting year was that pre-natal diagnosis of severe mental issues and the availability of abortion-on-demand are one incontrovertible blessing of modern medical science and politics. None of the clients tended that year had any remote prospect of living even semi-independent lives. Only the doctor's children enjoyed any measure of parental support (in that he built and partly financed the house) and even for those there was no meaningful family interaction. Families had abandoned the rest to state care, which, whether in large facilities or group "homes," amounted to warehousing.

To the extent that giving over such fundamentally damaged children to state care was a painful choice, the families certainly suffered. But what enduring good was served by the effort? And how could anyone consider abandonment of a child to state caretakers to be more ethical than abortion.

Babies born with severe defects are a sad thing, and society has a moral obligation to take care of them and help them. But when a fetus is severely damaged or a genetic mutation is almost certain to produce a damaged fetus, it is cruel to require that fetal life be sustained in a situation certain to impose harmful physical, emotional and economic consequences.

There is no decent, humane reason to do this. Usually it is a religious belief that justifies imposing life against all humane considerations. But when does the religion that sanctions this ever step up with support in any meaningful way? Oh, Pope Francis said sympathetically that the Church should "accompany" the pregnant woman spiritually through her trauma. How nice. This is condescending PR bullshit! Real support is left to the parents, if they are able, and to the larger community through taxes that provide human services.

The "reverence for life" religions, of course, don't even help by paying taxes. But what about families who willingly accept a pregnancy with serious birth defects, who then raise the child with love and care? One can only applaud their selflessness—until they justify it by saying that such children teach us to be compassionate, and by losing them to abortion we lose what they could have offered us.

Now think about that. They are saying that to be compassionate we must deliberately allow children to be born with severe physical and/or mental limitations. What kind of reasoning is it that says others must be brought needlessly into a life of suffering so we can show compassion? This is all so wrong!

Getting Government's Hands Off Women's Bodies

The obsessive drive to control women's reproductive decisions is neither pro-life nor moral. It is moral depravity. It relegates women's status to less than that of a corpse. A corpse has far more autonomy. You can't take its organs without the deceased's prior consent or the consent of the spouse, close family members or attorney for medical decisions. A living woman's body, if she is pregnant (and even before, through contraceptive limitations), is controlled throughout the pregnancy by specific government regulations.

Nothing about this can be justified from a secular, human-centered perspective. What would happen if there were no laws regarding abortion other than those that cover medical practice in general? Women would terminate pregnancies that were disastrous for them as the situation required, almost all during the first trimester, some in the second trimester (most often for medical reasons) and very rarely in the third trimester for severe medical reasons.

What valid (i.e., humanitarian) secular reason exists for overriding the woman's decision and forcing motherhood and all its lifelong ramifications on her? There are none. There is only the theocratic religious desire to have sectarian dogmas validated by our legal system. No one is harmed by leaving women free to have an abortion that she feels is in her interests. The fetus neither knows nor cares. A few women may regret their abortions, but they should take this up with the clergy who guilt-tripped them, not their legislators.

As for society, far more damage is done in terms of social welfare costs and dysfunctional families by prohibiting abortion. Only abortion for sex selection is socially harmful when it is done to avoid having girl children in societies that devalue and mistreat girls. But the problem is patriarchal sexism and the solution must address that.

Where are these churches when it comes to bearing the social costs of unwanted children—so often due to religion-based restrictions on access to contraceptives? The objection by Catholic and fundamentalist churches to reality-based sex education, contraception and abortion is well known. The costs are not.

In 1991, the Minnesota Women's Consortium published an analysis of the public cost over a five-year period of one unintended pregnancy and birth in Minnesota. The costs included counseling, prenatal care, the Women-Infants-Children (WIC) nutrition program, childbirth, the Aid to Families with Dependent Children (AFDC) program, food stamps, medical assistance for mother and child, public health nurse, and the Head Start pre-school program. The total came to $58,446.48. The report noted that one St. Paul high school had 55 girls pregnant in February of 1991. The five-year cost to the taxpayers for those girls and their babies would be $3,214,530. This analysis has not been updated since 1991. However, costs of everything have doubled, so we can assume these have too. Teenage girls still get pregnant. Although some get abortions, many go on welfare.

We are adding 80 million people a year to the planet. By 2100, world population will reach 10 to 14 billion if nothing stops it. Of course, something will. Earth can sustain only so many people and at some point the consequences of overpopulation will become evident and frightening enough to override every form of opposition to birth control and abortion. We can only hope the override won't be draconian and a catalyst for genocidal wars.

Besides population growth control, there is another civilization-saving benefit to ending the mistreatment of women. Stephen Pinker writes about this in his insightful book, *The Better Angels of Our Nature*, about the general decline in violence through the ages in all areas of life.

Relevant to the topic of this chapter, here is what he says, quoting one of his sources:

> Potts and his coauthors argue that giving women more control over their reproductive capacity (always the contested territory in the biological battle of the sexes) may be the single most effective way of reducing violence in the dangerous parts of the world today. But this empowerment often must proceed in the teeth of opposition from traditional men who want to preserve their control over female reproduction, and from religious institutions that oppose contraception and abortion. (p. 688)

Pinker notes how women's empowerment and increasing influence have been an important factor in the decline in violence he documents in chapters such as "The Pacification Process," "The Civilizing Process," and "The Rights Revolution."

None of this violence-reducing empowerment has come from authoritarian, theocratic religions. It has come in spite of them. At some point the respectful, pandering, social-political charade that is propping up archaic, morally depraved beliefs about women as social property has to become abhorrent enough to enough thoughtful citizens that we finally tell these emperors they have no clothes and be done with them.

6

Dogma-Driven Healthcare: The Witch Doctor Standard

*"We have legalized the ability for medical professionals to honor their
religion and their conscience over law. We have legalized anarchy."*
— Niles Ross, former pharmacist;
retired pharmaceutical industry professional

It appears that the Trump administration is almost certain to make our healthcare decisions more financially and personally restrictive, especially in their conformance to religious beliefs. Very little is likely to be positive, other than, perhaps, some progress on the marijuana controversy that keeps stirring the pot (so to speak) in many states.

Donald Trump campaigned on the promise to repeal and replace Pres. Obama's Affordable Care Act (ACA), which mandated coverage by healthcare insurance policies and provided subsidies to make it affordable for everyone. The ACA covered everything except abortion (for the usual religion-coddling reasons). Adjustments were needed for some of the self-employed but on the whole it was working well. The Republicans hated it for political and ideological reasons. Since the 2016 election gave them control of Congress they have tried to do some kind of repeal and replace but without success and have turned their attention to tax reform instead.

However, according to news reports the certainty of increasing restrictions had the effect of sending large numbers of women to Planned Parenthood and other women's clinics for long-term contraceptives. Those contraceptives are good for several years and without the ACA would cost a woman about $1,000.

Whatever cutbacks the Republicans come up with will be legally challenged. Americans United for Separation of Church and State, with other state-church separation groups, announced on Nov. 10, 2017, that they are suing the Trump administration for ruling that no employer will be required to cover contraceptives in employee healthcare insurance plans contrary to their religious beliefs. (See americansunited@au.org.) So far so good, but more lawsuits may have to be filed because the outcome for reason-based healthcare is bleak. For the January 22, 2018 anniversary of the *Roe v. Wade* ruling, Trump pumped up his anti-abortion base by announcing a plan to more aggressively enforce the right of medical personnel to refuse to provide care that conflicts with their religious beliefs. There would be a new "Conscience and Religious Freedom" division of the Department of Health and Human Services civil rights office. To call this the witch doctor standard of care is hardly an exaggeration when everything related to sexuality, contraceptives, abortion, reproductive technology and end-of-life decisions is subject to the irrational beliefs of individual medical personnel. It invites the anarchy called out in this chapter's opening quotation.

That being said, this chapter should be useful for evaluating insurance coverage proposals as they come up. Of all the topics in this book, none have the potential to compromise your health and wellbeing like religion-driven health care. You can't escape it because you are unlikely to know where the pitfalls are. For example, most people are aware that Catholic hospitals will not do abortions or provide birth control services, but there's a lot more to it than that.

Children suffer needless pain, become disabled, spread contagious diseases, and die of medical neglect because we have laws that say faith healing is health care. Medical personnel may legally refuse to provide standard—even life-saving—medical care if it is contrary to their religious beliefs. Your healthcare insurance coverage may shift from secular to religious control. Reality-based sex education is limited, and critically needed contraceptives, such as the morning-after pill, are kept as inaccessible as possible—especially for young girls who need them the most. Even reproductive technology to achieve a wanted pregnancy is compromised by restrictions. End-of-life decision making is constrained by beliefs that only "God" can determine when you die and that "suffering is the kiss of Jesus," as Mother Teresa said. Stem cell research continues to founder on the rocks of legally sanctioned religious beliefs about protoplasmic "personhood."

All of these restrictions could be challenged as state-church violations when the religion-based providers are tax exempt and government-funded. However, even if the entire healthcare system was privatized and taxed, we would still be up against conscience exemptions. They override all other laws. They override your humanity, your right to control your body, your right to live and your right to die—all to validate mystical unverifiable religious beliefs.

Marijuana and the No-Evidence Bureaucratic Trap

Many people want pot legalized for both medical and recreational use, and some states allow that to some extent. Generally, the secular/liberal left favors legalizing it and the religious/authoritarian right is opposed. Neither has a good reason because good reasons come from good evidence and there is none. All we have are anecdotes, although—such as they are—they seem to support legalization.

We can't get the evidence because marijuana is classified as a Schedule 1 drug, meaning very addictive and dangerous. Restrictions on use prevent it from being tested properly. So why not declassify it? It's not that simple. Researchers need reliable samples to work with and they are hard to come by. That's because most nations don't allow the medical use of marijuana and therefore don't allow testing. It's bureaucratic fine-print nonsense, the most difficult roadblock ever devised to hinder the progress of civilization.

How did it start? As far as I could find out, it was a right-wing congressional panic following World War I about the horrors of recreational drugs. From what I read, some congressman saw a hysterical article about marijuana in a gossip tabloid (I remember seeing a copy of it in a class on social issues) and got the weed listed as a Schedule 1 drug with no evidence whatsoever. There it stays. Some users claim it has significant medical benefits; others say it's a gateway to hard drugs. Without well-structured scientific testing, this is only what some people say. But the problem started because people found smoking pot to be pleasant. In typical religious-right thinking, if it's pleasant there must be something evil about it. Meanwhile, without scientific testing we have social testing state by state. We'll see how that works out.

Conscience Exemptions Trump All Other Laws

Conscience exemptions may sound like a laudable human rights concept, but they are a major roadblock to having health care based on your own needs rather than someone else's religion. As so often happens, they are the unintended consequence of good intentions. They were a response to the post-World War II Nuremberg Trials and the Nazi defense that "I was just following orders."

Conscience exemptions were seen as a way to legally protect people from being forced to commit atrocities, such as the Nazi practice of doing medical experiments on Jews. It made "I was just following orders" no longer a legitimate defense and made one's conscience a barrier against unjustifiable, inhumane orders. Unfortunately, this well-intentioned exemption became a protection for those who refuse to provide justifiable and humane medical care. It even covered what is otherwise considered the minimum standard of care when that care does not conform to the provider's religious beliefs.

The 1973 *Roe v Wade* decision legalizing abortion was the catalyst for the first national conscience exemption in the United States (some states already had them). Immediately after that decision, Sen. Frank Church, from Idaho, introduced an exemption bill that passed 92-1. It protected private hospitals that were receiving federal tax support through the Hill-Burton Act and government programs (such as Medicare and Medicaid) from being required to provide reproductive services that did not conform to their religious beliefs. These services have come to include abortion, contraceptives, sterilization, referrals to other providers, some fertility treatments and the use of stem cells. Many states followed with their own conscience exemptions and some pharmacies have allowed "pharmacists for life" to refuse to fill prescriptions for contraceptives.

The only protection for patients was an informed consent clause that prohibited medical personnel from giving fraudulent information about a procedure they refused to do, such as claiming harmful side effects. This has not worked well, as unjustified fear mongering continues to deter patients from seeking needed reproductive health care. In some cases, laws have been enacted requiring that false information be presented to patients.

With conscience exemptions, it may not always be the medical facility that is the problem as it is the personnel working there. Here is a personal account provided to me for publication by Niles Ross, a medical professional:

> Suppose there is a hospital that is non-sectarian, and is well known to perform abortions. Each individual OB-GYN physician is *not* obligated to perform them, even if the "hospital" performs them. Each individual health professional—doctor, nurse, pharmacist, X-ray technician—has his or her own individual religious-and conscience-directed right not to perform a procedure.
>
> It is now 1970, and I am working in what is my final job as a pharmacist before I go on to other things in my career—although at the point of this story that is not on my radar screen. I am working in a private, non-profit, non-sectarian hospital in New York State. It is at that time that New York State legalized abortion prior to the United States Supreme Court doing so.
>
> The Chief Administrator of the hospital is making a tour of every single department. He has now just walked into the pharmacy and he states (by paraphrase and memory): "Starting Monday, this hospital will perform abortions. We are open 24-hours a day, and we will perform abortions as needed, which might mean 24 hours a day. If there is any pharmacist who cannot dispense the drugs, let your supervisor know, and you will be exempt from that. However, we ARE open 24 hours a day, and the drugs WILL be dispensed 24 hours a day."
>
> So back then, the conscience exemption was well known and alive and well. It happened that we had two Catholic pharmacists. Neither of them expressed objection, and they did dispense the drugs. This alleviated a big potential problem. We had only one pharmacist on the night shift—a Catholic. He preferred the night shift and, of course, we all preferred that he preferred it. Had he voiced objection, the entire shift system would have collapsed. Nothing happened, but it could have. So the issue is not only the institution, it is the individual person. The chain of providers involved in you exercising your

right to have the procedure you need is only as strong as the weakest link, and that is the conscience exemption. This was evident in the Nancy Cruzan "right-to-die" case as individual nurses objected to care that was other than "keep her alive into infinity."

There are pockets of the country where religion-controlled, non-Catholic hospitals and health care providers are also part of the problem. I emphasize that religion plays a special role in health care, but it is not only Catholicism. It bears the brunt of the discussion because of the number of Catholic hospitals, but the *person* can also pose the problem because of the conscience exemption.

I am now living in another state. My personal physician is an employee of a Methodist hospital. He is fine and dandy with my living will, but he may not be able to honor it. This is why: The Methodist hospital has a "hospital within a hospital." This is a sub-hospital for very ill, long-term patients (burn unit, as an example) and there are specially trained physicians who are employed to work in that sub-portion of the hospital. The hospital gets those physicians from a medical contracting company that supplies physicians of this sort to hospitals all over the country that want to contract with them. That contracting company is a Catholic institution.

The Methodist hospital, as an institution, will honor my living will. However, there is no Methodist hospital treating me. There are only physicians, and nurses, and pharmacists, and X-ray technicians. Therefore, it is the conscience exemption, being applicable to specific people apart from the specific institution that makes things very difficult. A patient cannot interview every single health care provider. The inpatient, particularly, is subject to whoever shows up at his or her bed at the particular moment of need, with the patient vulnerable at that particular moment of physical, medical, and emotional difficulty. Even with the strongest health care advocate—and my lawyer is— the health care advocate cannot be there every single moment to be available when an emergency occurs. (Note the discussion of 24-hour abortions—hospitals treat on a 24-hour day.)

It is at that moment that the conscience of the individual health care provider kicks in. Nor will it help that my lawyer will threaten legal action at the moment the health care provider decides to plunge some device into me to keep me alive. A valid Supreme Court ruling in my favor is of no use to me. Terri Schiavo lived seven years.

What this comes down to is that a medical facility and/or its conscience-driven staff members can refuse to perform a legal—even necessary—procedure if it is against their religious beliefs. They can even refuse to tell you of its availability elsewhere. Even so, there may be nowhere else to go if you are in an HMO or an employer-provided healthcare plan that limits you to that facility or if you live in a rural area where it's that facility or none. And there is not a damn thing you can do about this.

The issue Niles raises is serious. Conscience exemptions have created a veritable anarchy in medical care, with patients vulnerable to whatever religious belief drives the medical caregiver at hand. Furthermore, if a patient dies or is otherwise harmed by irrational conscience-driven treatment, the hospital and/or its staff cannot be sued. Oh, they can be sued for malpractice, but there is no such thing as conscience malpractice in the medical field. Cut off the wrong leg and you're in trouble, but let a woman die rather than perform a life-saving abortion and you're home free.

Obviously, the consciences of others can sometimes be dangerous to your health. Yet there are no standards for what constitutes a legitimate conscience exemption. There should be, and they should be secular and evidence based, with the patient's desires and needs given priority. No one's conscience should be allowed to deny the morning-after pill to rape victims or permit medical neglect of a child to satisfy the parents' faith healing beliefs or deny physician aid in dying to end irremediable suffering or compromise the treatment of any of the other diseases and conditions and circumstances some religions believe must be subject to theological control. For the hopelessly ill and suffering person, the medieval mindset has come full circle. The rack of the Inquisition is now one's deathbed. Still in the name of religion. Still just following orders—from God.

Here's a test case for setting conscience exemption standards, as reported by the Associated Press, Dec, 21, 2010, and in *The Humanist* magazine, March-April 2011: In 2009, Sister Margaret McBride, an administrator at St. Joseph's Hospital and Medical Center in Phoenix, Arizona, authorized an abortion as the only way to save the life of a woman in her 20s who was 11 weeks pregnant and near death from pulmonary hypertension. The abortion was forbidden by Catholic doctrine, as spelled out in the U.S. Conference of Catholic Bishops' "Ethical and Religious Directives for Catholic Health Care Services" that governs health care in Catholic hospitals in the United States. Bishop Thomas Olmsted of the Roman Catholic Diocese of Phoenix excommunicated McBride, claiming her action was a source of scandal for the Church. The diocese also ended the hospital's affiliation with the Church.

It's hard to see this as punishment. I would think McBride and the hospital would want to say, "Good riddance." But the pull of religious belief can be strong. McBride and the hospital were heroic in rejecting that pull so they could save a life. McBride was, in fact, given an award by a Catholic lay group called "Call to Action." The members had been excommunicated in 1973 but apparently adopted a "good riddance" attitude and continued to object to inhumane dogma.

The hospital president, Linda Hunt, defended McBride's actions, say-ing, "If we are presented with a situation in which a pregnancy threatens a woman's life, our first priority is to save both patients. If that is not possible, we will always save the life we can, and that is what we did in this case." Bishop Olmsted said the mother's disease (with death nearly a 100% certainty, according to the doctors), ". . . needed to be treated. But instead of treating the disease, St. Joseph's medical staff and ethics committee decided that the healthy 11-week-old baby should be directly killed."

Noooo, it was *not* a "healthy 11 week-old baby." It was a fetus at barely more than two months gestation and impossible to save under any circumstances. But such are the emotional word games that infuse anti-abortion propaganda. No such sympathy-seeking language is ever used to describe the alive and sentient young women whose lives are considered disposable by the demands of theology.

So the question is, which conscience-driven action operating at St. Joseph's Hospital should realistically fall under the exemptions law—McBride's for saving the young woman's life or Bishop Olmsted's for wanting to sacrifice the woman's life to save an un-savable fetus just to uphold his Church's "sanctity of life" (for fetuses only) theology and avoid an abortion "scandal" for the Church?

As the law stands, both saving the woman for demonstrable humanitarian reasons and letting her die for irrational theological reasons are conscience-driven actions. Accepting both as valid leads to medical anarchy. The solution is to apply the exemptions only to actions that are evidence-based, demonstrably humanitarian, and supportive of the patient's wishes.

Hospital Mergers and Secular vs Religion-Based Care

The economics of hospital management have led in recent years to a proliferation of mergers and affiliations to gain greater market power and achieve cost efficiencies. Trouble arises when one of the hospitals is controlled by the Catholic Church. In these circumstances, Catholic theology must prevail and all staff in the merged institution must agree to adhere to the "Ethical and Religious Directives for Catholic Health Care Services." They apply to everyone, Catholic or not. Here is what the Directives say about such mergers, taken from Part Six, "Forming New Partnerships with Health Care Organizations and Providers":

69. If a Catholic health care organization is considering entering into an arrangement with another organization that may be involved in activities judged morally wrong by the Church, participation in such activities must be limited to what is in accord with the moral principles governing cooperation.

70. Catholic health care organizations are not permitted to engage in immediate material cooperation in actions that are intrinsically immoral, such as abortion, euthanasia, assisted suicide, and direct sterilization.

71. The possibility of scandal must be considered when applying the principles governing cooperation. Cooperation, which

in all other respects is morally licit, may need to be refused because of the scandal that might be caused. The diocesan bishop has final responsibility for assessing and addressing issues of scandal, considering not only the circumstances in his local diocese but also the regional and national implications of his decision.

72. The Catholic partner in an arrangement has the responsibility periodically to assess whether the binding agreement is being observed and implemented in a way that is consistent with Catholic teaching.

This means that, if the only hospital near you is Catholic or in a Catholic-secular partnership, you're in trouble. No contraceptives, no abortion (or even a referral for an abortion) even if your life depends on it, no removal of a life-threatening ectopic pregnancy, no prenatal diagnosis if there is any hint that it may lead to an abortion, no vasectomy or tubal ligation, no morning-after pill even if you've been raped, no *in vitro* fertilization or other doctrinally off-limits fertility technology, and no aggressive end-of-life pain remission. Here is what the Catholic bishops say about that, from Part Five of the Directives, "Issues in Care for the Seriously Ill and Dying":

61. . . . Since a person has the right to prepare for his or her death while fully conscious, he or she should not be deprived of consciousness without a compelling reason. Medicines capable of alleviating or suppressing pain may be given to a dying person, even if the therapy may indirectly shorten the person's life so long as the intent is not to hasten death. Patients experiencing suffering that cannot be alleviated should be helped to appreciate the Christian understanding of redemptive suffering.

If you can't understand why suffering is good for you, too bad. And we all pay for this "Christian understanding" with higher taxes because these hospitals are tax-exempt and get federal funding besides. Therefore, a hospital that refuses to provide a standard service for doctrinal reasons is actually being paid by the taxpayers for doing nothing. There is no recourse for the patient. Hospitals can't be sued if they have an arbitration clause in the admitting documents (who reads them?) and a recent Supreme Court ruling prevents people from bringing class action suits against corporations

Defunding Family Planning Insurance Coverage

The ACA required all health care plans to include contraceptives and sterilizations without co-pays or deductibles. This outraged the Catholic bishops, who claim their religious liberty is compromised if they are forced to provide such services to the employees of organizations the Church controls. They forced Obama to eliminate coverage of abortion and then put coverage of contraceptives on the chopping block. Obama hoped to defuse the controversy in 2012 by allowing exemptions for strictly religious entities, which IRS calls the "integrated auxiliaries" of churches. That left the female office workers and housekeepers who staff them out of luck. Obama insisted that religion-controlled facilities, such as hospitals, colleges and social service agencies that serve the general public, be covered. There are 600 hospitals and more than 200 colleges controlled by the Catholic Church, plus numerous social service agencies, such as Catholic Charities—all tax exempt and funded largely by the taxpayers through government grants and contracts. There are millions of employees in these hospitals and social service agencies and about 900,000 students in the colleges—all with widely varying religious beliefs, and 98% of the Catholics among them use contraceptives.

Not good enough, the bishops said. They insisted that their religious freedom [to force their beliefs on those millions of religiously diverse employees and students] was under attack. So Obama backed down again—somewhat—trying to compromise. He said all Catholic-run organizations would be exempt from providing the coverage, but the insurance companies would provide it instead, still at no cost to patients. That left the bishops' medieval "conscience" clear for public relations purposes.

Still not good enough, the bishops said. Even this separate and indirect contraceptive involvement in insurance coverage was too much of an infringement on their religious liberty. Almost immediately, a private company in Colorado, Hercules Industries, whose owners happen to be Catholic, made the same claim and a judge issued a temporary restraining order to prevent "imminent irreparable harm."

Since then, efforts have been underway to protect such "religious liberty" at the expense of everyone else's freedom by allowing employers and healthcare insurance providers to exclude any coverage they consider to be immoral or in violation of their religious beliefs. The Trump administration has issued a ruling supporting this.

Where would this end? Could coverage be denied for any sex-related condition some employers considered immoral or contrary to their religious beliefs? HIV testing? Cancers transmitted by sexual activity? Childbirth for unmarried women? How about blood transfusions (Jehovah's Witnesses) or almost all medical care (Christian Scientists)? There would be no end to the religion-generated chaos. Just such an amendment was offered by Sen. Roy Blunt (R-MO), but the U.S. Senate voted to table it on March 1, 2012. The vote was 51-48, frighteningly close for such a potentially destructive law. These cases almost always end up at the Supreme Court and the Court almost always rules in favor of the bishops.

The Long Battle Against Faith Healing Laws

This is an issue with which I have been personally involved, so I will report what I know and what I have leaned from CHILD (Children's Healthcare Is a Legal Duty), the only organization dedicated to protecting children from faith-based medical neglect. CHILD has recently reorganized as CHILD USA and merged with a civil rights organization headed by legal activist Marci Hamilton that covers a wide range of child abuse cases.

CHILD was founded by Rita and Doug Swan, former Christian Scientists, whose 18-month-old son died of meningitis when the Swans relied solely on prayer to heal him. The tragedy brought reality home to them and they have since worked relentlessly to repeal laws that validate faith healing as legitimate health care. These laws exist in many states at the request of Christian Science lobbyists. Apparently, legislators never have sense enough to ask what the Christian Scientists intend to do that they need protection from prosecution.

When CHILD began its work, Nebraska was the only state without a religious exemption in its child abuse or neglect laws, thanks to the legislative initiative of Sen. Ernie Chambers. Nebraska is the only state in the country that has never had a religious exemption pertaining to medical care of sick children. Today six more states have removed such an exemption: Oregon, Hawaii, Massachusetts, Maryland, North Carolina, and Tennessee. Other states have at least made significant improvements. In the past 20 years, Oklahoma is the only state that has added a religious exemption.

Two states, Mississippi and West Virginia, have no religious exemptions from immunizations. Only Mississippi allows a religious exemption from metabolic testing. (This simple test on a newborn can indicate a condition that causes mental retardation if not treated quickly, yet Mississippi permits parents to refuse it for religious reasons.) The worst states are those with a religious defense to a manslaughter or negligent homicide charge. They are Ohio, Iowa, Idaho, Arkansas, and West Virginia. In essence, Mississippi, Louisiana, and Nevada may also have a religious defense to manslaughter.

Other states have an unsatisfying mixed bag of exemptions and non-exemptions. For example, Washington state requires parents to provide "medically necessary health care" as part of its criminal mistreatment law. However, it then says, "It is the intent of the legislature that a person who, in good faith, is furnished Christian Science treatment by a duly accredited Christian Science practitioner in lieu of medical care is not considered deprived of medically necessary health care or abandoned." Astonishingly, this says in effect that, 1) prayer is equivalent to medical care, and 2) Christian Science prayers are exclusively endorsed as equivalent to medical care.

In defense of the Washington state legislature's overall sanity, if not due diligence, this exemption was added secretly in a conference committee's reconciliation of House and Senate bills covering health care. It was then accepted *pro forma* by the legislature with no sign indicating awareness of the addition. Sadly, the secretly added exemption was used as a defense by a couple who let their son die slowly and horribly of a ruptured appendix in 2009. They were members of the Church of the Firstborn and claimed the law's exemption for Christian Science should apply to them also. The parents were charged with manslaughter but ended up getting probation.

One has to wonder how any state could allow this barbaric abuse of children. I found out when a faith healing death in Minnesota caused me to become a lobbyist for CHILD as they challenged the state's faith healing laws. Below is the story. It is discouraging.

What It's Like to Challenge Faith Healing Laws

"We have a statute that says *that?!*" That stunned comment by Mary Jo McGuire, a state legislator (now a county commissioner), was one of the few rational responses I got when I began a no-brainer (I thought) lobbying campaign on behalf of CHILD to repeal Minnesota's faith healing statutes that exempt faith healing parents from prosecution for medical neglect of children. It became a five-year slog through mind-numbing legislative cluelessness.

It started in 1989 and ended with very little success in 1994. The project was a response to the death from diabetes of 11-year-old Ian Lundman when his Christian Science mother and stepfather relied solely on prayer to treat his illness. I was joined in the lobbying effort by CHILD member Steve Petersen, who worked diligently on almost a daily basis, and by George Erickson, also a CHILD member, with assistance from the American Civil Liberties Union-Minnesota.

Rita Swan warned me not to expect much from liberal legislators, although one would think they would be supportive. I found both the liberal left and the conservative right to be more concerned with protecting parents' religious beliefs than the lives of children. There were exceptions, of course, as illustrated by the quotation in this section's opening paragraph. I did get two top-ranking liberal Democratic legislators to sponsor our bill to repeal the statutes. Sen. Jane Ranum sponsored it in the Senate, and Rep. Phil Carruthers did the same in the House. They were tenacious. We also had the support of Sen. Bill Luther (later elected to Congress, now retired from public life), who helped with lobbying and witnesses' testimony.

Rita and Doug brought witnesses to testify about the tragic consequences of having statutes that give parents permission to let their kids die by relying solely on prayer. Ian Lundman's biological father, who had been living in another state, came to testify, carrying his son's baseball glove. His and the others' testimony was wrenching, but did no good. Compassion and common sense went out the window when religion came in the door. For example, Rita was asked to describe Christian Science beliefs. She was professional and gave an unemotional, straightforward, textbook account of the belief system. (It consists of not admitting that disease exists. The "treatment" for an illness is a prayer that refuses to acknowledge the illness, for only by acknowledging it can it come into existence.) The legislators listened—and then one of them accused her of bashing religion! One legislative staff member said to me, "Well, doctors don't cure everyone either." (No, but their track record beats a system that denies illness exists!)

I saw the medical examiner's photos of Ian's body. He was like a corpse dragged out of a Nazi extermination camp. Yet, when Ian's grandmother testified, she said, "I was with Ian the day before he died, and he looked just fine to me." No doubt he did. Her religion had so deadened her to reality that she could not see it right in front of her, and so she didn't.

Our bill had to get through two committees, one chaired by Sen. John Marty (still in office) and one by Sen. Allen Spear (now deceased). Both were very liberal but both were immovable and could not bring themselves to infringe on the beliefs of well-meaning Christian Science parents. . . Not even when one Christian Science woman pleaded with legislators to not repeal the faith healing statutes because, if they did, she would not be allowed to fail—not be allowed *to let her child die!* This astonishing statement did not horrify the legislators at all. That children in faith healing families were being denied the equal protection of the law regarding medical care seemed not to concern them. Neither committee recommended passage of our bill.

Our sponsors, Sen. Ranum and Rep. Carruthers, tried very hard to get something useful passed. In the end, against opposition from legislators determined to protect religious beliefs, they achieved a partial victory when faith healing parents were made mandated reporters of a sick child. How those parents were to do that without acknowledging that the illness existed, I have no idea, but at least they were made accountable.

The political power of this small religion is astounding. Christian Science has too few members to affect the outcome of an election. Yet, legislators readily accede to their requests for preferential statutes. And it doesn't stop with one request. The Christian Science lobbyists then approach the insurance companies and ask for coverage for their prayer "treatment" based on those validating statutes. And they get it! Then they go back to the legislators for stronger exemptions based on the insurance coverage. And they get it! During the 2009-10 debate on health care reform, they came close to getting covered for prayer "treatment" that consists of refusing to admit that disease exists! That provision was removed after pressure from CHILD members but attempts to include it continued at the state level as local essential benefits packages were developed.

As part of the ACA, the government offered states a number of plans from which to select a "benchmark plan." This was a template to be used by a state's insurance carriers. At least one of the policies each carrier offered had to be identical to the benchmark plan. One of the plans was the Federal Government Employee Health Association Plan. It included coverage for Christian Science prayer "treatments"—treatments based on the notion that disease does not exist! Colorado had already chosen it as one of its three plans. The governor was lobbied by the Christian Science Church to choose it as its benchmark plan. With 50 states available, it is highly probable that payment for prayers was part of a good number of state plans. Not many people pay attention to this part of the plan, and not many legislators stop to think how this state validation of prayer alone as medical care encourages faith healing parents to rely solely on it, with the inevitable tragic results.

Then there are the Christian Science nursing homes. They provide only basic custodial care. They don't take temperatures or do anything else that might suggest a disease exists. Yet patients get this care at no cost through Medicare, whereas they would have to pay several thousand dollars a month in any non-Christian Science facility because Medicare covers only skilled nursing services—except for Christian Science facilities. Christian Science did suffer a temporary setback in 1997 when U.S. Attorney General Janet Reno opposed tax support for Christian Science nursing homes. Another temporary setback came when a federal court ruled that Medicare-Medicaid payments for Christian Science nursing homes were "unconstitutional, invalid, unenforceable." However, Christian Science advocates in the U.S. Senate continued to seek tax funded faith healing and in 1998 they prevailed. In 2000, CHILD lost the battle entirely when the Supreme Court ruled that faith healing is "a subset of medical care." Both the 8th and 9th Circuit Courts of Appeals upheld Medicare funding for Christian Science nursing homes and the U.S. Supreme Court has refused to hear constitutional challenges from those cases. So, absurd as it is, yes, we have statutes that say that! They are in many states and at the federal level, providing tax support for Christian Science custodial care and for prayer that denies illness exists, while exempting from prosecution those who allow children to die for this hocus pocus.

End-of-Life Decision-Making

You may think you have a right to make your own end-of-life decisions—after all, who knows your situation and your mindset better than you? Well, there are people who are sure they know better, and they are determined to have that "know better" insight reflected in the laws you must follow. Here's what "know better" looks like, taken from the "infallible" (even though entirely speculative) doctrines spelled out in the U.S. Catholic Bishops' "Ethical and Religious Directives for Catholic Health Care. It's in Part Five under "Issues in Care for the Seriously Ill and Dying":

> The truth that life is a precious gift from God has profound implications for the question of stewardship over human life. We are not the owners of our lives and, hence, do not have absolute power over life. We have a duty to preserve our life and to use it for the glory of God, but the duty to preserve life is not absolute, for we may reject life-prolonging procedures that are insufficiently beneficial or excessively burdensome. Suicide and euthanasia are never morally acceptable options.

So you see, you don't own your life, the bishops do, and you just have to take their word for it that they are authorized by God, through the pope, to dictate the conditions of this ownership. They think suffering is good for you in a spiritual way, and they will do their best to see that the laws of our land don't allow you to end that suffering on your own terms. Fortunately, the laws of the land are changing, but we still have a long way to go before our end-of-life decisions become our own and not the bishops'. Not too long ago, there were seldom any end-of-life decisions to make. Nature made them for us. Pneumonia was once called "the old man's friend" because it ended a suffering person's life fairly quickly. Then came medical advances. They did a great job of controlling and even curing many diseases, but sometimes had the unintended consequence of allowing one's dying to be extended with an endless array of often-unwanted life-support equipment and medications. Release into death was impossible because our laws denied that physicians could reasonably have a duty to help their patients die when it was no longer possible to help them live.

Organizations promoting physician-assisted dying began forming. Some people took matters into their own hands by assisting a suffering loved one's death. Some were prosecuted for this, but sympathetic juries tended to go light on punishment. In the 1970s, Derek Humphry, a British journalist, helped his cancer-ridden wife die peacefully. He escaped prosecution and went on to organize the Hemlock Society (now called Compassion and Choices) to work for physician-assisted dying. Other groups followed. Humphry has since published a best-selling book, *Final Exit*, which describes ways to do a self-deliverance.

In the 1990s, Dr. Jack Kevorkian, a Michigan pathologist known for supporting voluntary euthanasia (Greek for "good death"), opened public debate on the issue in an attention-getting way. He developed a "death machine" that ensured a quick, painless, self-administered death from inhaled chemicals. Dr. Kevorkian advertised his services and charged no fees. He assisted about 130 desperate people during a ten-year period. After defying many legal attempts to stop him, he was finally arrested after appearing on the CBS Television show, "60 Minutes." On that episode he showed a videotape he made of the self-deliverance of Thomas Youk. Although the death was clearly voluntary, wanted, and rational (as Youk attested on the video), Dr. Kevorkian was charged with second degree murder and the delivery of a controlled substance. He was tried in 1999 and sentenced to 10-25 years in prison but released after eight years. He died an unassisted death of natural causes in 2011.

An HBO movie, "You Don't Know Jack," accurately dramatizes his stubborn insistence on the right to die on one's own terms, and his willingness to break the law and pay the price for forcing the issue to public attention. Dr. Kevorkian did succeed in raising public awareness and increasing public acceptance of a physician assisted death. Along with that came increased membership in organizations for physician aid in dying. Most worked to change state laws, but one—Final Exit Network (FEN)—focused on helping people do a self-deliverance because their need was urgent and it would be years before the laws changed—if they ever did.

The Court had ruled earlier that states could experiment with "death with dignity" laws, although getting state legislators to allow physician-assisted dying has been almost impossible. The issue is clouded by religion-instigated propaganda about slippery slopes and Nazi-like euthanizing of disabled people. To date, only Oregon, Washington and Montana have such laws. The Oregon experience, with its popular appeal, successful implementation, and problem-free track record made it easier for other states to follow—although with resistance from authoritarian religions all the way.

A short-lived inclusion of Georgia in those "other states" came on November 4, 2011. The state had arrested four volunteers from Final Exit Network on a charge of assisting a suicide. (This was nothing more than giving advice and emotional support to someone who wanted to do a self deliverance, was mentally competent, and whose medical condition had been verified as serious, debilitating and irreversible.) In addition to arresting the four volunteers, the state froze Final Exit Network's assets and persuaded law enforcement authorities in Arizona, Maryland and Ohio to raid the homes of other Network volunteers and confiscate their computers and records.

In Maryland, in December of 2014, state regulators revoked the medical license of Dr. Lawrence D. Egbert, the medical director for Final Exit Network, for engaging in "unprofessional conduct." This consisted of reviewing the medical records of six people, recommending them for FEN's assistance, attending the self-deliverance rehearsal, talking with them and holding their hands. Dr. Egbert was 87 and had practiced medicine for over 60 years. He has since died.

So there it stood, but not for long. Charges against the Final Exit Network volunteers were dropped. However, as expected, the Georgia legislature acted quickly to pass a restrictive law that would be constitutional. Attorney Robert Rivas explained it in the Spring 2012 Final Exit Network newsletter:

> . . . The ruling opened for Georgia the opportunity to enact a law criminalizing assisting in a suicide, like those of many states. The General Assembly of Georgia set out to pass such a law at lightning speed, compared to their usual snail's pace, and Georgia lawmakers thanked the Catholic Conference and Georgia Right to Life for their help in hurriedly drafting the new statute. . . . The draft defines "assist" as "the act of physically helping or physically providing the means" to commit suicide. This definition, clearer than defining words in other states, would protect Final Exit Network's volunteers from being charged in future Georgia cases. . . . In contrast, the laws of some states are obtuse when they prohibit "aiding" or "assisting" in a suicide. Some state laws provide definitions that are downright hostile or threatening to FEN's mission. Minnesota, for instance, makes a criminal of anyone who "intentionally advises, encourages, or assists another in taking the other's own life," language that would be unconstitutionally overbroad if it is interpreted to prohibit FEN from providing information, education, and emotional support to members in the hour when they most need it.

And that is what happened in the Minnesota instance. In May 2012, Final Exit Network and four of its volunteers were indicted on 17 counts of assisting the suicide of a 57-year-old Twin Cities woman who self-delivered in 2007. The woman was in great pain from an irreversible, untreatable condition and left a letter explaining her determination to end her agony. She called on FEN for information and guidance, which they provided. FEN has had to spend thousands of dollars defending their right to extend compassion to those who ask for it, need it and desperately want it.

Somehow this is considered criminal. By December 2017, FEN had lost an appeal and the Supreme Court declined to review it, so the case will go to a federal district court as a civil action based on denial of free speech. Meanwhile, those who called in the police [Why? Because they loved the woman so much they wanted to see her suffer as long as possible?] will not be charged for invading her privacy and dishonoring her desire to die on her own terms. Only those who cared about her enough to help her are being dragged through the court system.

And of course there are other laws impeding one's right to die with dignity. People who are able to do a self-deliverance without a doctor's help can certainly do so, but there are insurance laws that can make it impossible without the survivors' being penalized financially. Also, emergency medical personnel are required by law to revive a person who is clearly trying to do a self-deliverance but has not yet succeeded. Tattooing "Do Not Resuscitate" on your chest is no protection. Only a medical form for that, signed by a doctor, and readily at hand for the paramedics, will work.

The Basic Right to Bodily Autonomy

We need a T-shirt that says, "Get Religion Out Of Medical Care." Of all the healthcare issues discussed here, where is the secular justification for laws that deprive someone of the right to control how their body is treated? What is a valid conscience exemption? Some awful things are done by following one's conscience. Anti-abortion zealots murder doctors who dare to provide abortions. Faith healers let their children die of medical neglect or allow them to infect others by being unvaccinated. Can a Jehovah's Witness nurse refuse to give a blood transfusion?

The Nuremberg laws were passed to ensure that "I was just following orders" is no longer a defense. The "medical experiments" the Jews were subjected to were plainly torture. Yet now, for end-of-life procedures, we are subjected to torture at the hands of others who are "just following orders" based on their personal religious beliefs. Along with legalizing "conscience" driven anarchy, we have also legalized the evil we sought to outlaw—we have legalized torture.

When does the conscience exemption become not only barbaric but absurd? Conscience exemptions should apply only if demonstrable harm can be shown by performing a service. That was their intent following Nazi medical experiments on Jews, and it should remain the sole intent.

If beliefs are so important to some believers that they can't do their job, they should find a different job. The United States would do well to adopt the position of the health ministry in Norway. Faced with "conscience" demands, it has refused to budge. As the secretary of state at the health ministry, Robin Kåss, said, "If you're a pacifist, you can't work as a police officer. If you refuse to perform a blood transfusion, you can't be a surgeon. If you deny a patient contraception or a referral for an abortion, you can't be a general physician."

As for hospitals, none of them, whether owned or affiliated with a religious organization or not, should be permitted to deviate from the medical standard of care. Similarly, why treat faith healing as legitimate health care? It has been demonstrated over and over again that prayers for healing don't work. Why legitimize nonsense?

Is there any rational reason to defund Planned Parenthood or any reality-based family planning services? The motivation is based purely on religious beliefs about the "ensoulment" ("personhood") of fertilized eggs. These doctrines are neither rational nor practical.

End-of-life decision-making should be a civil right, unimpeded by laws that serve only to support doctrinal beliefs that suffering has spiritual merit. Reality and personal autonomy have to count for something. Religion-based health care denies both. It should find no enforcement or validation in our secular laws.

Postscript: A Death With Dignity

I am including this story because Annie Chase asked me to publicize it and because it is satisfying to see that the human species really does include people like Annie—grounded in reality, intelligent, decent, caring and thoughtful . . . who know how to live, and how to die . . . who bring meaning and purpose into a meaningless universe.

Annie Chase (born March 19, 1946; died March 8, 2010) is now, in her words, "one lucky stiff," after achieving her self-deliverance on Monday, March 8, 2010. Annie wanted her story told to encourage open discussion of the right to a self-directed death. She began writing her thoughts in January of 2010 and completed them with an audio recording as her failing eyesight made using a computer difficult. Her last recording was on March 8 as she prepared her self-deliverance. Her material consisted of nine pages of text and two 90-minute audiotapes. She gave it all to me to condense and compile into what became a 32-page booklet to promote the right to a self-directed death: *My Purpose Driven Death: How I Became One Lucky Stiff.* It is available from Atheists For Human Rights, Minneapolis MN. Contact mac@mtn.org, or julianagengast@yahoo.com for more information.

The following is an excerpt from Annie's last recording. Because of religion-based laws, Annie had to die alone to avoid legally jeopardizing those she loved. . . . but her family and friends were with her in their thoughts, and she knew that.

Hello from the "Other Side"

January to March 2010. HELLOOOO FROM THE "OTHER SIDE"! Annie Chase here. As I write this I am pretending to speak from the Great Beyond. No afterlife is involved, just a literary construct to help me address a topic I've found is difficult to discuss because it involves unpreventable sadness and loss. The topic is Death. Because many people are not at ease discussing either their own death or someone else's, they miss the opportunity to shape their final stage of life to their own desires and ethics, and to convey their wishes to those who love them. This is a sad but preventable loss.

From my perspective, I could see death's necessary inevitability as part of the terrible, wrenching beauty of life. The choice isn't whether to die. No one is exempt from that One-Death-Per-Birth rule. I am that lucky stiff who got to choose some of the specific features of the experience. I wanted to make it a fulfilling, consciously enacted final stage of the only life I would ever have. Metaphorically speaking, I didn't want my approaching union with the debonair Mr. Oblivion to be solemnized in a hasty 2 a.m. shotgun wedding, with a few glum family members in their bathrobes looking on. I didn't want my one-and-only death to be a forcible abduction by a barely-glimpsed stalker who sneaked up and conked me on the head before dragging me off to his rude hovel.

I got inklings that my life's "best if used by" date was becoming gradually decipherable, like the fortunes that float murkily up to the little window in a Crazy 8-Ball oracular device. In 2005, after years of occasional, sudden and puzzling symptoms, I was diagnosed with Wegener's Granulomatosis, a degenerative disorder similar to lupus. When in an active phase, it can flare up in sporadic, unpredictable periods of debilitating fatigue, dizziness, joint pain and weakness; extreme sensitivity to light, noise, heat and cold; rapidly-growing and randomly appearing tumors; and sometimes, as in my case, loss of sight. About a year ago, the unmistakable signs of rapid reduction of my visual capacity made it necessary to consider whether to continue To Be or Not To Be. I also had to decide how soon I must act or how long I could safely wait to do so, since I would need my eyes to research and carry out my exit plan.

I owned my body. As long as I was of sound mind, and acting of my own volition in my own behalf, and as long as I was not endangering anyone else in the process, no one but me had the right to decide anything about what I did or didn't do with that body of mine. I was single and fiercely independent, with no one reliant on me for support. Beginning with my life-long, voracious appetite for books, almost all the activities that were meaningful to me depended on the use of my eyes. I had no willingness to re-learn every small, daily survival skill to live as a non-sighted person, bereft of reading and art and dance performances and fall color and unfettered mobility. That was my decision, and mine alone to make. Others may choose a different destiny, and I had the greatest admiration for those who found fulfillment in dealing courageously with a debilitating disease or physical impairment. They deserve full support, respect and love.

In recent years, some people had begun talking openly about end of life options, including the right to die and the recent availability in some states of medically assisted death. That was a start, but it didn't cover what I wanted to avoid—suffering, loss of control over my body and life circumstances or allowing some outside "expert" or a panel of them to dictate the terms of my experience of the all-important last stage of my life. I wanted practical information and a dependable method of ending my life. The book *Final Exit* by Derek Humphry was invaluable—straightforward, simple and reassuring. It offered several dignified procedures and explained why some methods many people (including me) first called to mind were not good at all. I recommend that everyone obtain that book. How in the world could the right to die not be a basic human right? I saw how badly the right-to-die movement was needed but, of course, there was a huge oppositional movement that said only God gets to strike us down or take us home to his eternal loving bosom, or both.

In May of 2009, it became clear that I was losing my sight and it was time to plan it being my last trip around the sun. As I peeled away the onion layers of accumulated possessions, I also simplified my finances. I turned most of my valuable things and accounts into cash. I knew how much I needed to live on for the remaining time. Wow! I was rich! It turned out that being rich didn't have anything to do with how much money it was. It was the sense of ease and freedom because I had more than I needed. What I had enough for was to make the money and treasured possessions emblematic of almost another form of immortality. My resources went a long way and covered a lot of needs when it was divided into chunks of a few hundred, or a thousand, or in a couple of cases, even a few thousand dollars, all directed to helping—to having the joy of helping—mostly younger people get a better start.

It turned out to be so much fun. What bliss, what freedom, an absolute sense of being on a total lark! A hugely enjoyable part of my life began at that point. I started cherishing everything, thinking in terms of the last trip around the sun. I started looking at the seasonal things I was enjoying and experiencing for the final time. Everything from the last ride on one of the best roller coasters at Valley Fair. . . . the last time I would see the fall leaves change color. . . . the last time I would eat a Colorado peach. . . . the last really good watermelon. . . . the last Michigan cherry.

When I realized the plan needed to go ahead there was a tiny bit of relief because I realized that I'd made this plan and it was mine and I really did want to be able to carry it out and I really did want it to be an emblem of what can happen if you take matters into your own hands. I knew I was down to about the last month that I would be here. I had to make some decisions—about my son, for example. He had not wanted to hear much about this. His body language told me he was resistant to the information that I was going to be leaving, but I wanted to consciously have those last parts of my time with him. I decided to tell him the specifics of the plan, but not the day and time.

One of the most wrenching things for me was on the day I carried out my plan. My son had stayed with me the night before. We had talked about it and I knew he at least accepted the reality of what I was going to do. He hadn't fully accepted that it was entirely necessary, but he seemed to be OK with it. We got up that morning, my last day, and I needed to pretend it wasn't my last day, and I needed to not break down when (I thought) he's blissfully unaware that his mother is hugging him for the last time.

There were some sad things—unavoidably sad things—but even those sad things were so much easier to handle when I was deciding to handle them. What is true is that everybody who is born will die. And what is true is that, during the time between the being born and the dying, our lives and the lives of everybody around us can be profoundly affected by our smallest actions, our smallest decisions, our smallest little meannesses and holding back, our smallest acts of kindness and generosity. They all matter. They all matter so much. And, realizing what a precious incredible privilege it was to have a human form, to be in human form—though painful as hell—I wouldn't have missed it for anything.

During the last two weeks I realized it was time to tell more people. It was an emotional last two weeks because people were breaking down and crying, and I was breaking down and crying for them—*for them*—in their sorrow.

And yet, for me, a healing sort of detachment had begun to set in. I felt more keenly than ever—although it had been a factor during all that last year—my freedom. I realized I didn't need to be concerned about anything that was going to happen. I knew I was engaged in the pain of other people's having to release me, but I felt released, I felt wonderfully released with each such encounter.

MARCH 8, 2010. Now I've finished talking as a disembodied spirit from the "great beyond." This is me now. This is me, Annie Chase, on my last day of life at about a quarter to 5 in the afternoon on March 8, 2010. I woke up this morning, ate a light breakfast and prepared for what I would be doing in the evening. In about another hour I'm going to eat a light meal so I have something on my stomach, nothing too heavy. I'm going to write a letter to my grandson in the next hour or so, telling him how much he's been a bright light in my life, and telling him I hope he is not angry at me for not making clear when our final goodbye was.

Now I'm down to the last few hours of my time here on Earth. I have a certain anticipation, a little bit of apprehension, kind of a fluttery feeling in my stomach. It's a little bit like the time my sister kept barring me with her arm from getting on the roller coaster until we could be in the very front seat. I'm in the very front seat of this roller coaster. It hesitates at the top of the hill so I can have a last look over the whole sun drenched, shimmering active world of this amusement park. I look around and I see I've already been on the Laugh in the Dark ride. I've already gone in the Fun House and looked at myself in a whole bunch of—I hope—distorting mirrors. I've been scrambled on the Scrambler ride. I've been caught in the grip of the Octopus ride.

I've been saving the roller coaster for last. The biggest thrill. The wheels on the front of this roller coaster are just about to go over the little bump at the very top of the hill. I know that as it starts to plunge down and gather speed I will surrender to it. I'll surrender to the free fall. At the end of the free fall will be—nothing. Nothing. David Byrne's song about heaven said, "Heaven is a place where nothing happens." I'm not scared. I'm not scared of that kind of nothing. I know *that* nothing really is *not* something.

. . . Love to you all.

7

SCIENCE, CENSORSHIP AND
THE COST OF IGNORANCE

"Ignoramus, there you are, sitting in your hopped-up car;
and your brains ain't up to par, and your ears stick out too far."
— Song parody by Allan Sherman, from "The Dropouts' March"

Something strange and unexpected came into the social milieu with the Trump administration. Protest marches have been common throughout our history, so Trump's election generated marches for women's rights and other civil rights . . . but this was the first time we had a March for Science.

We have to march for facts??!!

It would seem so. Trump's appointment of Scott Pruitt (Oklahoma's Attorney General) to head the Environmental Protection Agency (EPA) reinforced his campaign rants against science and environmental regulations and the facts of climate change—which Trump called a "hoax." Almost immediately after taking office, Trump signed an Executive Order that nullified a large part of Pres. Barack Obama's Climate Action Plan. Pruitt is fully on that page.

Trump has taken the United States out of the landmark 2015 international climate agreement, saying he was elected to represent Pittsburgh, not Paris. But climate change affects the entire world and Pittsburgh's coal fired smokestacks, the nation's agricultural pesticides, and global warming's rising seas and erratic weather know no boundaries, least of all lines drawn on maps. With this scientific-evidence-be-damned attitude in force, the EPA has been heavily staffed with climate change deniers, has rejected scientific studies that show the danger of deregulating some chemicals, has found no environmental problems with continued use of fossil fuels, and in general has done things that only weaken the agency.

There is no interest in the science about our environmental problems. In the fundamentalist circles influencing the Trump administration, there is no need to do anything about climate change because "God" is in charge and will not let his human creations suffer.

Among the EPA's fundamentalist staff members is Michael Dourson, a toxicologist. Trump put him in charge of the EPA's chemical safety and pollution prevention department. Dourson has written a series of Bible based books titled *Evidence of Faith* that attempts to combine religious beliefs with science. In the books he claims that both the Bible and science are true because they both have "God" as the author. According to Dourson, it seems the Bible can be taken literally and still be true by accepting that the language used was simply what was appropriate at the time. (Of course this doesn't make sense but it's all the fundamentalists have to work with.)

There is pushback on these attacks on the EPA, even among some of the Republicans in Congress, so how much damage will be done is impossible to even guess, especially with Trump's mental twitchings changing or trying to change EPA and other science oriented policies almost daily.

Most religion-based ideas about how the world works have been abandoned by the vast majority of people in developed countries, except in certain fundamentalist circles. The most contentious notions still with us are about zygote personhood, genital complementarity, and the fanciful biblical theory of creation. All are front-burner political issues and will remain so until the realization sinks in to the voting public that these are sectarian religious doctrines that have no place in the laws of our secular government.

Scientific Facts and Evolution vs. Creationism

Ever since Charles Darwin proposed the theory of evolution as an explanation for the origin of species, proponents of the biblical version of creation have waged a relentless battle to keep evolution from being taught in public schools. *Church & State*, the magazine of Americans United for Separation of Church and State, reports the latest in this battle in every issue.

With courts consistently ruling against creationism, religious fundamentalists have tried to get it into science classes indirectly. When calling
it "balanced treatment" failed, they renamed creationism as "intelligent
design," hoping to disguise its biblical foundation with an unspecified
designer. Since that also failed, they have been trying to weaken the
theory of evolution by having textbooks designate it questionable, with
scientists supposedly divided or unsure of its validity. In Tennessee,
the legislature passed a bill allowing evolution to be discussed in ways
that could undermine it in favor of religious beliefs. Essentially the same
thing has gone on in Florida, Texas, Missouri, Kentucky, Oklahoma, New
Mexico and Louisiana.

Although, due to the Supreme Court's rulings, these bills go nowhere,
they still cause considerable damage by inciting controversy and requiring expensive taxpayer funded state litigation to defend them. Some
science teachers discuss evolution reluctantly and minimally or not at
all to avoid stirring up controversy. As a result, the United States ranks
poorly in scientific literacy. As *Church & State* reported in its July-August
2011 issue:

> . . . Polling data has consistently shown soft support for evolution
> in the United States. A Gallup poll issued late in 2010 found that
> 38 percent of Americans backed what might be called "theistic
> evolution"—the idea that humans developed over millions of
> years from less advanced forms with guidance from God. An
> additional 16 percent said they believe in development over
> time with no input from God. The remaining 40 percent backed
> creationism and said they believe "God created human beings
> pretty much in their present form at one time within the last
> 10,000 years or so."

To put those figures in perspective, the United States ranks next to
last in support of evolution among 34 countries, only slightly better
than Turkey, which ranked last in a survey by *Science* magazine, Vol.
313, 2011. The top dozen countries were Iceland, Denmark, Sweden,
France, Japan, United Kingdom, Norway, Belgium, Spain, Germany,
Italy, and The Netherlands. The dozen at the bottom of the barrel were
Slovak Republic, Poland, Austria, Croatia, Romania, Greece, Bulgaria,
Lithuania, Latvia, Cyprus, United States, Turkey.

You're wondering how the United States could rank that low? Consider that, for the 2012-2013 school year in Louisiana, Gov. Bobby Jindal signed a bill that allows some school voucher money to be transferred from public schools to Christian fundamentalist schools whose "science" curriculum suggests that the Loch Ness Monster exists. One wonders what Turkey must be teaching to beat that one to earn its bottom of the list booby prize.

Despite this embarrassing ranking and Supreme Court rulings that creationism by any name is a religious belief and cannot be taught in public school science classes, the battle continues with ever more creative schemes. This is not helped when 60% of biology teachers in public high schools are already reluctant to teach evolution in a straightforward way. One of the serious problems with creationist attacks on evolution is that *all* science is thereby attacked. To question evolution is to deny the facts of physics, chemistry, geology, astronomy and all the rest, because all are related.

Scientific Knowledge and Stem-Cell Research

Stem cell research holds a promise to cure Parkinson's disease, diabetes, spinal cord injuries and other afflictions, but religion-based laws have restricted it severely. Why? Because of the belief that an embryo—a microscopic cluster of undifferentiated cells—is a real human being with an immortal soul. Destroying these nearly invisible specks is called murder. This is human imagination run amok while sick people pay with their health and their lives. Would finding useful alternatives to embryonic stem cells resolve the controversy? Perhaps . . . but with the unacceptable consequence of establishing a precedent for allowing religious beliefs credibility in matters relating to scientific research.

As with attacks on teaching evolution, opposition to stem cell research compromises the future of scientific research in the United States. In South Korea, a global center for embryonic stem cell research has been set up that is attracting scientists from other countries (including the United States) who don't want to deal with irrational and pointless restrictions on their work. The center has been accepting thousands of applications from people willing to participate in tests of stem cell treatments.

The bottom line with stem cell research is that it has a pro-business appeal that may eventually override religious mysticism. Consider the business community's response to an anti-cloning bill introduced in the Minnesota legislature in May of 2011. Neal St. Anthony, a Republican and CEO of a global biotech company, saw the bill this way, as quoted in the May 2, 2011, Minneapolis Star Tribune:

> I'm concerned about the ambiguous language in the bill. This whole thing started as a way to prevent reproductive cloning. I agree that reproductive cloning is not appropriate under any circumstances. But I'm concerned the same bill could also ban therapeutic stem-cell research . . . potential cures for Alzheimer's, diabetes or even certain cancers. . . . I would one day like to move [our] research office to Minnesota to join the rest of our U.S. operations, . . . but this proposed bill makes me nervous about the future of biologic research in Minnesota.

Scott Fischbach, the head of the anti-abortion organization Minnesota Citizens Concerned for Life, insisted that research would not be affected, saying in the same newspaper report:

> . . . The bill says researchers should not kill life to create it. There's nothing ambiguous about this. We're not focused on 12 jobs in California. I represent 70,000 Minnesota families, and they all work and play in Minnesota. Here in Minnesota, we respect life. We don't kill each other in pursuit of a dollar. The scientific research industry wants to do whatever it wants to do. They want no bounds.

Researchers at the University of Minnesota agreed with the business community, noting the bill would inhibit work on regenerative medicine and even "criminalize" it. The bill went nowhere but efforts to restrict the research continue. There are thousands of sick people who might not think stem cells qualify for the "kill each other in pursuit of a dollar" category. Just as there are abortion opponents who picket clinics, then bring a daughter in to have an abortion because it's a different story when it's your own family, there are opponents of stem cell research who welcome a cure derived from stem cells when they need it for themselves.

A good example is a story in the *Washington Post* reprinted in the *Minneapolis Star Tribune* April 17, 2012, about Timothy Atchison, a 21-year-old Alabama man who faced lifelong paralysis from injuries suffered in a car accident. He volunteered for a test using embryonic stem cells to see if they could repair his spinal cord. The results have been promising and Atchison is regaining some movement. Because of his religious beliefs, he had opposed abortion and stem cell research—until stem cells offered him a way to overcome an otherwise greatly restricted future. Different story now, he said—these cells were suddenly "different." They were leftover from fertility treatments, weren't going to end up in someone's uterus, would probably be thrown away, etc., etc. He explained it all:

> I am adamantly against abortion in any form. It did cause me some searching and researching biblically what is the proper answer. I don't really see a baby's life was destroyed for this to take place.

So much for embryonic personhood, which is not mentioned in the Bible. (But neither is abortion in any restrictive way.) As the news article noted:

> Atchison's story reveals provocative insights into one of the most closely watched medical experiments, including what some may see as an irony: that a treatment condemned on moral and religious grounds is viewed by the first person to pioneer the therapy, and his family, as part of God's plan.

Now if only Atchison could get pregnant . . .

Sex Education: Abstinence-Only vs. Facts-Only

The Obama administration put in a number of government programs to promote fact-based sex education in public schools. They have been highly effective in reducing teen pregnancy, especially among those living in poverty, disadvantaged in many ways and with few resources to help them build productive lives.

Then the Trump administration pulled much of the funding and severely crippled or eliminated the programs. According to a July, 2017 report by Jane Kay for *ReveSal News*, " . . . Several grantees were told by officials at the Department of Health and Human Services Office of Adolescent

Health that the decision to eliminate funding came from the office of the assistant secretary for health. Last month, President Donald Trump appointed a new chief of staff there, Valerie Huber, who favors abstinence as the solution to teen pregnancy."

How well does that work? Andy Kopsa, who writes for AlterNet, posted the results of research he did on abstinence-only sex education programs in October 2011. It is typical of many such reports that show these programs simply do not work. According to Kopsa, the United States has wasted $1.5 billion over 15 years funding abstinence-only sex education programs. Pres. George W. Bush contributed to the funding with his Community Based Abstinence Education grants. Pres. Barack Obama tried to get rid of this useless expenditure but a Republican controlled Congress included $250 million for the same failed programs in the Affordable Health Care Act.

Here are some details from Kopsa's report (see http://www .alternet. org/story/152755/as_attacks_on_planned_parenthood_aim_for_ sexed_funding%2C_let%27s_remember_how_bad_religious_backed_ abstinence_only_programs_are, Oct. 16, 2011).

> Study after study has revealed the ineffectiveness of abstinence-only programs in reducing teen pregnancies and the spread of disease. . . . Abstinence-only programs come under fire for questionable instructional methods and curricula as well. The Sexuality Information and Education Council of the United States (SIECUS) periodically releases reviews of abstinence-only programs and finds they often rely on fear and shame to encourage abstinence, and promote biased views of gender, marriage and pregnancy options.. . . I have covered two abstinence-only groups in the past year: Project SOS in Florida and WAIT (Why Am I Tempted?) Training, now known as the Center for Relationship Education (CRE), based in Denver. I investigated their methods, connections and over $14 million combined in federal and state grants.

Kopsa reports that the Title V program recommends that grant recipients be inclusive of LGBT students and non-stigmatizing. WAIT/CRE applied for funding saying they had been vetted for inclusiveness by the

American Psychological Association Gay and Lesbian Issues Team. However the APA denied having ever approved of the WAIT/CRE program. Kopsa says:

> Project SOS and WAIT/CRE are unfortunately representative, but they don't even scratch the surface when it comes to outing the legion of discriminatory, shaming and medically erroneous abstinence-only programs.

Kopsa is right in saying the programs he investigated are only representative. Abstinence-only sex education is one of the most lucrative sources of government pork barrel funding, as Marty Klein demonstrates in *America's War on Sex: The Attack on Law, Lust and Liberty*. (See Marty Klein, Ph.D., *America's War on Sex: The Attack on Law, Lust and Liberty*, "Battleground: Sex Education—Where Children Come Second," pp. 15-16.) Here is Klein's breakdown of how extensively government subsidizes religion based abstinence-only sex education.

> Most of the $200,000,000 that goes to promote abstinence-only-before-marriage each year is awarded to agencies over which there is no oversight whatsoever. A huge amount of this taxpayer money goes to frankly religious organizations. Here are a few examples:
>
> **Pennsylvania:**
> Catholic Social Services $46,000.00
> Lutheran Social Services $231,000.00
> St. Luke's Health Network $92,000.00
> Shepherd's Maternity House $50,000.00
> Silver Ring Thing $400,000.00
> **California:**
> Catholic Charities of California $361,605.00
> **New York:**
> Catholic Charities of New York $2,500,000.00
> **Illinois:**
> Roseland Christian Ministries $800,000.00
> Lawndale Christian Health Center $461,278.00

To see which agencies get abstinence funding and how much in your state go to http://www.siecus.org/policy/states/. Almost one billion dollars has been spent on abstinence-only-until-marriage programs . . . . Remember, their goal is persuading young people to not have sex until they marry, not as a means to an end (to take care of themselves), but as an end in itself (*the only way* to take care of themselves). And since almost three-quarters of high school kids have sex before they finish high school, much of this one *billion* dollars is aimed at telling kids who have already had sex that they shouldn't start, or if they've started, they should stop.

This religion-based abstinence-only sex education is ludicrous to anyone old enough to remember when contraception was unreliable and no one ever admitted to having sex outside of marriage. Eight-pound babies born suspiciously soon after a marriage were acknowledged by saying, "The first one can come any time. After that it takes nine months." Truthfully, I can say that we didn't need abstinence—only sex education in those days. We girls were terrified at the prospect of getting pregnant and did our best to avoid it. Not always successfully. Nature's imperative could defeat the best intentions, resulting in a quick wedding or a secretive stay in a home for unwed mothers or a visit to a "back alley" abortionist where, sometimes, the girls died.

No, we did not need abstinence-only sex education. Far more terrifying than the preachers' threats of hellfire were the realities of unwed pregnancy. If such traumatic inducements to chastity didn't work very well then, why would this silly abstinence-only stuff work now? At least the taxpayers weren't billed for the reality-based terror inflicted on us by nature's mindless sex drive.

According to a United States Centers for Disease Control (CDC) poster I have, teen birth rates are highest in the South, where abstinence-only sex education is playing teens and taxpayers for suckers in its cruel and costly con game. Here are teen birth rate for 2006:

U.S. average teen birthrate for 15- to 19-year-olds: 41.9 births per thousand females. For South Dakota, Minnesota and Nebraska: 18-30 per thousand, with New Hampshire lowest at 18.7. For the northern tier of states and the west coast: 31-40 per thousand. For the middle tier of states, including the District of Columbia, Delaware and Arkansas: 41-50 per thousand. And for the southern tier of states: 51-68.4 per thousand, with Mississippi highest at 68.4. (Mississippi also leads the nation in rates of STD transmission.)

On the bright side, the news from the CDC is better—there has been a significant decline is teen birthrates. In the U.S. since 2010. The drop is credited to an increased use of contraceptives, comprehensive (NOT abstinence-only) sex education, and Planned Parenthood's peer education programs. It's all about self-respect, responsibility, and knowledge. It's about knowing how to control nature's mindless imperative so we are benefited by it, not victimized.

Censorship: Who Says What Can Be Said?

It's been said that the strongest drive is not love or hate, but the drive to censor another's opinions. A lot of truth there. Of course, the first thing that comes to mind when censorship is discussed is sex, not opinions. Sex has been a major target of censors throughout the centuries—at least in the Abrahamic religions. But free speech has fared even worse (except where religious proselytizing on government property is claimed as an exercise in free speech). All societies have allowed prostitution in one way or another, but few if any have allowed people to speak critically of their rulers or the culture's religious beliefs. That was generally a criminal act.

To get the full flavor of how bad things used to be—and to understand where the current remnants of censorship in our laws originated—here is an example of the pronouncements of the Catholic Church in the wake of the Enlightenment. (Protestants were just as extreme, but not as extravagantly verbose.) This information was provided for this book by William Sierichs Jr., a Baton Rouge LA journalist and historian of Christianity, who writes a column, "Christianity in its Own Words" for *The Moral Atheist* magazine, which I edit, published by Atheists For Human Rights.

> In a Nov. 25, 1766, encyclical on the dangers of anti-Christian writings, Pope Clement XIII told church officials: "The well-being of the Christian community which has been entrusted to Us by the Prince of shepherds and the Guardian of souls requires Us

to see that the unaccustomed and offensive licentiousness of books which has emerged from hiding to cause ruin and desolation does not become more destructive as it triumphantly spreads abroad. . . . unless We lay the scythe to the root and bind up the bad plants in bundles to burn, it will not be long before the growing thorns of evil attempt to choke the seedlings of the Lord Sabaoth.

"[Through bad books] They have not restrained their impious minds from anything divine, holy, and consecrated by the oldest religion of all time; rather in their attack they have sharpened their tongues like a sword. They have run first of all against God to their pride. . . . They do not respect His providence nor do they fear His justice. They preach with a detestable and insane freedom of thought . . .

". . . Finally, who can avoid deep sadness when he sees the bitter enemy exceed the bounds of modesty and due respect and attack with the publication of outrageous books now in open battle, now in dissimulated combat the very See of Peter which the strong redeemer of Jacob has placed as an iron column and as a bronze wall against the leaders of darkness. . . .

"Therefore since the Holy Spirit has made you bishops to govern the Church of God and has taught you concerning the unique sacrament of human salvation, We cannot neglect our duty in the face of these evil books. . . . It is necessary to fight bitterly as the situation requires and eradicate with all our strength the deadly destruction caused by such books. The substance of the error will never be removed unless the criminal element of wickedness burn in the fire and perish. Since you have been constituted stewards of the mysteries of God and armed with His strength to destroy their defenses, exert yourselves to keep the sheep entrusted to you and redeemed by the blood of Christ at a safe distance from these poisoned pastures. For if it is necessary to avoid the company of evildoers because their words encourage impiety and their speech acts like a cancer, what desolation the plague of their books can cause. . . ."

It goes on and on like this, pronouncement after pronouncement, one pope after another—and the effort to impose those religious views on everyone continues today. Sierichs' lengthy historical report includes the following dispatch from our culture war. After noting the unsuccessful efforts of U.S. Rep. Ernest Istook (R-OK) to add a "religious liberty" amendment to the U.S. Constitution, Sierichs says:

> Yet another such amendment was proposed in September 1999 in a Washington DC church by a group of Republicans in the U.S. House of Representatives. Rep. Tom Delay of Texas, the Republican whip, later House majority leader, and a radical Christian extremist, argued: "We as a nation must take a stand for authority and against disorder. And, as we all know, the highest authority is God. In the battle for our culture, we all need to understand that you cannot just stand up for America, you need to kneel down for America." Majority Leader Rep. Dick Armey of Texas agreed, "Our laws should at every turn be a complement to, and encouragement for, those laws of the Lord God Almighty."

> ... The attempts by Christians to overthrow the U,S, Constitution stem in part from raging paranoia, in part from the movement's fundamental authoritarian attitude and in part from ignorance. Many Christians don't know the history of their movement or why America's Founders wanted religion kept out of government. Deception by church leaders is part of the problem—such as claiming that the courts banned prayer in school when only organized or coercive prayer is barred, not individual students quietly, voluntarily praying. Censorship, to keep Christians ignorant of embarrassing facts or opposing viewpoints has also played a major role.

Although the battle to put religion in government goes on, we no longer have laws against criticizing government. Such talk stopped being censored early in this country's history and has actually become a highly popular activity. Just listen to talk radio.

There's a reason why it's so heavily and blatantly right wing and uncivil. In the early 20th century, at the onset of public broadcasting, the federal government declared that the airwaves belong to the public and broadcast media were to serve the public interest. Views had to be balanced (the "fairness doctrine") and "propaganda stations" were not allowed. These were the conditions for being granted a broadcasting license.

President Ronald Reagan changed all that. The Fairness Doctrine was rejected in favor of whatever the marketplace would support. That led to Rush Limbaugh and a proliferation of similar in-your-face talk show hosts, along with one-sided news reporting and the general incivility that has come to prevail and to be picked up by Internet users. It appears to be another divisive aspect of the culture war. How much of this would be possible if we got rid of laws based solely on sectarian religious beliefs? Very little.

Outright censorship in the United States (not just dumbing down or hiding information) is now focused primarily on sex. The infamous Comstock Laws, first enacted in 1873, are still on the books. The laws targeted sexually explicit paintings and literary works as well as publications and advertisements for contraception and abortion.

Because of public resentment of the Comstock Laws, Congress has deleted all of them—except for abortion-related information, even though *Roe v. Wade* made that unconstitutional. The penalties for disseminating such information have even been increased and expanded to include dissemination via the Internet. Unenforceable now, but ready to be enforced if *Roe v. Wade* is overturned.

Books still get banned by censorial zealots, although not as aggressively as they once were. (Realizing that high profile banning could turn a little-known book into a bestseller might have something to do with it.) The targets are mainly those that say anything straightforward about sex, sexuality, homosexuality, and four-letter words we all hear every day. The issue seems to come up entirely in public schools when a school library shelves a book religious fundamentalists don't like. The National Coalition Against Censorship regularly publishes reports on what the censors are up to. As it says:

> While rarely in the national news, book censorship is an everyday event in the U.S. It takes only one person to launch a challenge: because a book contains "sex" or "violence" or a character is a "bad role model" or because it "denigrates religion" or "undermines parental authority" (and on and on). The goal, invariably, is to remove the offending material and keep all students (in a class, grade, school or district) from reading it.

The Catholic Church's well-known *Index of Forbidden Books* is now ignored, but its censors get occasional satisfaction banning the more publicly visible arts. In October, 2010, the Smithsonian was forced by Catholic political pressure to remove a video from an exhibition in the National Portrait Gallery titled, *"Hide/Seek: Difference and Desire in American Portraiture."* It included at video titled *"Fire in My Belly"* by David Wojnarowicz, who had died of AIDS. There were 11 seconds showing ants crawling across a crucifix. The Catholic League objected that it offended Catholic sensibilities. Republican politicians were contacted, including Rep. John Boehner (House Speaker) and Eric Cantor (Majority Leader). Government funding for the Smithsonian was suddenly in jeopardy and the video was pulled.

A more insidious censorship is the hiding of information in libraries through misleading cataloging. My informant for all things censorial in libraries is Sanford Berman, the now retired former chief cataloger for the Hennepin County library system in Minnesota. Sandy tells all about this. He regularly takes the Library of Congress to task for not cataloging material under headings the user might actually look for. It does no good to use technical or clinical terminology for sexual topics, he says, when users are familiar only with the street language. Crude as it may be, that is how it should be cataloged (with cross references to other terms) if the goal is to have the user find it.

Berman also objects to cataloging historical topics in a way that suggests an interest in whitewashing unpleasant facts about wars, invasions, massacres and the like. He gives the example of a long out of print book, *1492: What it Means to Be Discovered*, about the conquest of America by the Spanish. Along with the history, it has reproductions of woodcut art depicting the horrific tortures and brutal murders inflicted on native people. It was cataloged under "Fine Arts." . . . hardly where someone might look who was seeking information about the European treatment of native people in America.

Berman has had dozens of his suggestions for accurate subject headings accepted, but dozens remain. These are forms of censorship that hide information. Why is this done? Berman thinks it could be bureaucratic lethargy, individual bias, political sidestepping or failure to recognize the significance of a topic. Regardless, he says, libraries have a responsibility to the public to do better than that.

Censoring Critics of Politically Predatory Religion

Throughout this book I have shown how religious beliefs form the basis of many of our laws, yet objections to the harm done by those laws is seldom if ever based on those beliefs. Religious right proponents of predatory religion-based laws are called social conservatives rather than advocates for a theocratic society, which they are. Sometimes advocacy for religion-based laws is said to be based on "moral conviction" to make it appear that religious belief is not the motivating factor. The issues the religious right supports are opposed by liberals as unfair or discriminatory, almost never as a violation of the Establishment Clause, which they are.

Objective criticism of religious beliefs that affect our laws is denounced as religion bashing, rather than a legitimate topic for public discussion. Criticize religious beliefs in this country and (on the off chance such criticism is allowed to be made public) editorials, columnists and letters from readers will jump all over the critic, no matter how relevant the topic to contemporary issues. We can't talk about ensoulment in a discussion of "personhood," abortion or stem cell research because the ludicrousness of the belief underlying the laws restricting abortion and stem cell research would be exposed. The defensive reactions to criticism of religious beliefs are driven by the Catholic Church's canon law #1369:

> A person is to be punished with a just penalty, who, at a public event or assembly, or in a published writing, or by otherwise using the means of social communication, utters blasphemy, or gravely harms public morals, or rails at or excites hatred of or contempt for religion or the Church.

That takes care of everyone outraged enough by dogmatic religion's misanthropy to speak out, including humanistic believers, atheists and any public officials who put their duty to support the Constitution ahead of dogma.

Censoring Sexual Expression

It doesn't take much watching of television and movies to see there's very little sexual expression left to censor, so for those with a taste for graphic sex, the religious right war against sex has been lost as far as what people can watch. But only on film. You still can't get live sex for personal viewing or see thong bikinis at Daytona Beach or drink liquor in a club with nude dancers.

Yes, there are regulations, such as they are. Prostitution—defined as paying someone for sex or offering sex for payment—is against the law, but paying porn stars to have sex in front of a camera to make a film that people will buy to watch is legal. So prostitution is not OK, but doing the same thing to create a porn film is just fine.

Such is the status of sexual censorship laws in this country. Take, for example, what is known as the 2257 Regulations. They are supposed to protect minors from exploitation as performers for sexually explicit material. It's a minefield of requirements for extensive record keeping of performers, with indexing and cross-referencing every one for every depiction of sexuality in every medium possible, going back to 1995. It has people in their 60s still being tracked. So much for controlling child pornography in any meaningful way. And it only tracks material produced in the United States—as if it can't be obtained from other countries.

Sex clubs are another target for regulation. Admittedly, the idea of places such as swing clubs and S/M clubs does not appeal to everyone, but they are what they are and if they are not causing trouble why not leave them alone? But that's not what the moral busybodies do. Whatever goes on there, no harmful criminal behavior or abuse of children has ever been reported (unlike the goings-on in Catholic rectories—and I am far more than a little repelled by what has been going on there). Yet consensual sex in private venues seems, in the minds of the religiously uptight, to need regulation. Bottom line: Do as you will, but harm no one.

8

Public Schools:
Facing a Religious Transformation

"[. . . the school's purpose is] to equip minds and nurture hearts to transform the world for Jesus Christ." — Mission statement of Holland Christian High School, Holland, Michigan, the private school from which Betsy DeVos graduated

One of the most serious attacks on our civil rights and liberties advanced by Donald Trump has been his appointment of billionaire Betsy DeVos as Secretary of Education. DeVos is a long-time staunch advocate for the public funding of private/religious schools. The role of the Secretary of Education is to support and advance the nation's public school system, something in which she has never shown any positive interest. She has never attended a public school nor taught in one nor held any administrative position in one.

Our public schools are responsible for the education of 50 million children. DeVos is no more capable of handling that job than Trump is of being president. There is every indication that what DeVos wants is to destroy the public school system. There is every reason to expect DeVos to advance religion-supportive goals, and to have strong support from the Republican controlled Congress, state legislatures and governors.

For just one example (as of August 2017), the Georgia State Board of Education has mandated teaching the meaning of our national holidays. The mandate leaves how to teach the subject up to local jurisdictions. Is anyone clueless enough to think such teaching will be objective and not an excuse to promote "Christian nation" ideas?

Fortunately, the Jewish community is objecting to this—they have 2,000 years of experience with Christian religious aggression and are not stupid. They have political clout so we can hope they use it to stop this attempt to distort history for religious purposes. The Atlanta Freethought

Society reported this in their August 2017 newsletter and gave a list of state officials to call. That is a good idea, but see the "To the Barricades" chapter for information on how to stop this right wing political carnage at the source.

Getting Taxpayers to Subsidize Religious Education

The battle to get taxpayers to fund religious education has been going on since public schools were established in this country. They weren't really established until after the Civil War, and then only minimally. It wasn't until well into the 20th century that they became a fixture in society with mandated attendance. Regardless, public schools, however partially or fully established, have been seen as missionary territory for religions, and they have fought for control over them.

America in the early years of European colonization was made up predominantly of white, Anglo-Saxon Protestants, so their cultural and religious views were expressed in school activities and curricula (as well as the nation's laws, too many of which we still live under). In effect, the public schools were Protestant schools. Increasing immigration brought religious diversity, particularly Catholicism, into the schools, and it didn't go well. Catholics objected to Protestant prayers and Protestant Bible reading. At one point, in 1844 in Philadelphia, hostilities got so out of hand that there was a bloody riot that lasted three days. Thirteen people were killed, homes and stores were set afire and a Catholic Church was burned down.

The Catholics decided to build their own schools and, from 1850 on, have wanted government funding for them. At the time, it seemed reasonable, given the publicly funded *de facto* Protestant nature of the public schools. But anti-Catholic sentiment ran high, and state-church separation became popular—at least where public funding of Catholic schools was concerned. Pres. Ulysses S. Grant made stirring speeches in favor of strict state-church separation and taxing churches. (A lot of good information about these early years is in Lawrence Lader's book, *Politics, Power & the Church: The Catholic Crisis and its Challenge to American Pluralism.*)

This inspired a proposed constitutional amendment in 1876 when U.S. Congressman James G. Blaine (R-Maine) offered the Blaine Amendment.

It prohibited any tax money from going to any religion for any purpose. Although it failed at the federal level, almost all states picked it up and added it to their constitutions, with language noting religious schools especially as being denied funding.

As far as putting it into practice, some states did but others ignored it and continued to allow prayers and Bible readings. The text of the state Blaine Amendments follows closely the proposed federal amendment, which said:

> No State shall make any law respecting an establishment of religion, or prohibiting the free exercise thereof; and no money raised by taxation in any State for the support of public schools, or derived from any public fund therefor, nor any public lands devoted thereto, shall ever be under the control of any religious sect; nor shall any money so raised or lands so devoted be divided between religious sects or denominations.

With many states banning prayers and Bible readings in public schools, the U.S. Supreme Court began taking up the legal challenges in 1947, thus making such religious observances unconstitutional nationwide. First it was *Everson v. Board of Education* (1947), then *McCollum v. Board of Education* (1948), then *Engel v. Vitale* (1962), then *Abington Township School District v. Schempp* (1963).

Although these cases should have ended the efforts to have religion in the public schools, the battle continues. It's waged primarily by Protestant fundamentalists because the Catholic Church still wants its own taxpayer funded schools. (Shamefaced disclosure: When the *Schempp* ruling was announced, I cheered—as the devout brainwashed Catholic I was at that time—even though the case included a companion lawsuit filed by an atheist, Madalyn Murray O'Hair. I managed to overlook that because I was happy that those heretical Protestant prayers were out of the public schools.)

School prayer amendments in one form or another have been introduced in Congress every year since 1963, but have gone nowhere. Their purpose appears mainly to be a bullying tactic by letting it be known publicly that this is a Christian nation, nonbelievers should just suck it up, and to oppose the religious intrusion is a mean-spirited attack on religious liberty.

More promising have been the strategies to get government funding. To avoid the restrictions of the Blaine Amendments in state constitutions, most have been voucher schemes for state-provided tuition that can be used at schools of the parents' choice. Almost all have failed because voters have tended to favor their public schools, especially in suburban and rural areas.

Meanwhile, indirect funding has been acquired by lobbying legislators to provide such things as bus transportation and non-religious textbooks. These are claimed to be benefits for the parents or the child, *not* the school. (But then why aren't these benefits given to the private schools favored by wealthy families?) They are therefore deemed constitutional— even though they reduce a religious school's operational costs while increasing the cost of public school education. Ironically, these increased costs sometimes incite taxpayer complaints that public schools do not operate in financially efficient ways and suggest that more taxpayer support should go to allowing children to attend the more "frugal" religious schools.

Every issue of *Church & State* (the newsletter of Americans United for Separation of Church and State) and of the Americans for Religious Liberty newsletter carries articles and news items about the latest schemes for getting government to fund religious schools through vouchers and special benefits. The campaign is nationwide and never ends.

Along with this has been denigration of public schools, public school teachers, and teachers' unions. (These were apparently OK for decades until suddenly, in a religion-heavy election year, they were not.) It was a constant drumbeat in the run-up to the 2012 presidential election and still is. Teacher tenure is attacked as protecting incompetent teachers and preventing the hiring of unlicensed teachers who are supposedly more experienced in a particular subject.

Of course, there is more to teaching than knowing the subject matter, important as that is. It's knowing *how* to teach. But without teacher tenure school systems are likely to lay off the tenured teachers at the top of the pay scale and replace them with young, lowly paid and inexperienced beginners.

And so the quality of public education suffers as the drive to dismantle it in favor of private/religious schools advances. Meanwhile, programs to help children from deprived environments become learning-ready get no focused attention, even though that is the problem. Weakening the public school system only puts more of our education in the hands of the religious right.

This problem is not confined to red states. Here's an example from my own liberal blue-state city—Minneapolis. The facts are as stated. I was there. I was fully involved. I published reports in local and national atheist periodicals, in an atheist history booklet, and in my previous book, *Culture Wars*. There were news media reports at that time, and official records of the case are in the files of the Minnesota chapter of the American Civil Liberties Union and the Minneapolis School Board.

Due to the passage of time I have not included the family name of those who were victimized. I have lost track of them and do not know if that information is still accurate or might inadvertently cause them harm if publicized. What is important and essential here is how they stood up for their rights in the face of religious tyranny. They can forever be proud of what they did.

The Persecution of a 6-Year-Old Boy

In 1994 I got a call from Mary Lou. She had been watching our atheist public access TV program and wondered if we could help. The story she told was so hard to believe I wondered if I was getting all the facts. I was. Here they are as Mary Lou told them to me. None of them were ever disputed.

In 1990, Mary Lou's son Michael (then 6 years old) started first grade at an elementary public school in Minneapolis. His teacher had replaced the public school curriculum with one from the Catholic schools. She held regular prayer time and brought religion into class activities. Michael knew his family didn't pray so he told his mother, a regular volunteer teacher's aide at the school.

Mary Lou spoke to the teacher, who said she had been doing that for 12 years and no one complained. She said she thought Michael "needed a little God in his life." Mary Lou told her what she was doing was unconstitutional and told Michael he didn't have to pray in school. The teacher ignored Mary Lou's complaint and Michael refused to participate in the prayers, so the persecution began and, with the connivance of the school principal, escalated.

Throughout the school year, Michael often came home crying. He was ridiculed by the teacher and punished with time-outs for not praying. Forced to make a religious bookmark, he drew a crying face on it. (Mary Lou showed it to me.) Some parents refused to let their kids play with "that atheist kid." Some classmates would not go near or touch his desk for fear of something having to do with "satanic contamination." He was suspended for an "unprovoked attack" even though the "victim" denied vehemently that he had been attacked. During a Boy Scouts recruitment the teacher said all the boys could join "except Michael, because he doesn't believe in God." He was refused placement in a class for gifted students with the teacher's disdainful remark, "What makes you think you're so smart?"

Michael always earned the highest grades and learned to read and write in six weeks. At 9 years old, he tested at the 8th grade level. The final blow came when Michael was refused placement on the class math honor roll although his grades were far above the eligibility level. The teacher said it was because God knew what Michael was thinking and he was not thinking good thoughts so didn't deserve to be on the honor roll. That was the last straw for Mary Lou, so she took the case to the Minneapolis Civil Rights Department.

The Minneapolis School Board and the school district's legal firm began stonewalling tactics so nothing was resolved. For three years Mary Lou wrote letters, made phone calls and tried to get appointments with school officials to no avail. Everything she tried failed. That's when she called me for help. She had been relying on the Civil Rights Department and was not aware that the Minnesota Civil Liberties Union (MCLU) might be more effective. I put her in contact with them and they were effective. As Matthew Stark, then president of MCLU, said at one of our atheist meetings, "The facts are not in dispute" and the school board had no choice but to settle.

I wondered why the school board had been so resistant to settling the issue. After all, every member claimed to be dedicated to civil and constitutional rights. All opposed voucher systems. None was a fundamentalist Christian. However, it seems that liberal and moral principles can become negotiable when adhering to them might create bureaucratic problems. I found this out when I called a school board member. After acknowledging that he knew about the case, he said, "Do you realize it costs over $140,000 to fire a tenured teacher?" Apparently, that cost overrode the need to protect a small child from abuse. The only punishment the teacher got was five days suspension without pay; the principal received no punishment at all.

And where were the media in all this? I sent out numerous news releases but they were ignored. Mary Lou's attorney got some coverage in a weekly free paper. Several of us atheists went to a school board meeting to express our outrage. For that we got a small news item in the mainstream paper and a brief mention on TV and radio. We couldn't help but wonder what would have happened if Michael had been a mistreated racial minority. It would have been front page news—and rightly so—with public apologies and perhaps some election defeats. But what happened to a little atheist boy was apparently not considered newsworthy.

The case was easy to settle quickly. Mary Lou got a token monetary settlement of $10,000, out of which the MCLU took $2,000. The school board also had to acknowledge the facts of the case (but not admit guilt) and send a notice to all teachers in the system restating the school board's policy forbidding religious proselytizing. Had Mary Lou refused the school board's offer and taken the case to federal court, she might have gotten more money. However, she said she wanted Michael to learn right then, while still a child, the importance of standing up for one's rights. She said that dragging the case through federal court could take years and by the time it was settled Michael would be too old to care any more.

Michael was finally awarded his honor roll certificate as furtively as possible. His classmates had received their honors in a public ceremony. Michael was handed his three years later by an assistant superintendent at 11:30 a.m. on Tuesday, February 1, 1994, in an empty room in the school administration building, with a few of us atheists there to lend emotional support. The presentation was unapologetic and perfunctory. Michael was given his certificate not because it was right but only because it was legally required. To memorialize the event Michael had his certificate printed on a T-shirt—and in ever larger sizes year by year as he grew. The certificate is dated as earned in 1990 and presented in1994.

Mary Lou went to the next school board meeting with Michael and challenged the board to explain themselves as they faced an audience of citizens. After each question, only a long, heavy silence hung in the room. Following Mary Lou, I spoke, as did an atheist colleague), calling the board members to account for their shameful behavior.

After I published the story in *Secular Nation* magazine, two members of Atheists United in California (the largest local atheist group in the country) organized a "High Fives for Michael" fundraiser to buy him a complete computer system—the best available at the time—to show the atheist community's support.

Some time later, I was on a committee to screen school board candidates for party endorsement. I asked about this case. One candidate knew exactly what I was talking about. All she would say was that the school board had fired that law firm, which had insisted on stonewalling Mary Lou. That advice, as I was told by those involved, cost the school board $30,000 in legal fees.

How Secular Are Secular Charter Schools?

Publicly funded secular charter schools have proliferated to fill perceived gaps in traditional public school educational curricula or strategies, but the result has been an opportunity for infiltration by religious groups. The mandated secularity of a charter school is often compromised when a curriculum that started out legitimately enough slides into a blatant promotion for a religious viewpoint.

For example, the June, 2012, issue of *Church & State* had an extensive report on the national situation. Life Force Arts and Technology Academy in Tampa, Florida, was under investigation for teaching Scientology, meanwhile collecting $800,000 a year in taxpayer support. Likewise, the Ben Gamla charter schools in south Florida, which evidently were deep into unconstitutional involvement in Judaism. In Pennsylvania, the

Pocono Mountain Charter School was in trouble for allegedly funneling taxpayer supplied school money to a local church. In Texas, a charter school organization called Cosmos was accused of financially favoring Turkish Muslim teachers and contractors. And all over the country, Catholic schools that were no longer financially sustainable became public charter schools. But with the same teachers and administration, what are the chances that the religious views would be abandoned? Especially when effective monitoring for compliance doesn't have a good track record.

It goes on and on. Worse yet is that the Center for Research on Education Outcomes at Stanford University, after studying 2,403 charter schools, found that, "37 percent deliver learning results that are significantly worse than their students would have realized had they remained in traditional public schools." On math scores, the study also showed that 47% of charter school students did about the same as students at regular schools and 37% did worse.

But then the U.S. Supreme Court stepped in, possibly settling the controversy over taxpayer funding of religious education the worst way possible with a decision that allows funding religious schools through tax credits. It's a money laundering scheme (there is no other term for it) that is impressive in its legalistic subterfuge and far reaching implications.

On April 4, 2011, in a 5-4 ruling in the case of *Arizona Christian School Tuition Organization v. Winn,* the Court upheld an Arizona law that allowed tuition-support organizations to collect money from parents, then send it to the school of the parents' choice as a tuition payment. This amount could then be taken on the parents' tax return as a credit. The private or parochial school gets the money, the parents get reimbursed by the government, the public schools are weakened by underfunding, and the taxpayers get the shaft, since somewhere down the line taxes have to be raised to make up for the tuition-reimbursed shortfall. The amount of laundered money was limited to $500 per individual and $1,000 per couple. Would it go higher? Will the sun rise tomorrow? Worse yet, *taxpayers cannot sue to stop this!* Why? Because Supreme Court Justice Anthony Kennedy said it's not taxpayer money, it's the parents' money and they can donate it to a tuition-support organization if they choose. And of course the tuition support organization can donate it to whatever school it chooses.

The Justices were divided ideologically as expected: Chief Justice John Roberts, Justices Antonin Scalia, Clarence Thomas, Anthony Kennedy and Samuel Alito formed the majority. In the minority were Justices Stephen Breyer, Sonia Sotomayor, Ruth Bader Ginsburg and Elena Kagan. Kagan (with Breyer, Sotomayor and Ginsburg) wrote the following strong dissent blasting the ruling, saying in effect that states seeking to aid religion no longer need to develop constitutional work-arounds to get cash grants—just ask for tax credits:

> Today's decision devastates taxpayer standing in the Establishment Clause cases. . . . The Court's opinion thus offers a roadmap—more truly, just a one-step instruction—to any government that wishes to insulate its financing of religious activity from legal challenge. Structure the funding as a tax expenditure, and *Flast* [the 1968 *Flast v. Cohen* ruling that allowed some taxpayer challenges to expenditures under the Establishment Clause] will not stand in the way. No taxpayer will have standing to object. However blatantly the government may violate the Establishment Clause, taxpayers cannot gain access to the federal courts.

Religious Occupation of Public Schools

When prayers and other religious observances were ruled unconstitutional, Protestant fundamentalists tried another tactic—using public school property after hours to express their beliefs and recruit new members. Katherine Stewart has written a detailed report on this strategy in *The Good News Club*. She has followed that up with damning details about charter schools in an article published in the Fall 2017 issue of *The American Prospect* titled "The Proselytizers and the Privatizers," subtitled "How religious sectarian school voucher extremists made useful idiots of charter movement."

It started with the formation of the American Center for Law and Justice (ACLJ), guided by attorney Jay Sekulow, as a counterpoint to the American Civil Liberties Union (ACLU). Sekulow picked up on a 1981 Supreme Court ruling, in *Widmar v. Vincent*, that a state university had not violated the Establishment Clause by denying a religious group the right to meet on campus—it had violated the group's free speech rights; therefore the group's right to meet was constitutional. There was only one dissent by Justice Byron White. With a clear perception of what the Court's ruling might mean for the future, he wrote:

> I believe the proposition is plainly wrong. . . . Were it right, the Religion Clauses would be emptied of any independent meaning in circumstances in which religious practice took the form of speech.

That is what happened when the ACLJ and Sekulow began mounting challenges to claims of Establishment Clause violations by saying religious speech is free speech, devoid of any particular content. Using *Widmar* as a precedent, Sekulow's first legal success was securing the right of a group called Jews for Jesus to hand out pamphlets in airports. The strategy has been building and being refined ever since. In a speech to ACLJ supporters in 1990, Sekulow said:

> Our purpose must be to spread the gospel on the new mission field that the Lord has opened—public high schools. Yes, the so-called "wall of separation" between church and state has begun to crumble.

As Justice White predicted, the Establishment Clause of the First Amendment has become almost meaningless where religious proselytizing by public school students is concerned. One of the more notable, but typical, examples of this has been the "See You at the Pole" movement. As Stewart describes it:

> Like many of the religious initiatives now taking place in America's public schools, "See You at the Pole" represents itself as a student-led program. It began when a group of students gathered around a flagpole in 1990 in Burleson, Texas, a small town just south of Fort Worth, and now claims to reach two million students at 50,000 schools. The events take place annually, usually at 7 a.m. on the fourth Wednesday of September at schools across the nation, and students often bring sophisticated sound systems, rock bands, and other accessories of the mega-church movement onto their public school campuses.
>
> The ceremony involving nailing pieces of paper [with the name of a non-Christian classmate] to a cross has been recorded in at

least one other instance, at a high school in Kaufman, Texas. In the technical terms of the public school missionary movement, "See You at the Pole" is an example of "peer-to-peer evangelism." The important thing about peer-to-peer evangelism is that, from a legal perspective, it is "private speech" by students, of the sort protected by the Free Speech Clause of the First Amendment. So, as the national leaders of the movement are fond of repeating, it's perfectly legal.

The event is said to be student sponsored and led, but Stewart points out the heavy involvement of "pastors, teachers, administrators and parents" in organizing and setting it up. And it's not harmless. Sometimes students who refuse to participate are humiliated and bullied.

Going further than "See You at the Pole" has been the formation of public school student Fundamentalist groups such as the Fellowship of Christian Athletes (FCA), complete with pre-game prayers and praising Jesus in a public way that promotes their Christianity. The Supreme Court has allowed such activities by assuming they are all arranged by the students, and not recognizing the coercion of non-participating students that is bound to occur, as anyone who has ever been to high school knows.

One victim reported by Stewart was Nicole Smalkowski, a 15-year-old Jewish student and gifted athlete. The persecution was relentless, with efforts to get Nicole and her family to leave town, and one teacher telling her, "This is a Christian country, and if you don't like it, get out." The family refused to leave town but Nicole doesn't participate in sports any more. Such treatment occurs all over the country (including homophobic bullying as an expression of Fundamentalist free speech), but only a few who are courageous enough to object publicly make the news.

A growing feature of this evangelical move into public schools is the Good News Clubs, on which Stewart's book is based. They are a function of the Child Evangelism Fellowship (CEF), a proselytizing movement that is well organized nationally and well funded. It is aimed at the "4-14 Window," referring to the ages of the large group of children in the world considered to be prime subjects for religious proselytizing. Again, it was a Supreme Court decision that opened the public school doors for it with its June 11, 2001, ruling in *Good News Club, et al. v. Milford Central School*. The case involved Milford Central School's denial of meeting space for a Good News Club because its purpose was a purely religious service. The Good News Club prevailed by arguing that its free speech rights were violated, and not the Establishment Clause. In summary, the ruling was this:

> Restrictions on speech that takes place in a limited public forum must not discriminate on the basis of the speaker's viewpoint and be reasonable in the light of the forum's purpose. Because the school's exclusion of the Good News Club violates this principle, the school violated the Club's free speech rights guaranteed by the First Amendment. Furthermore, the school's claim that allowing the club to meet on its property would violate the Establishment Clause lacked merit and thus was no defense to the club's First Amendment's claim.

Justices voting in the majority were William Rehnquist, Antonin Scalia, Clarence Thomas, Sandra Day O'Connor, Anthony Kennedy, and Stephen Breyer (in part). Dissenting were John P. Stevens, David Souter, and Ruth Bader Ginsburg.

So what do Good News Clubs do? Stewart goes into great detail documenting their activities. They are in 3,500 public elementary schools. Stewart says, "Today there is more religious activity in American public schools than there has been for the past 100 years." (p. 2) They claim to be nondenominational, yet promote only the Fundamentalist biblical worldview. They claim to hold Bible study classes focusing on history and a broadly religious perspective, but it's actually sectarian indoctrination. They insist that their program does not involve the school in any way, yet gives children the impression of school sponsorship. They claim to reinforce the beliefs of the parents who send their children to these clubs, yet work to undermine those beliefs in favor of their Fundamentalist agenda. They claim to focus only on the children who join the clubs, yet use their rapport with those children to recruit others.

They ultimately create a divisive student environment. Their goal, as Jerry Falwell (one of the movement's leaders) said, is this: "I hope to see the day when, as in the early days of our country, we don't have public schools. The churches will have taken them over again and Christians will be running them." Another movement leader, Robert Thoburn, said, "I would imagine every Christian would agree that we need to remove the humanism from the public schools." He also encouraged Christians to run for school boards, saying, "Your goal must be to sink the ship."

And sinking it is. In August of 2012, the U.S. Court of Appeals for the 8th District not only ruled in favor of CEF's incursion into Minneapolis public schools, but required the Minneapolis school district (aka the taxpayers) to pay CEF's legal fees of $100,000. The school district had created after-school community partnerships with local organizations to augment a school's efforts to boost student achievement with programs that (as stated in the Court of Appeals document) "encourage social, mental, physical and creative abilities, promote leadership development and improve academic performance." The district had accepted CEF as a community partner on the basis of what it assumed were secular activities similar to what was offered by the Boy Scouts, Girl Scouts, Big Brothers/Big Sisters, and Boys and Girls Clubs of the Twin Cities, which were also community partners. It removed CEF from the after-school program and filed an injunction against them when the prayer and proselytizing surfaced.

The group was allowed to continue meeting at the school, but only at the end of the 3 p.m. to 6 p.m. period. This meant CEF no longer had access to the school's bus and food services. Attendance dropped to five students, down from 47, so CEF appealed the injunction, charging viewpoint discrimination based on the religious content of its speech. The appeals court agreed, citing previous federal court rulings that religious speech is private speech when not school sponsored. So now, as reported in the *Minneapolis Star Tribune* on Oct. 11, 2013 (see also the ruling of the 8th Circuit Court of Appeals, No. 11-3225, *Child Evangelism Fellowship of Minnesota v. Minneapolis Special School District No. 1*, filed August 29, 2012):

> Dave Tunell, the Child Evangelism Fellowship's state director, said he hopes three or four more after-school clubs could emerge from summer events conducted by churches in city parks.

Religion in public schools is on a roll. Child Evangelism Fellowship was returned to its status as a community partner with the school, complete with free literature distribution to recruit attendees, and free bus and food service (not free to the taxpayers, of course).

But wouldn't that make it school sponsored? Even though the school says it does not sponsor it? Even when the school's teachers may also teach the CEF classes? If this is not sponsorship, it would be interesting to see what real sponsorship is. As for the Minneapolis school district, it is not going to appeal for fear of getting hit with more and larger fees from religion-friendly rulings. If it wants to avoid a complete religious takeover of its schools, it has no choice but to discontinue all of its otherwise-valuable after-school education-enhancing activities, thanks to a judiciary that increasingly sees anything other that full support for religion as hostility toward religion.

Added to this is that these child evangelism groups do not have churches. They don't need to. They can meet and hold services and proselytize for minimal costs out of public school classrooms. No mortgage, no maintenance costs, no utility bills, no liability insurance, and free parking besides. All thanks to a Supreme Court and a free press that seem to have lost all interest in doing the job the Constitution assigned to them. But how about the ultimate protectors of our democratic freedoms—the ordinary citizens who watch their rights being eroded and do nothing as long as their religious beliefs are validated? How many ordinary citizens would it have taken to stop what happened to 6-year-old Michael? Two or three would have done it. Yet in 12 years of outrageous unconstitutional proselytizing by a Catholic fanatic, there was only one person, Michael's mother, willing to speak up.

Citizens are closer to their schools than to any other government institution. The parents who are horrified if a school library book mentions sex do not hesitate to speak up. Where are the rational parents when religion is being pushed on students in a public school?

Public Education: Where the Sacred Has No Place

There is no good reason to fund religious education in the many ways we do through constitutional run-arounds. Why should any religious or private K-12 school be funded by the taxpayers, directly or indirectly? Public schools have a long and laudable history of educating children well. Where they fall short, the cause is always external, in the child's environment—poverty, emotional deprivation, physical abuse, poor parenting, health problems, and so on.

Those causes must be addressed; transferring education funds from public schools to private and religious schools will not do it and cannot do it and has never done it. It can only make matters worse by encouraging an increasingly divisive society, both at the playground level and in political skirmishing for more (and more selectively preferential) government funding of religious schools.

It is sometimes claimed that private/religious schools do a better job of educating students; therefore, all students should have the choice of attending one, regardless of income status. No study has ever shown this to be true. If a private school does do a better job, it's because they can be selective about the students they accept, whereas public schools are not allowed to discriminate.

But there is one possible non-educational advantage to attending a private school, as I learned from a politician I once campaigned for. Although he supported public schools, he sent his children to private schools. Why? Because, he said, it enabled them to meet and become friends with children from wealthy families—something that could be a great advantage to them later on in establishing a career. But these were a politician's kids, already with advantageous social connections and able to afford a private school. How many career building upper class friends would the vouchered-in children of a welfare mother find?

The argument that tax support for religious schools can be justified because they relieve the government of the cost of educating the religious school student does not hold up when one considers the loss to the state from religious tax exemptions.

Also, educating students at a religious school is a choice, just as installing a home swimming pool is a choice, yet this is no argument for taxpayer support for private swimming pools, even though it relieves the state of the burden of providing more public swimming pools. But schools and swimming pools are in different categories of need. So what is the need for religious schools?

Here is the Catholic perspective, probably shared in their way by all religions that seek public support for their schools. The belief may be sincere—or not—but it is hardly something the taxpayers should be funding. It certainly has no secular value. This if from the old Catholic book I've referenced in other chapters—the 3-volume *Radio Replies* by Rumble and Carty. I have two of the volumes, probably the only copies still in existence—cover missing on one, pages yellowing, but the exposure of the Church's batshit crazy beliefs is invaluable. The books are from the 1940s when the Catholic Church had no fear of speaking nonsense plainly because there were no media available or willing to call that nonsense to public attention, as is now so easily done with the Internet:

> I would say to Catholics who send their children to public schools when there is a Catholic school within reach, that they are violating a grave law of their religion, and that no supposed temporal advantages can be sufficient compensation for that. Secondly, I would challenge their statement that their children will get a better education at state schools.
>
> Is it a "better" education to fit a child for this life by reading, writing and arithmetic than to fit it for both this life and the next by a solid formation in religion, reading, writing, and arithmetic? What is the use of bringing forth children to temporal life, if they are brought forth to eternal death? If a parent gives life, let him [*him*?!] give life indeed, not only in this world, but in heaven also.
>
> Education, to be complete, must embody the formation of the whole being, intellectual and moral, body, mind and soul. The spiritual atmosphere is entirely absent from the state school. My own education as a Protestant was entirely in state schools, and I know by experience the irreligious atmosphere that prevails. They are no place for Catholic children. Conversing with me recently, an Anglican clergyman deplored the fact that only about 10 percent of Anglicans practiced their religion. He blamed state school secular education. "We Anglicans," he said, "played the part of Judas when we handed our children over to the tender mercies of the state, and accepted the policy of free, compulsory, and secular education." And a Catholic parent who sends

his children to a state school without absolute necessity is also
playing the part of Judas.

Well! I went to Catholic schools for 9 years and to public schools for three
years plus four years at a public university. What I learned in Catholic
schools was how important it was to receive the Sacraments, follow
Church doctrine and admire the saints and martyrs for how much they
loved God. None of this had anything in particular to do with the humane
treatment of others or social justice. One nun's racism was memorable,
although so was another's human centered realism. There were good
ones and bad ones. (I think the good ones left the Church in the '60s
when the convents started closing as the supply of obedient "brides of
Christ" ran out.) In public schools it was different. Lots of stuff about
social justice and understanding the human condition. Very liberal, very
inclusive, very inspiring. The Catholic schools encouraged a slave mind;
the public schools encouraged a free mind. I leave it at that.

Is there any secular value in allowing religious Good News Clubs and
similar operations to use our public schools in ways that create division
and controversy? If we are stuck with the Supreme Court decision that
allows these clubs, we should restrict the after-school start time to at
least two hours after the last class or allow no public access before at
least 6 p.m. or only on Saturdays. We should also charge rent sufficient
to cover all maintenance costs plus a profit for the school's educational
expenses, *and* apply this policy equally for all groups that want to use
public school facilities in off hours.

9

TAXES AND RELIGIOUS EXEMPTIONS: FREELOADING AT ITS FINEST

"When a religion is good, I conceive it will
support itself; and when it does
not support itself, and God does not care to support it—so that its
professors are obliged to call for help of a civil power—it is a sign,
I apprehend, of its being a bad one." — Benjamin Franklin

Unlike the other topics in this book, taxes affect everyone. Every one of us ordinary non-privileged citizens pays to make up for revenue lost to unjustified tax exemptions, religious favoritism and corporate loopholes. Everything Trump and the Republican controlled Congress have been saying indicates that their reversed Robin Hood approach to taxes and social policies is only going to get worse.

At this writing, Congress has passed a tax reform bill along party lines—all Republicans in favor, all Dems opposed. They are making it sound good for the vast non-wealthy majority with promises of significant tax reductions and expanded credits. I can't say much about it at this time because all I know is what I read in news reports.

It's 500 pages of legalese that even tax experts find difficult to comprehend. It is known that there are numerous loopholes and special treatments, but no one knows to what extent fiscal misfeasance, malfeasance and nonfeasance lurks in all that fine print. One thing is certain: All of it will favor the wealthy and anything favoring the non-wealthy will only *sound* good. It's a Ponzi scheme.

Various news reports of what has been going on in negotiations indicate more funds for religion, more "religious freedom" of the Hobby Lobby kind, more restrictions on abortion and contraceptive rights, many people left without affordable healthcare, generous permanent tax cuts for the 1%— with more promised—and some for the 99% but with an expiration date.

The cost of these destabilizing tax reductions will add one and a half trillion dollars to the federal deficit, so the next generation or two will be stuck with paying higher taxes to reduce that deficit. Republicans are talking about finally getting their dearest wish—cutting back on Social Security, Medicare and Medicaid—what they call "Entitlements" (as though they are undeserved) but what those living in the real crap-shoot world of financial insecurity know as their Safety Net. The Republicans need a financially destabilizing debt load to get enough votes to shred that Safety Net.

This is the cynical exploitation of people's tendency to grab what they can for themselves while they can and not care that it shortchanges future generations. The burden that deficit will impose on their children and grandchildren is beyond their understanding.

As this tax gambit goes through, watch Trump's financially and morally clueless working class followers cheer. Hey! The child tax credit will be $2000 per child instead of $1000! What a benefit! And the Dems are screwed, along with their non-wealthy constituents, caught between a rock and a hard place. They will have to vote to keep the middle class tax reductions in place to stay in office. And so they will have to support Safety Net cutbacks to reduce the deficit—which will also jeopardize their chances of staying in office because that child's mother has reached retirement age (most likely well over 70 by then). Social Security has shrunk to chump change to pay down that $1.5 trillion deficit, and those 401K funds (If any) are at the mercy of the stock market, while the wealthy retain their tax breaks. There will never be a future-generations burden for them. Special-interest loopholes will take care of that, starting with elimination of the estate tax in the tax reform bill.

There's more to this scenario, and it's all bad news. The Dems will have to control the legislative and executive branches of government when this crap hits the fan to be able to recover from this fiscal mess. Good luck with that as long as this Ponzi scheme holds up. Of course, if they have political control and rational thinking is forced on them, they can save the fiscal day by elim-inating all tax exemptions for secular and religious nonprofits. That would take a lot of political courage, and how much have we ever seen of that?

Promises of tax reform helped boost Trump's popularity. We see now how that campaign promise paid off. The rallying cry became "Drain the

Swamp," but Trump's proposals have not been about draining the swamp but overloading it with more "swamp" recruits—wealthy cabinet members and agency heads intent on cutting benefits for people who have little and lowering taxes for those who have more than they know what to do with, as news reports tell me.

One of the problems with our tax system is that it's like a magician's blammo box that looks transparent but hides the trick. For example, during his election campaign Trump bragged about not paying millions of dollars in taxes by taking advantage of a pernicious loophole. The loophole was subsequently removed with the support of Hillary Clinton when she was a New York senator. It had been quietly inserted in the tax code years earlier as part of a larger bill.

Loopholes like this get sneaked in all the time, often in large bills and at the last minute with little if any legislative awareness of what is going on. If big donations influence legislation, the payoff may be obscure loophole language in a tax bill, not something noticeable where a legislator could be held accountable.

One source of revenue never mentioned by cut-my-taxes protesters is removing the tax exemption for churches and secular nonprofits. It's been in the news lately, but it was all about giving even more to churches by neutralizing the Johnson Amendment to the tax code. This amendment, proposed by then-Senator Lyndon Johnson and adopted in 1954 made nonprofit tax exemptions contingent on their being politically neutral, although they could discuss issues. (Yeah, like discussing issues doesn't make it clear which candidates a nonprofit prefers. But it helped control pulpit politics.)

Trump had signed an executive order directing the IRS to use "maximum discretion" (meaning "look the other way") in applying the Amendment to churches. He didn't mention secular nonprofits but they would have to be included to shield religion from being charged with violating the First Amendment. Trump announced this policy at the National Prayer Breakfast in February of 2017, calling it a protection of "religious liberty."

That policy would have allowed churches to become major donors to political campaigns. Since donations to churches are deductible as charitable contributions, church members would be indirectly contributing to those campaigns. There are many problems here and many churches as well as individuals were not in favor of politicizing religion and creating political infighting among church members. However, repealing the Johnson Amendment has not appeared in the current tax reform bill (maybe it's being held for future negotiations as Democrats challenge the bill's provisions).

Given the uncertainties of this issue, there is little more to say. The only thing certain is that Trump will keep doing his best to make "religious liberty" the hammer that chips away and eventually destroys whatever shred of state-church separation we have left in this country. It will continue to get worse if we allow it.'

Death and Taxes: Only One of Them Is Certain

Over the years, as a political activist, I have had discussions with politicians about religious tax exemptions. All understood the problem, even expressing eagerness to tax religious institutions and musing about ways to do it, but all concluded that (as one former U.S. senator admitted to me), "Anyone who told the truth about taxes could never get reelected."

There certainly are many non-religious aspects of our tax system that are questionable, and even politically treacherous, but given our First Amendment's religion clauses, we should not be paying higher taxes so religions can benefit from paying nothing. We need to be told the truth: Death *and* taxes are not certain, only death is certain. Taxes can be escaped by those who get classified as tax exempt. These are primarily religious, educational and charitable nonprofits. For religious organizations, there is not only escape but complete financial unaccountability. At least secular nonprofits have to file a financial report annually with the IRS; religious organizations do not.

Generally (there are state-specific variations), religious institutions pay no state or federal income taxes; no sales, gas, car or excise taxes; no user fees; no inheritance taxes; no taxes on investments, stocks, mutual funds and bonds; no capital gains taxes on the sale of property; and no property taxes to cover the cost of fire and police protection, libraries and schools.

They don't even have to verify to the IRS the church donations taxpayers claim on their income tax forms. Related businesses, such as religious bookstores, biblical and creationist theme parks, schools, hospitals, fitness centers, recreational facilities and campgrounds are tax exempt. These tax exemptions are bestowed on them just because they are religious. About the only things religious institutions have to pay taxes on are any completely unrelated commercial businesses they might own, such as shopping centers and hotels.

No Good Deed Goes Unpunished

The law of unintended consequences never applied so well as it does to the decision to exempt religious institutions from taxation. It leads one to think the cynical quip, "No good deed goes unpunished," has some truth in it. As our nation grew and state constitutions began to allow tax exemptions, churches were included, more or less as a charitable gesture, since in the early years most were too small and poor to pay taxes. As churches became financially stable, exemptions were considered justified because churches dispensed charity, augmenting that of community poor houses and county poor farms. But then, through bequests, business investments and gifts from wealthy donors, religious institutions began prospering immensely. With wealth came power and influence, and so, through political pressure, the exemptions grew and grew.

Today almost nothing churches do can be taxed, even when they generate millions of dollars of income and return nothing of value to the community, only dogma-driven harm. What began with some justification is now morally, fiscally and socially reprehensible.

How Did This Happen?

Efforts to bring this situation under control are as old as the initial tax exemptions, which began in the 1830s. Numerous pieces of state and federal legislation have been introduced since then to end the preferential treatment of churches, to no avail. In 1874, the issue had become such a matter of public concern that James Garfield (later President Garfield) addressed Congress on the matter. He said:

> The divorce between Church and State ought to be absolute. It ought to be so absolute that no church property anywhere, in any state, or in the nation, should be exempt from equal taxation;

for if you exempt the property of any church organization, to that extent you impose a tax upon the whole community.

In 1875, President Ulysses S. Grant also addressed Congress. He came bearing a 900-foot petition with 35,000 signatures of people opposed to tax exemptions for religious institutions. He said:

> I would also call your attention to the importance of correcting an evil that, if permitted to continue, will probably lead to great trouble in our land . . . it is the accumulation of vast amounts of untaxed church property. . . . In 1850, the church properties in the U.S., which paid no taxes, municipal or state, amounted to about $83 million. In 1860, the amount had doubled; in 1875, it is about $1 billion. By 1900, without check, it is safe to say this property will reach a sum exceeding $3 billion . . . so vast a sum, receiving all the protection and benefits of government without bearing its portion of the burdens and expenses of the same, will not be looked upon ac-quiescently by those who have to pay the taxes. . . . I would suggest the taxation of all property equally, whether church or corporation.

We have made a number of such efforts in my state of Minnesota, none of which have been successful. I believe they typify the tax situation around the country, so are worth including in this chapter.

Minnesota Governor Rudy Perpich proposed eliminating the sales tax exemption from nonprofits in 1987 and got nowhere. In 1988, Rep. Tom Osthoff sponsored a bill that, as reported in the *Minneapolis Star Tribune* on March 14, 1988, would have:

[R]emove(d) $4 billion in property tax exemptions, which would have raised $180 million and cut homestead taxes by an average of 7.3 per-cent statewide, according to a study by Minnesota House researchers. The bill would have taxed hospitals, nursing homes, nonprofit organiza-tions other than churches and schools, civic centers, arenas, auditori-ums, leased airport property, college property not used for education, and residential property owned by churches, educational institutions and governments. Church property was included in everything except possibly the civic centers, arenas, auditoriums and airport property. To no one's surprise, the bill failed.

In the 1970s, an amendment to Article X of the Minnesota Constitution to allow taxing the business operations of churches passed by over 70 percent. The amendment was supported by a coalition of business associations and labor unions. Despite the overwhelming popularity of this amendment, it has never been implemented. The most recent attempt to do so was around 1989 when I was involved in getting implementation language into the tax bill. The bill was pulled at the last minute (according to my legislative contact) due to political pressure by religious institutions.

In 2011, U.S. Senator Charles Grassley, a Republican representing Iowa, opened a Senate Finance Committee investigation of the financial irregularities of several mega-ministries, something he had been gathering data on for several years. These are organizations run by "prosperity gospel" televangelists who occasionally make the news by living over-the-top lavish lifestyles, with mansions, private jets, yachts, and other luxurious acquisitions. Grassley, although a religious-right supporter who shares the religious beliefs of his targets, tried to stop these tax exemption abuses. He succeeded only in publicizing their excesses, but that was a good thing in itself.

Grassley then shifted his focus. For one thing, he dropped the financial inquiries in favor of supporting legislation that allowed mega-ministries to engage in political activity while retaining their tax exemptions. For another, he started going after nonprofit hospitals, whose tax-exempt status is based on providing a certain amount of charity care. He appeared to have had some success in at least tightening the IRS regulations. An October 15, 2011, news report in the *Des Moines [Iowa] Register*, written by Tony Leys, detailed Grassley's efforts and the effect on taxpayers when nonprofits profit from unjustified tax exemptions. Leys wrote:

> For example, more than $1.9 billion worth of hospital property in Iowa is tax-exempt, state records show. If those hospitals were normal businesses they would pay more than $58 million in annual property taxes, which would help fix roads, hire teachers and keep police on the beat. The result: Everyone pays higher taxes because of such exemptions. [As for free care, Iowa's 46 nonprofit] hospitals made nearly $295 million after expenses, about three times the amount of free care provided to patients too poor to pay. Fifteen of the hospitals provided less than 1

percent of their overall expenses in free care to the poor. Only 11 hospitals provided free care equal to 2 percent or more of their expenses. . . . nonprofit foundations are required to spend 5 percent of their assets on charitable activities per year.

Churches, of course, are not required to spend anything on charity, despite the huge incomes of the larger churches. Any significant charity they provide is funded by the government under contract, and by other public entities such as the United Way.

The most serious obstacle to eliminating church and secular nonprofit tax exemptions has been the 1970 Supreme Court decision in *Walz v. Tax Commission of the City of New York*. The justices ruled 8 to 1 that exempting churches from taxation was a benevolently neutral accommodation—although neutrality by definition can be neither benevolent nor malevolent.

Part of the decision was based on the assumption that churches do charitable work and contribute to American culture. But many do little or no charitable work, and of those that do, anything significant is often paid for by government grants and/or private foundations and civic organizations such as the United Way. Many businesses do more good (as anyone who has faced a car breakdown or plumbing disaster knows) but they are not tax exempt.

As for culture, the most notable contribution from religious organizations in recent decades has been a divisive culture war. While churches may do some good, no one considers the harm many of them cause that far outweighs the good. Every topic in this book exposes a body of theology-based laws that victimize all of us in some way while causing our taxes to be raised to deal with the damage.

What is always overlooked about the *Walz* ruling is that it did *not* say that churches *must* be tax exempt, only that they could not be denied tax exemption if secular nonprofits were exempt. States were free to tax or exempt all or none. The states chose to exempt all. Because secular nonprofits want to keep their tax exemptions, religious organizations are no longer the sole cause of this unfair system, but they are a major player in keeping it going. They are, in fact, the one thing most likely to keep it going.

Although *Walz v. Tax Commission* did not say churches can't be taxed, the ruling is often taken to mean taxing churches violates the religious freedom clause of the First Amendment. Viewed this way, we have a schizophrenic First Amendment that, on one hand, prohibits an establishment of religion so no one is forced to carry these freeloaders, while on the other hand guaranteeing freedom of religion so everyone is forced to carry them. Such are the political contortions this nation struggles with to keep religious institutions appeased regardless of the burden on everyone, religious or not.

Property Taxes: We Pay More Because They Pay Nothing

Tax inequities show up most clearly and affect most people directly in how real estate is taxed. In every community, there are services government must provide: fire and police protection, road and bridge repair and maintenance, street cleaning, emergency services, education and recreational facilities—all these and more if we are to have what we call civilization.

Property taxes are assessed to cover these expenses, but only on some property. Those with a property tax exemption get all the benefits of the city's services but pay nothing. That revenue shortfall is made up by the rest of us, who pay more. Of this group, owners of business and commercial real estate can pass their tax costs on to customers and clients. Homeowners and renters cannot. For them there is no way out. They must cover the shortfall created by the tax exempt while also paying higher prices to cover the taxes on business property. This can be especially hard on senior citizens whose retirement income is far below their former employment income.

Given the difficulty of taxing churches, some proponents of tax fairness have suggested charging churches a service fee for the city services they enjoy at taxpayer expense. Some cities have tried this but the churches put up such a fight that the efforts have not succeeded. To their credit, there are religious organizations that, at least occasionally, will voluntarily pay a fee to cover their use of public services. For example, in 1967, the minister of the First Universalist Church of Minneapolis wrote a lengthy editorial for the (then named) *Minneapolis Star* pleading for his fellow religionists to reject church tax exemptions as a threat to their integrity and religious freedom. He detailed the instances of church wealth he personally knew about that he considered unconscionable. Nothing came of his efforts.

However, his views have had some support. In the 1988 *Star Tribune* report on tax exemptions referred to earlier, it was noted that Augsburg Publishing House (owned by the Lutheran church) donated about $325,000 between 1975 and 1988 to the City of Minneapolis for those services. Also, St. Olaf College and Carleton College in Northfield, Minnesota, were donating about $20,000 a year, in addition to larger amounts for special projects that included a hospital and an ice arena, to that city. I have heard of Unitarian-Universalist churches doing the same thing. What this does, of course, is indicate the huge amount of money available to fund city services and lower everyone's property taxes if all property is taxed.

How much lost revenue must homeowners and renters make up to cover that shortfall? In Minnesota, which is probably typical of the situation nationwide, tax exempt property statewide was valued at $84 billion in 2013. It has at least doubled since then. In Minneapolis and St. Paul, one-fourth of the property is tax exempt, This is probably typical among all the states, with exceptions such as Boston where half of the city's tax base is tax exempt. The taxes not collected due to tax exemptions must be made up by increasing taxes on taxable property.

An End at Last to Preacher Perks?

For decades the clergy have been getting property tax exemptions just for being clergy. This goes back to 1954, when Cold War hysteria caused our elected officials to put religious bigotry in many forms into law as a barrier against "godless communism." The legislator who proposed this exemption, Rep. Peter Mack Jr., a Democrat from Illinois, explained it this way:

> Certainly, in these times when we are threatened by a godless and antireligious world movement, we should correct this discrimination against certain ministers of the gospel who are carrying on such a courageous fight against this foe. Certainly this is not too much to do for these people who are caring for our spiritual welfare.

Not much of a secular purpose there, since it had no affect on the Soviet Union did. It did, however, affect U.S. taxpayers, who had to make up for the lost revenue. This benefit allowed clergy to buy several homes tax-free! For example, a millionaire minister who bought a $408,638 second home at a lake in Tennessee got the clergy exemption on that in addition to his first home, thanks to a favorable ruling by the U.S. Tax Court. Then there were the clergy housing allowances granted eight members (including five from the Robert Schuller family) of Robert Schuller's Crystal Cathedral Ministries in California that amounted to an annual total benefit of $832,000. Congressional budget records showed the cost to taxpayers for this largesse to be about $500 million a year. Some efforts were made to limit the benefit to one home and to question whether this benefit should even apply to millionaire clergy. The more important question is: why have this preferential benefit at all?

In November, 2017, the Freedom From Religion Foundation (FFRF) reported in its newsletter "Freethought Today" that it had won its second attempt to end these perks with a federal court ruling in its favor against strong religious opposition. In commenting on the ruling, it noted that U.S. District Judge Barbara Crabbe had objected to the unconstitutional preferential entanglement of government with religion. The report quoted *Christianity Today* as finding that "84 percent of senior pastors receive a housing allowance of $20,000 to $38,000 in added (but not reported) compensation to their base salary." Appeals to Judge Crabbe's ruling, and further rulings, continue to be made but have failed, so victory, while likely, is not yet certain.

What It's Like to Fight Property Tax Exemptions

Including all nonprofits in property tax exemptions has led to a proliferation of secular nonprofits, which join the churches to keep the exemptions. An example of this occurred in 1996 in Colorado, when a referendum to tax the property of all nonprofits was offered with business community support. Benefits to homeowners and businesses were substantial, with generous exemptions for smaller nonprofits, and the tax on other nonprofits easily absorbed. Despite this, the nonprofits joined the churches. Billboards urging "NO on 11" depicted a little broken heart and the plaintive cry, "Don't Hurt the Helpers." The referendum lost 4 to 1. A report by a pro-referendum activist, Jackie Marquis, in the Nov-Dec. 1996 issue of *Secular Nation* (provided at my request as editor) included this analysis:

Since 80% of the privately owned nonprofit properties in Colorado are owned by churches and religious organizations, . . . I would venture to say this was the real target. There were exemptions in the other 20% of nonprofit properties, so in reality only a few of these would be affected. Why did it fail? There were many reasons. Let me start with the opposition's strength and power.

Most nonprofits are big business and operate as big business. The opposition took in over $700,000 to fight this. Now you know where the money is. Nonprofits also have tremendous political power, just as corporations do. . . . They had many voluntary speakers everywhere. With their financial power, they were able to pay two full time campaign organizers and purchase hundreds of thousands of dollars worth of television, radio and newspaper advertising.

Their television ads were very compelling, implying that every kind of service they render and little churches were going to close down. Little old grandma and grandpa were going to be out on the streets. The homeless would not be able to be fed. Kids would lose their daycares. The zoo, the Humane Society, the blood banks, everything was going to have to close. . . . Politicians spoke out for them everywhere. They even have bill-boards now that say "Thank you from the helpers" with their little broken heart and a red circle with 11 on the inside with a red stripe through it. Their money is still being spent and of course not one red cent on taxes to help the taxpayer out.

. . . We spent $7,000, a drop in the bucket compared to our opposition. We did not get the funds we thought we would. We did not get the statewide media coverage we expected. . . . We had a letter of endorsement from the Business Coalition For Fair Competition, which is an alliance of 19 national trade associations. We could not get this letter of endorsement out to the public.

What amazed me was how we could not get the press to cover the misinformation on the opposition's flyers and TV ads. . . . The media would not let any of the various county tax assessors' inaccuracies out. There was blatant, huge figure-switching going on. The rearranging of figures all over the state was evident, like showing nonprofit school properties where there are no schools, and showing that El Paso County had more nonprofit properties in the 1980s than it does now in the 1990s. This of course is impossible, but would the media pick it up? No!

. . . The opposition kept saying homeowners' properties would go up. This was totally false. We couldn't even fight that, even when we had a letter from the El Paso County tax assessor saying the taxes could not be raised, even when we had our local tax watchdog state that could not happen. . . . In Denver, Mayor Webb said Amendment #11 would drive churches into extinction. Well, all I know is that the "American Dream" has become extinct for many Americans. Many can no longer even think of owning a car, much less a house. Many can barely pay their rent. No politician, no government entity, no corporation, whether profit or nonprofit, seems to care to help the taxpayer—they just keep adding taxes on our backs constantly. The greed is unbelievable.

Fighting the status quo and bucking the system is sure a challenging thing. None of [the liberal] organizations would back us. They stated that, while they think it is unconstitutional that churches don't pay taxes, they would not make a public stand for the Amendment. The cowards! Let's face it. They all protect their own pockets, even if it means they will be fighting the religious right for a lifetime.

I for one am not donating to any of these, ACLU, AU, People for the American Way, etc., any longer, because if they had taken a stand behind our small group against the religious right, it would have made our fight a lot shorter. Even Planned Parenthood is cut off by me now. They lie in bed with the Catholics who have denied women's reproductive rights for centuries and lie in bed with the prolifers while making in 1993 a $23 million profit, and paying two acting presidents $185,000 each for now two years. (The past president made $321,000.)

They certainly have used police protection many a time. They did not make a stand against their enemies who have murdered their doctors and others, and bombed their clinics. This is the element that has cost Planned Parenthood so much money, and then they lie in bed with their enemies to avoid a little property tax. I sure found out a lot about these nonprofits since this Amendment fight began.

Many said Amendment #11 went too far. In my opinion, it didn't go far enough, in that I think all these entities are businesses and should pay taxes as any other business or individual pays, with no special privileges for anyone. If you can afford to buy property and build, you should be able to pay the property taxes.

. . . Now the City of Colorado Springs is crying about funds (again) and has frozen the salaries of the police and firefighters and others (although the supervisors got raises) and is trying to figure out where to get more funds or which other poor working slobs they can cut. It is absolutely mind boggling! I bet many of them are wishing they had voted for Amendment #11.

Who Prospers From the Prosperity Gospel?

Churches fight to keep these tax exemptions and charitable perks— and to get more. The national Citizens for Tax Justice (www.ctj.org) founded in 1979, lobbies legislatures to ensure taxes are adequate to maintain social programs. Its coalition members and directors include religious organizations. In Minnesota, it works with the Joint Religious Legislative Coalition (www.jrlc.org) whose four sponsoring members are the Minnesota Catholic Conference, the Minnesota Council of Churches, the Jewish Community Relations Council of Minnesota and the Dakotas, and the Islamic Center of Minnesota. (It was founded in 1971 as the first interfaith public-interest lobby group in the United States. Since then, groups in other states around the country have been formed.)

Areas of legislative concern include the entire range of social welfare issues. Churches cite the need for fairness and bemoan the plight of the poor, yet none of them ever offer to pay any taxes themselves. I found a report in the *Minneapolis Star Tribune* for March 3, 1992, where the Joint Religious Legislative Coalition made specific proposals for raising taxes by $649 million on businesses and higher incomes to fund social programs, with no suggestion that their own tax free haven be tapped to help achieve this "need for fairness." The same effort continues when- ever budget crises arise.

Many of these programs are administered through churches, which contract with the government to do this or are paid from government sources such as Medicaid and Medicare. Recently, as illegal immigration has become a concern, churches have been highly visible as advocates for compassion and creating a pathway to citizenship. For example, in 2011, a coalition of religious groups issued just such an advocacy statement. It was signed by representatives from Jewish Community Action, the Interfaith Coalition on Immigration, and the Islamic Civic Society of America.

As for who would benefit from an increase in these social programs (although the compassion is no doubt genuine), underlying it all is that taxpayer funding is needed to implement them—and that religious institutions have been and would continue to be major providers of such services—paid for by taxes to which none of them contribute but all of them benefit financially.

The comfortable financial status of many religious institutions is fairly well known. Despite the Vatican's multi-million-dollar losses in court for shielding pedophile priests, it remains extremely wealthy, not just in its financial investments but in its collection of priceless works of art—a major tourist attraction in Rome. As for Protestants, the media regularly report on the lavish lifestyles of various televangelists, as documented by Sen. Charles Grassley in his now-aborted campaign to make lavish-spending churches accountable for abusing their tax exempt status.

In 1977, the *Minneapolis Star Tribune* did a multi-part investigative piece on the Billy Graham operations that revealed, among other things, that Graham had millions of tax exempt dollars deposited in foreign bank accounts while paying most of his employees minimum wages or less. Later, in 1987, the paper reported that Graham's tax free profits for 1986 amounted to $3.8 million. There is no reason to think the Graham operation, which has ministries in several countries, is any less profitable today. Graham's profits quoted here were in 1977 to 1986 dollars, and values have escalated. Certainly his organization can afford to pay taxes. It has since moved to Charlotte, North Carolina, Graham's home town, where a Billy Graham Library has been established. (Billy Graham died Feb. 21, 2018, at age 99, and the enterprise has for some time been run by his son Franklin.)

In 2011, Americans United for Separation of Church and State, a First Amendment watchdog group, reported the following multi-million-dollar annual budgets for several prominent religious right organizations noted for encouraging the erosion of state-church separation: Pat Robertson Empire, $412,581,050; Jerry Falwell Empire, $400,479,039; Focus on the Family, $130,258,480; Alliance Defense Fund, $30,127,514; American Family Association, $21,408,342; Family Research Council/FRC Action/ FRC Action PAC, $14,569,081; Coral Ridge Ministries, $17,263,536; Traditional Values Coalition, $9,888,233; Ethics and Religious Liberty Commission of the Southern Baptist Convention, $3,236,000.

Then there are the "prosperity gospel" evangelical megachurches—a huge national network inspired by Kenneth Copeland, "The Godfather of the Prosperity Gospel"—with acres of property and thousands of members. Most of these churches seem to be prospering nicely. Several were featured prominently in the *Minneapolis Star Tribune* in September, 2011. One of the examples given was the Substance Church, with an income that has been growing annually, from $150,000 in 2004 to $2.5 million currently. The church has accomplished this by preaching from Bible verses such as this, from Proverbs 11:24-25: "One gives freely, yet grows all the richer; another withholds what he should give, and only suffers want. Whoever brings blessing will be enriched, and one who waters will himself be watered." The "evidence" that such giving is rewarded came from those occasional reports by churchgoers who gave when it was difficult, then recovered financially, always certain their god was rewarding them, never realizing that it is a mathematical certainty that some of those donors will get something they can see as a reward.

One might argue that, even though a religious organization's financial activities are questionable, donors are free to support them regardless. Maybe so, but what if those activities cause considerable harm? We seldom see reports from those who gave and gave with no recovery. But some do surface to shed light on the reality of this particular aspect of tax exemptions. Chuck Gallagher, who has a web site where he bills himself as a "Business Ethics and Fraud Prevention Expert," recently took on the Kenneth Copeland Ministries (KCM). The following is from Gallagher's web site (see "Kenneth Copeland—Godfather of 'Prosperity Gospel'? Why Not Comply with Grassley?" at http://www.chuckgallagher.com, filed under: Business and Personal Ethics, Choices and Consequences, and Religion and Ethics).

CBS Evening News recently did [an article] on Kenneth Copeland Ministries and the related public investigation launched by Senator Charles Grassley [since ended]. . . . The senate investigation relates to compliance with the tax laws governing non-profit organizations. The question is whether the ministry resources are being diverted into for-profit businesses that the Copelands own or have control of such as aviation, real-estate development and Texas and gas wells. A portion of the article is reprinted here:

'It's a business, it's a bottom-line business,' said a former ministry employee—who feared being identified. The employee answered hundreds of prayer requests a day, most sent in with donations, before quitting, feeling 'betrayed' by Copeland's gospel of prosperity.

Michael Hoover, who worked for Kenneth Copeland Ministries for five years, quit in 2005 over disagreements with the church. He says he witnessed other employees doing work on behalf of for-profit businesses tied to the Copeland family. 'In my viewpoint, I believe that they were using a lot of the ministry's assets for personal businesses,' he said. 'The nonprofit activity and the for-profit activity are so intertwined that you can't, you can't separate them,' said Ole Anthony of the Trinity foundation."

Kenneth Copeland recently stated: 'You render unto the government what belongs to the government. And you render unto God what belongs to God,' he said, according to the newspaper. 'You can go get a subpoena, and I won't give it to you,' Mr. Copeland continues. 'It's not yours, it's God's and you're not going to get it and that's something I'll go to prison over. So just get over it.' Here's the question: what would keep the Kenneth Copeland Ministries from being fully compliant with the Senator's request?

Gallagher's web site also includes comments from visitors about this article. Most said they agreed with the Copelands, noting that "rappers and thuggish figures" and other high living celebrities make millions and fly corporate jets and nobody investigates them. The fact that those celebrities paid taxes while FCM was tax-exempt and abusing that privilege did not seem to occur to them. But there were other comments. This one says it all. It's from a woman who tried to get an accounting of all the money her mother gave to FCM. She asks who has a right to this information:

> . . . I believe with all my heart, we should let the ones affected most by this money making scam have a say in determining the answer to those questions: 'I had a home,' 'I had a life,' 'I had faith,' 'I had a family,' 'I lost a loved one,' 'I have no clue what the truth is any more!' 'I will never trust any form of religion.' These are merely a handful of endless testimonies coming to light nationwide. Ranging from all walks of life, their heartbreaking testimonies can be found throughout the web, yet inconceivably, victims are being labeled as fools, ignorant, and basically downright blind for not seeing the truth behind the Prosperity Gospel's falsehoods.

Being only human, our quest for health and wealth regrettably does lead some in the wrong direction. Promises and guarantees, made by the Prosperity Gospel ministers, give people that have not obtained these blessings on their own a second chance at achieving their goals in life. An important discovery I made while reviewing testimonies revealed that numerous victims had very little knowledge of the Prosperity Gospel's dark side. These unfortunate victims appear to be equipped with only a small portion of the web of deceit these ministers weave.

Picture yourself being raised in a small country town, with a population of only a few hundred, the closest city only a population of a few thousand. Computers, Internet, cable, satellite TV and other high tech gadgets are not needed or desired. You are living a simple, solemn life you wouldn't trade for any amount of cash. After your working day is done, you gladly remove your shoes, kick back in your easy chair, and relax without a care in the world for a while. After flipping on the TV to view the local evening news, you are reminded to give thanks that you don't have the worries that accompany life outside the haven of your home and community. Religion is your safeguard, your faith is strong, and you have no doubts about the truth behind your beliefs.

This was my life, before KCM. Prosperity Gospel ministers enter the homes of many victims through a 30-minute Sunday morning worship service on a local broadcast station. Growing up in Jigger, Louisiana, truly located in the middle of nowhere, I can testify that we only received on a clear day about three or four channels. Warnings of dangers associated with Prosperity Gospel ministries made by critics, ministers, and victims go unheard; therefore, tragically for many, when the realization of this scam is discovered it is already too late. Families have lost their homes, life savings and some even their lives due to Prosperity Gospel doctrines.

Unfortunately, my mother was not one of the lucky ones. Her faith in this false Gospel ultimately cost her her life. After more than a decade of programming her mind to believe and think the Prosperity Gospel way of life she lost her battle with cancer. By refusing medical attention, she sealed her fate, but the programming she acquired from Kenneth and Gloria Copeland proved strong all the way to her last breath.

A diary she left revealed the horrific tale of her life from 1992-2002, the top of each page titled with Kenneth Copeland, Gloria Copeland or BVOV. Some mistakes in life we cannot undo, and good intentions don't always go as planned. These victims are simply following misleading promises of health and wealth. The use of miraculous healing confessions and newly found wealth testimonies are their sales pitch. Sadly, my mom among many others are proof that their sales pitch works.

The possibility of these megachurches misusing finances for personal luxuries is what brought this scam to the public's attention, not the loss of life, the financially bankrupt, and numerous victims that have been left in the wake of this devastating hoax. So, do we continue blaming the victims or do we stand up for them, learn from their mistakes and put an end to these senseless tragedies? Even I, being a victim's daughter, have many lingering questions, such as: How is it that some see the truth and others do not? What leads these victims to believe the unbelievable? Are some more vulnerable to these sorts of money-making schemes than others?

When all is said and done, perhaps they will be tagged, not as the Prosperity Gospel, but the false Gospel. One quote from

Copeland should erase any doubts of KCM innocence: "It's not yours, it's God's and you're not going to get it and that's something I'll go to prison over. So just get over it!"

Preaching a Prosperity Gospel is not the only way to take advantage of trusting people. For months, in 2011, "Doom's Day" was once again prophesied—this time to occur on May 21st, 2011. Although widely publicized, it never happened, of course. Just one more recurrence of a continuing religious theme that has endured 2,000 years.

This time it was promoted by "Rapture" prophet Harold Camping, from Alameda, California. If this foolishness were treated as just that, we could dismiss it with a few jokes and irreverent end-of-the-world parties. But it's not. Many people take these predictions seriously.

Camping's national promotion through billboards and other media resulted in people inflicting great harm on themselves and others. Some liquidated their assets to donate money to publicize the event, or incurred heavy debt to finance purchases and vacations in the expectation that they would be gone to Glory on May 22nd, or they quit their jobs; some even killed themselves and/or their loved ones to avoid the post-Rapture Tribulation.

Camping's tax-exempt organization, Family Stations, which produces radio shows, is a multi-million-dollar enterprise. Donations amounting to $100 million apparently helped finance the "Doom's Day" campaign. Shouldn't it be considered fraudulent to promote a money-making scheme that promises something the promoter knows will not be delivered? (Camping made no personal preparations for being Raptured.) At the very least, it is difficult to see what justifies preferential tax treatment here. This sort of thing happens every time someone promotes a Doom's Day scenario.

An Equitable Tax System: No Exemptions

How equitable are these religious tax exemptions? Many claim they are justified because of religion's supposed moral influence—but families are not tax exempt, and they are the basic source of moral guidance. One of the original reasons for the religious tax exemption was that churches offered a support system for dealing with economic hardships. But it was overwhelmingly a system in which churches helped only their own members—and

sparingly at that. For those who did not get this help, the dreaded alternative was "over the hill to the poor farm." Now we have government
programs such as Social Security, Medicare, Medicaid, Unemployment
Compensation and welfare assistance that are far more effective.

Would paying property taxes—or any taxes—be a significant hardship for
churches? Apparently not, since many nonprofits lease their property, and
pay taxes indirectly as part of the rental price, with no apparent financial
distress. Why would paying taxes be any worse for churches than for
homeowners? Homeowners pay property taxes, and ordinary taxpayers
pay income taxes, sales taxes, and taxes on interest, dividends and capital gains, while church income, sales, and investments are tax-free. Most
corporations are taxed on money or property bequeathed to them, while
churches get inheritances tax-free. Businesses pay income and property
taxes on nursing homes, publishing houses and other enterprises, while
churches that do the same thing are tax-free. In bankruptcy proceedings
in Minnesota (and perhaps in other states), money tithed to churches is exempt from being allocated to satisfy creditors. Adding insult to injury, some
churches will even demand compensation for the use of their buildings
as polling places, although they owe much of their ability to provide large
parking lots and handicap accessible facilities to their tax exempt status.

The tax exemptions that encourage this have resulted in a proliferation
of religious, charitable and educational nonprofits, some worthy, many
questionable and none that could not afford to pay their fair share of
taxes. We have churches that seem focused almost entirely on providing private jets and mansions for their preachers—often in communities
where the public schools are deteriorating for lack of sufficient funding.
We have nonprofit charities that seem interested primarily in socializing
(fraternal organizations with membership bars and dance halls come
to mind). We have educational nonprofits whose purpose appears to
be to convince the public to think as they do and to use their financial
resources to affect election outcomes.

Why exempt any of them, even those that provide worthwhile services?
If they can buy and maintain property, pay their utility bills, and hire
high-salaried CEOs, they can pay taxes like any other business. What
if all nonprofits were treated like any other business for tax purposes?
Taxes would be based on ability to pay, so small organizations would

not suffer any financial hardship while large ones would easily afford the extra expense. As with any business, a nonprofit would succeed or fail based on its ability to attract supporters. And those supporters would be in a position to contribute to the religious or secular nonprofit of their choice because their property tax burden would be eased by virtue of it being shared equitably.

It may be argued that there should be exceptions for nonprofits whose primary purpose is to provide a full time social service under contract with the government. However, many for-profit companies also provide goods or services to the government under contract, often as their primary activity. Such a contractual arrangement does not exempt them from taxes; neither should it exempt the nonprofit contractors.

Would taxing religious institutions violate the First Amendment? No more than government is involved in taxing citizens in general or in requiring secular nonprofits to file a 990 form. Does making newspapers pay income and property taxes violate freedom of the press? Does making a privately owned meeting hall pay property taxes violate freedom of assembly? Does making lobbying firms pay income taxes violate the right to petition government for redress of grievances? No freedom is jeopardized by reporting one's taxable income and its source or by having one's property assessed.

One of the tradeoffs for being tax exempt is that religious and secular nonprofits are not allowed to take political positions or endorse candidates, although they can discuss issues. Would that change if tax exemptions were removed? Of course. But would that be significantly different from what is already going on? Don't activities like the Catholic Church in Minneapolis and St. Paul sending out thousands of DVDs opposing same-sex marriage tell voters something? Don't the Protestant fundamentalists' voters' guides distributed to "moral values" voters tell the recipients something? Don't pro-choice rallies organized by Planned Parenthood tell voters something?

10

Our Most Favored Welfare Recipient Keeps on Taking

"Of all good words in prose or rhyme,
the greatest are these: I've got mine!"
— Hagar the Horrible, a marauding comic strip Viking
buffoon gloating over his loot (created by Chris Browne)

I wrote this book to call attention to the damage the election of Donald Trump promised to do to our civil liberties and values. For this chapter it seemed little more could be said because the damage had already been done and Trump could only make it marginally worse. But on January 2 of 2018, according to a report by American Atheists published in the Atlanta Freethought Society's January 2018 newsletter, *Atlanta Freethought News,* FEMA (the Federal Emergency Management Agency) decided to include, for the first time, the building and furnishing of houses of worship and other religious facilities in its disaster relief program. We can now consider the margin erased and taxpayers will be supporting the trappings of religious mysticism at the expense of helping people with real-world needs.

No administration, Democratic or Republican, has shown either an understanding or respect for the social and political value of keeping religion out of government. All I can do in this chapter is point out the problem with religion-friendly welfare and hope that somehow the general public will eventually see it too and take steps to stop it. Allowing religion into public life and feeding it and coddling it and accommodating it does not work. It is socially useless, financially wasteful and inherently dismissive of the First Amendment's attempt to maintain a healthy separation of religion and government.

Much of the credibility and respect that surrounds religious organizations is due to the perception of them as charitable institutions. They are seen as fulfilling a Gospel mission to feed the hungry and shelter the homeless. To some extent this is true, and to that extent it is admirable. Unfortunately, that extent has seldom if ever reached very far. Religious charity has always been a day late and a dollar short. Historically, those in need have never received much from religious institutions, although they always seem to have vast amounts of money available to build and maintain extravagant cathedrals, acquire priceless works of art and, more recently, buy mansions and private jets for televangelists.

Until well into the 20th century it was generally left to government-run poor houses and poor farms to feed the hungry and shelter the homeless where families were nonexistent or unable to help. What changed this was large-scale federal government involvement beginning in the 1930s. Social Security and many housing, employment, medical and welfare programs began lifting people out of destitution. With all that assistance available, religious institutions began finding it financially effective as well as biblically cosmetic to feed the hungry and shelter the homeless.

I experienced the Great Depression and know what it's like to live in severe poverty. I remember how it was when those government programs were just getting established. There were churches all around but no help came from any of them. (Well, except that the Catholic school tuition was reduced to a token amount to reduce the number of kids escaping the indoctrination for cost reasons.)

The real help came from a New Deal program that sent us canned food and decent bedding and established "neighborhood houses" that provided all kinds of wonderful community and family activities. In Catholic school I heard nothing about social justice and a lot about the "truth" of the Catholic Church and the hellfire and brimstone cost of committing a sin. It was only when I got to a public high school that I started hearing from my English teacher Miss Blessin and my History teacher Miss Dougherty about the importance of social justice as a basic human value—with not a word about religion.

Who Feeds the Hungry and Shelters the Homeless?

Several years ago I was doing public relations for a religious non-profit that provided health-related services. It was an excellent organization and its services were of the highest quality. Although it was run by a church, it operated in an entirely secular manner. When I was hired, their attorney emphasized how strictly they adhered to state-church separation principles. I was not even to refer to "our mission" in describing their work because of the religious connotation. I was to refer to "our programs" instead. I wrote newsletters, press releases and heartwarming booklets promoting the organization—all entirely true. My normally-required skill at writing public relations B.S. was not needed there. It was a joy to write honestly. My boss and I were both atheists and the management (ordained ministers) didn't care. We did a good job and we were appreciated.

When an anniversary celebration was planned I researched and wrote about their history, going back well into the 19th century. It was more informative than I had expected. The church had always tried to provide charitable services, but (as with churches generally) the help could cover only a small number of their own members.

Then the federal social welfare programs began, enabling impoverished people to pay for more of the things they needed to survive. That newly available revenue allowed the church's social services to expand and grow. . . and grow. . . and grow. By the time I was hired the operation had become very large, with several buildings serving hundreds of people from the general population in varying stages of need. And it was almost all publicly funded in one way or another. While I was there I saw how this religious nonprofit got a government grant to buy and maintain vehicles to transport their clients, all thanks to those federal programs.

To the church's credit, they were doing an excellent job—efficient, honest, professional, caring and respectful—with no religious proselytizing anywhere. However, the highest paid employee was the person who went around to families of the clients, primed with my booklets full of heartwarming stories about the wonderful work the church was doing. (The stories, as I said, were absolutely true!) The families were encouraged to remember the church in their estate planning.

And why wouldn't they? All the buildings and vehicles carried the church's name—everyone could see what the church was doing. So the church got remembered and prospered. But it was primarily the taxpayers who funded it all, while the church got the credit. My pleasant job ended when the church closed down our P.R. department. They were getting too big, they said, and we were attracting more public attention than they wanted. So no more public relations.

The job taught me a lot about how religious charities are able to provide the social services that generate such widespread public respect. If their good works don't come about because of funds available through social safety net programs, they come via direct contracts with government agencies to provide services on the government's behalf (such as Catholic Charities and Lutheran Social Services) and from secular public or private grant-making foundations.

To take an example from Illinois (reported in the liberal Catholic magazine, *Conscience,* in Vol. 2, 2012), from 60% to 92% of the revenue Catholic Charities received in five of its six dioceses came from the state. However, the bishops were closing most of the Catholic Charities affiliates rather than conform to state requirements that same-sex couples not be discriminated against as adoptive or foster parents. Although the bishops offered to refer such couples elsewhere, the state's Department of Children and Family Services declined, saying, "Separate but equal was not a sufficient solution to other civil rights issues in the past either." A commendable position.

To be fair, there are churches that do provide charity using their own money collected from members and fundraising activities. Although this is laudable, it is never enough to develop a significant charitable project. There is nothing wrong in principle with what these religious organizations—if operated by secular standards—are doing. It is probably cost-effective for government to farm out some of its social service responsibilities to churches, since the infrastructure, administrative skills and volunteer resources are already in place.

However, it is wrong to allow the public to be misled (whether intentionally or not) into assuming churches do this with their own money and therefore deserve respect and honor and preferential tax exemptions. They may be feeding the hungry and sheltering the homeless, but the taxpayers, private foundations and publicly supported organizations such as the United Way are footing the bill. The churches would not be doing this work otherwise.

Even more wrong—and dishonest—is the arrogance of religious social service providers that agree to provide necessary secular services under government programs, then refuse to provide those that conflict with their belief system (as the U.S. Catholic bishops have been doing with their drive for "religious liberty"). To demand the right to deny clients and patients—even employees—those services, while continuing to demand government funding for them, is to demand to be paid for work they refuse to do. It is dishonest.

So any significant church charity is funded largely by government agencies. And who are the recipients? Most visibly, it's poor people in dire need of help. They get Social Security, welfare, housing, medical assistance and more. Not so visibly—and arguably benefiting *far* more—it's religious institutions in no need whatsoever of help. They get tax exemptions, subsidies, grants, service contracts, and giveaways of all kinds that keep their revenue stream flowing. It's a business, with little or no financial accountability.

A Look at Charitable Giving

Roy Sablosky is a science researcher who evaluates the accuracy of sociological studies. He wrote a paper on his findings regarding religion-motivated generosity. While it was going through the peer-review process, he gave me permission to use some of his material for this book. The title is "Does Religion Foster Generosity?" For information about the data cited, see roy.sablosky@sablosky.com.

What he found is that studies on religious generosity tend to be unreliable. Much of it consists of self-reports and there is no independent standard against which claims of religiosity can be measured. Social desirability also skews any studies because people tend to say what they are expected to say. There is also the problem of terminology. "Charitable" does not always mean "generous." All charitable donations are tax deductible, but not all charity is generous. Sablosky cites several behavioral and economic experiments on generosity that avoid a connection to religiosity, however that is defined. In all cases, the results show that religious beliefs or the absence thereof have little or no observable effect on the subjects' responses to tests of generosity.

How much charitable giving, when defined as generous, is going on out there? Sablosky notes that churches are estimated to collect about $100 billion every year in donations. However, only 2% of that goes to humanitarian projects. The rest pays for buildings, maintenance, staff salaries, clergy housing, and so on. Donating money to a church is like paying a membership fee to a clubhouse, but it's all tax-deductible as a "charitable donation."

An interesting and apparently carefully researched investigation of charitable giving was conducted by Ryan T. Cragun, Stephanie Yeager and Desmond Vega over several months prior to publishing "Research Report: How Secular Humanists (and Everyone Else) Subsidize Religion in the United States" in the June/July 2012 issue of *Free Inquiry* magazine. Included in the documentation is a comparison of religious and corporate charitable giving. The Mormon Church, while touting its generosity, actually donates only about 0.7% of its annual income. Other churches generally do better, but still come in far lower than (for example) Walmart, which donates "about $1.75 billion in food aid to charities each year, or twenty-eight times all of the money allotted for charity by the United Methodist Church and almost double what the LDS [Mormon] Church has given in the last twenty-five years."

And how about organizations such as the Red Cross? Their donations, which directly help people in distress, amount to 92.1% of their income, leaving 7.9% for operating expenses. Assuming a generous 50-50 split between charitable donations and operating expenses in assessing whether an organization's function is primarily charitable, how many religious organizations would even come close to qualifying as charitable? Probably none. According to "Research Report," one of the authors' sources calculated the operating expenses of 271 churches and found them to average 71% of total revenue, mostly for clergy salaries.

One of the problems with defining religious charity is that religious activities, such as providing worship services, administering sacraments and attending to various other ritualistic tasks, are considered "spiritual charities," supposedly making them charitable activities. But they are not, as "Research Report" points out. When you provide charity, you give something, you don't exchange something. "Spiritual charities" are activities that clergy are hired to do. That is not charity, it is paid labor.

To be charitable for tax purposes implies that, if the charity were discontinued, the government might have to take over and provide it. Here is what "Research Report" says about that:

> There is one other argument religions could use to claim they are "spiritual charities." When religions pray for rain for the local community or when they baptize the dead to assure them salvation—as is done by the Mormon Church—isn't this a form of spiritual charity in the sense that even people not donating to the religion benefit? These acts certainly seem closer to charity, but they don't meet the criteria of what it means to be a charitable organization for tax purposes: If the function or service the charity provides were discontinued, would it result in a legal requirement for public funds to continue the function? Religious soup kitchens would probably meet this criteria but would praying for rain or baptizing dead people? Although Texas Governor Rick Perry may have prayed for rain and Mitt Romney may want past presidents baptized, we think most people would agree that government has no interest in addressing such "spiritual concerns."

> In summary, religions spend a relatively small portion of their revenue on physical charity, and while they spend a larger portion of their revenue addressing spiritual concerns, most of that qualifies as labor, not charity. What little qualifies as "spiritual charity" would not be replaced by government if discontinued. In short, religions are, by and large, not engaged in charitable work. . . . [R]eligions are more like for-profit corporations providing entertainment (such as movie theaters or amusement parks) rather than charities.

Underlying the imprecision and unaccountability that go with religious tax exemptions and subsidies is a deeper problem that should raise some concerns. Since the IRS cannot require a religious institution to disclose the identity of its donors or the amount received from them, the opportunity for fraud has to be irresistible for some people. The IRS isn't even allowed to determine what is or is not a church. It pretty much has to take the organizer's word for it and grant the religious tax exemptions and subsidies. So the donations come in, with no way to account for where they came from or where they went. The "church" could be a front for all manner of illegal operations. For example, here is an item from page 14 of the May 2012 issue of *Freethought Today*, the newspaper of the Freedom from Religion Foundation (FFRF) in Madison, Wisconsin:

Study. Church Scams Total $35 Billion

The *Wall Street Journal* reported May 7 that of the $569 billion that churchgoers and others are expected to donate to Christian causes worldwide in 2012, about $35 billion or 6% of the total will end up in the hands of "money launderers, embezzlers, tax evaders or unscrupulous ministers living too high on the hog." The article cites a study by the Center for The Study of Global Christianity at Gordon-Conwell Theological Seminary in South Hamilton, Mass. The article notes that churches aren't required to file IRS Form 990 that other 501(c)(3) nonprofits must file.

Given the ease with which "church" frauds can be pulled off, surely there have been, and are, illegal businesses that have set themselves up as churches. They are not taxed, not investigated, not required to report anything they do. What group of schemers would not take advantage of this to launder profits from drug-running, prostitution and gambling enterprises—or just to live high off the tax deductible "charitable dona-tion" hog by exploiting the gullible? And it's not just criminals who might take advantage of this open door. Any corporation that wants to fund some political activity anonymously could arrange to make charitable donations to a like-minded church (genuine or set up for the purpose) that would take it from there. We all pay higher taxes to make up for the revenue lost to those "charitable donation" tax deductions.

Subsidies, Grants and Giveaways

Entire books could be (and perhaps have been) written on this topic. My own research for this book has produced a small mountain of material, far more than I am able to deal with. Every example, instance or report has a great many similar ones behind it. Huge amounts of taxpayer dollars end up here. The Tea Party might want to check this out. Government subsidizing of religion is widespread in both direct and indirect ways.

The "Research Report" cited above includes a detailed account of the many ways the taxpayers are subsidizing religion for no particular reason other than that it is religion. Much of this is covered in the chapter on taxes, but the "Research Report" provides a table summarizing the nature of the subsidies and putting them in perspective.

Estimated annual government subsidies in the U.S.

Federal income tax subsidy	$35.3 billion
State income tax subsidy	$6.1 billion
Property tax subsidy	$26.2 billion
Investment tax subsidy	$41.0 million
Parsonage subsidy	$1.2 billion
Faith-Based Initiative subsidy	$2.2 billion
TOTAL	**$71.0 billion**

Subsidies not estimated

Local income and property tax subsidies
Sales tax subsidy
SECA exemption subsidy
Donor tax-exemption subsidy
Increase in donations from donor tax-exemption subsidy
Related business income tax subsidy
Fund-raising subsidy
Volunteer labor subsidy
TOTAL: probably billions more

Given our inability to estimate some of the subsidies, we are fairly confident that our estimates are on the conservative end of the subsidies provided to religions by government in the United States. To put this into perspective, the combined total of government subsidies to agriculture in the United States in 2009 was estimated to be $180.8 billion. Religions receive at least 40 percent of the subsidy that agriculture does in the United States.

Another way to illustrate the size of the subsidy may be to illustrate how much tax revenue would increase at the state level if religious institutions had to pay property taxes. In Florida, where the state government's budget was $69.1 billion in 2011, the amount of tax revenue lost from subsidizing religious property

was $22.2 billion or 3% of the state budget. The additional reve-
nue would have mostly prevented the $1.1 billion cut to firefighter
and police retirement plans and the $1.1 billion cut to public
schools.

It doesn't appear that these subsidies include government funded religious work that is done overseas. It's considerable. I have a report
from 2001, which, though a bit dated, is still useful. Foreign aid work by
religious organizations is subsidized by hundreds of millions of taxpayer
dollars a year. In the 2001 report, Catholic Relief Services got a 57%
subsidy. The National Association of Evangelicals' World Relief agency
got 47%. Seven religious charities combined got over a third of the government grants, totaling $409 million. Religion was a factor in some of
the aid provided. Catholic Relief Services refused to provide condoms
to prevent AIDS, and World Vision (a Protestant agency that got a 19%
subsidy) hired based on the applicant's religion. Interestingly, Oxfam
America, a well-regarded secular international development agency,
does its work without taking any government money. The report did not
explain why they could do that successfully while religious groups apparently couldn't. Worth thinking about.

Despite the constitutional violations inherent in government funding
of religion, the situation seems only to get worse. President Obama's
campaign rhetoric was strongly supportive of a wall of separation between church and state, yet his administration continued its destruction.
It has been undermined, leaped over and punched through so often
and so badly that it is more of a sieve than a wall. There is hardly a
religion-favoring proposal that doesn't get through. For example, the
February 2012 issue of *Mother Jones* magazine says:

> When it comes to religious organizations and their treatment by
> the federal government, the Obama administration has been
> extremely generous. Religious groups have benefited hand-
> somely from Obama's stimulus package, budgets, and other
> policies. Under Obama, Catholic religious charities alone have
> received more than $650 million, according to a spokeswoman
> from the U.S. Department of Health and Human Services, where
> much of the funding comes from. The USCCB [U.S. Conference
> of Catholic Bishops], which has been such a vocal critic of the

Obama administration, has seen its share of federal grants from HHS jump from $71.8 million in the last three years of the Bush administration to $81.2 million during the first three years of Obama. In fiscal 2011 alone, the group received a record $31.4 million from the administration it believes is virulently anti-Catholic, according to HHS data.

Reinforcing that assessment, the liberal Catholic magazine, *Conscience*, devoted much of its First Quarter 2011 issue to examining the extent to which Obama not only ignored his campaign promise to reverse the Bush administration's violations of the Establishment Clause, but maintained and even expanded them. Administrative decisions that looked good, such as new requirements to address constitutional concerns about the faith-based initiative funding under the Office of Faith-Based and Neighborhood Partnerships (OFBNP), were simply not implemented.

Religious organizations continued to receive funding that goes directly to churches, even for church building repairs, instead of to their supposedly secular—and separate—social programs, with no serious attempt at oversight. Non-discriminatory hiring policies were not only not mandated, they were deliberately kept off the agenda of the advisory body charged with making the OFBNP function within constitutional guidelines. There are, of course, strict rules against using OFBNP funds to proselytize, but no one was minding that store, especially in small towns and rural areas where social service recipients would be fearful of complaining in any case.

One of the necessary social services that government contracts out to nonprofit groups, for which it provides funding, is low-income housing. This can come with strings attached—the strings being the religious interests government agencies are asked to accommodate. Catholic organizations especially, due to their doctrinal rigidity, are most noted for this.

For example, below is an excerpt from a February 2012 fundraising letter sent by Americans United for Separation of Church and State:

The [Catholic] bishops' involvement in Proposition 8, a ballot referendum that repealed same-sex marriage in California in 2008, is well known, but in Washington, church officials often engage in subtler forms of lobbying to alter Americans' rights. Church leaders and lobbyists have argued, for example, that the "religious liberty" of believers is violated when governments recognize same-sex civil marriage—even though not a single church is required to sanction or perform such ceremonies. Last year, Catholic hierarchy lobbyists went so far as to ask the Department of Housing and Urban Development (HUD) to drop a proposed regulation that would have added sexual orientation as a protected class against discrimination in HUD programs. If adopted, this rule could have led to some people being literally left out in the cold with no place to stay.

Government involvement with religion at the local level seems to go on all over all the time. In 2000, Congress passed the Religious Land Use and Institutionalized Persons Act (RLUIPA), which seriously restricts local governments from controlling how, when and where religious institutions can locate and expand. So the institutions expand into a residential neighborhood, creating traffic congestion or they expand into an industrial area,, removing prime land for industrial development from the tax rolls. For cities to object would be to impose a "substantial" burden on the practice of one's religion. If local governments sue and lose, they must pay the plaintiff's attorney fees. Since the prospect of winning against a religious institution is seldom good and the costs of losing high, local governments tend to let the religious institutions have their way.

Publications that advocate for state-church separation are often filled with reports of what sometimes appears to be a total lack of separation. Recently, the government has started to fund Historic Preservation projects for churches. For at least a hundred years, such work was always privately financed. In 1900, repairs to the National Cathedral in Washington D.C. were made at a cost of $65 million, all private money. In 2011, repairs cost $700,000, this time paid with a government grant. Two other churches also got grants for repair work, one for $178,615 and the other for $700,000.

That is how church preservation is financed. All it took was a reinterpretation of a Supreme Court ruling. The 1971 *Tilton v. Richardson* ruling held that public money for restoration could be provided only if the building was not used for religious purposes. In 1995, the restriction was cited as no longer binding under the National Historic Preservation Act, and government funding was allowed. At first, the funding was provided only to churches of clear historic interest, but that was soon watered down to allow funding for almost any church building. Church-state separation finally hit bottom when the Supreme Court decided, in *Hein v. Freedom from Religion Foundation*, that citizens, as such, had standing to challenge government funding of religion only if the funding was authorized by a legislative body. Therefore, any funding from a government agency's discretionary funds could be used to fund any religious activity desired. Legislative bodies have no problem allocating discretionary funds to whatever agency they choose or to the president. That horse has left the barn.

The Establishment Clause seems never to be a hindrance to government support of religion any time a legislative body wants to do that. For example, here is an account of one effort I made to keep my City Council from giving high tax producing land to the Catholic Church. I have worked on projects like this so often and with so little success that I feel like Sisyphus pushing that rock up the hill. Here it comes rolling back down again. And again.

In 1989, the Minneapolis City Council gave away prime downtown land, worth between $5 million and $10 million, to the College of St. Thomas for a school of business administration because the college said it could not afford to buy it. The Council tried to find a way to get around the constitutional problem of publicly funding a religious institution and finally succeeded with a convoluted scheme that can only be called money laundering. Our mayor at the time, Don Fraser, was strongly opposed to the funding and gave me information to use in my efforts. However, Minneapolis has what is called a "weak mayor" system that prevents mayors from acting without substantial support from the Council. It left Fraser extremely frustrated.

There were letters to the editor from the Minnesota chapter of the American Civil Liberties Union and other state-church separation supporters, but they had no effect. A Wisconsin colleague, Paul Keller, wrote coherent, well reasoned letters to Mayor Fraser and State Attorney General Skip Humphrey (son of the late Vice President Hubert Humphrey) urging opposition to the giveaway. Humphrey's response only advised

Keller to take the matter up with the City Council. Mayor Fraser wrote a supportive reply outlining his efforts to prevent the giveaway. All of this was to no avail.

This multi-million dollar property now generates no taxes because it is owned by a religious institution. One of the arguments in favor of the give-away was that several scholarships would be given to low-income inner city students. However, those scholarships come with religious strings attached: No student can graduate from St. Thomas without completing at least three courses in religion. This is enforced indoctrination, cour-tesy of the taxpayers. In 1990, the business section of the *Star Tribune* had an article praising St. Thomas for its business success, but it came courtesy of the City Council's land giveaway underwritten by the city's property tax payers.

The College of St. Thomas school of business was always touted as operating in a secular manner. Yet, one friend of mine, who was taking a course in accounting, told me that the first day she came to class, when the instructor walked in, he asked the class to rise. Then he began to lead the class in prayer. My friend says she abruptly sat down and did not pray. She wondered if that would have an effect on her grade. It apparently did not, but these things are inherently coercive—with taxpayer support.

The hubris of religious institutions can be astonishing. They seem to feel entitled to government support for anything they want to do, with no concept of fairness. Here's an example of a situation that started in 2012 (*St. Paul Pioneer Press*, June 10, 2012) and is still going on as of this writing (*Minneapolis Star Tribune*, July 16, 2017):

In June, 2012, three churches in downtown St. Paul, Minnesota, decided they were charged unfairly for street maintenance. The city's fee for cleaning and maintaining downtown streets was $16.62 per linear foot for every building, regardless of its length, height, depth, purpose or amount of use. After all, street cleaning is street cleaning. Outside the downtown area, the fee was lower because there was less cleaning and maintaining to do. The three churches said they were treated unfairly because churches outside the downtown area paid less, so they wanted to pay less too, just because they were churches. They wanted to be placed in their own special category that ignored the "street cleaning is street cleaning" concept that treated all buildings alike for a service that was identical for all.

After some legal wrangling, the attorney for the churches, Scott Nordstrand, came up with what he insisted was a fair solution, and here it is, from the 2012 news reports:

> Nordstrand said a logical alternative might be to once again fund routine street maintenance through the general fund, which would eliminate street assessments but raise property taxes overall. Nordstrand crunched the numbers and believes he has a good handle on how much the overall burden would go up or down for various properties.

And no doubt Nordstrand's number crunching revealed that his fair alternative would leave the churches paying absolutely nothing, because they pay no taxes into the general fund (or anything else) and no property taxes either. But overall property taxes would be raised, with everyone paying more so the churches could pay nothing. And they really do think that is fair. As of news reports in 2017 the legal wrangle has become all about the right of the churches to be exempt from all fees. The original controversy over varying fees was apparently dropped. Nordstrand's 2012 "logical alternative" that the churches pay nothing eventually prevailed with a court ruling that the fees were actually taxes. Since then the city has been trying to work out a system where tax-exempt nonprofits voluntarily pay something to help maintain the city services from which they benefit. Of course, the churches are saying they might then have to cut back on all the social good they do. What that is remains unspecified.

City councils generally are opposed to these religious tax exemptions. They need the money for more productive purposes, but seldom prevail. One of our suburbs tried limiting the number of churches that could be built because of the loss of property tax revenue. That idea worked for a while but religious pressure soon ended it. My city council tried putting a fee on street lighting based on square footage instead of linear feet because churches tend to take up a lot of square footage, often entire blocks, while commercial businesses generally take up only linear feet along the roadway. Religious pressure shot down that idea too. Cities are prevented from removing property tax exemptions from church property because state laws don't allow them that level of control.

Some government preferential funding for religious activities is so ludicrous as to be embarrassing. Kentucky, for example, which already touts a Creation Museum devoted to assuming the Genesis account is actual history, now, in 2017, has a Noah's Ark theme park in Williamstown. Taxpayers put up the financial incentives covering 25% of the costs for the nonprofit (tax exempt of course) group Answers in Genesis to develop the (profitable of course) multimillion dollar tourist attraction. The Ark is 500 feet long and wooden (just like the Bible says, so of course it's authentic). And it will be educational, having among its passengers replicas of dinosaurs (but maybe just babies due to space limitations) and live animals including baby giraffes. The Tower of Babel will be there too.

Such noble intellectual efforts! And some people never seem to appreciate them! The National Center for Science Education objected that "students who accept this material as scientifically valid are unlikely to succeed in science courses at the college level." (What makes the NCSE think such students will even qualify for a high school diploma, much less college?)

Then there's P.Z. Myers, the notoriously outspoken biologist and evolution's one-man S.W.A.T. team. Here is his tail twisting analysis, from his blog, "Pharyngula":

> I'm going to be a contrarian here. I think the Kentucky legislature has made a perfectly sensible budget decision. Here's the deal: in the current budget, a couple of interesting decisions have been made.
>
> Funding for K-12 education, reduced by $50 million.
> Tax breaks for the Ark Park, $43 million provided.
> Highway improvements for the Ark Park, $11 million provided.
>
> Almost perfectly balanced: all the money handed over to creationists is taken away from education. And it makes perfect sense too. It's not as if the next generation might need a high

school diploma to take advantage of the employment opportunities provided by Answers in Genesis. In fact, it's probably a selling point to the creationists to have an especially ignorant work force already in place. Good work, Governor Beshear!

The latest development in this saga of self-dealing among religious "non-profits" is that the city, badly in need of funds for basic services such as police and fire protection, put a 50¢ "public safety" fee on tickets sold for the theme park. The creationists, not interested in giving a little when they could be taking it all, sold the park to themselves for $10 to avoid the fee. They called the fee a tax and said they should not be taxed because they are a church, even though their theme park was making a good profit.

Speaking of education and government-assisted creationism, I received the following discouraging email forwarded from George Erickson (source unidentified) on June 19, 2012. It reminds us that creationist fantasies are not confined to the fundamentalist Bible Belt. They are everywhere:

> There is a creationist facility in southeast Wisconsin called Timber-lee. Believe it or not, a number of Wisconsin school districts take kids there on an overnight field trip, which takes place on regular school days. I saved a program on tape a number of years ago. It was essentially a fundraising appeal for Timber-lee—they aspired to be "the showplace for creationism" in the Midwest. The individual promoting Timber-lee was Don Jacobs (Jacobson?), a radiologist who taught at the medical college of Wisconsin, but didn't believe in radiometric dating. Go figger. They have expanded and progressed to the point that these "field trips" have become a regular feature. One of the schools allowing it is the Racine Public School District.

Tax-Exempting the Sacred; Tax-Burdening the Secular

Is there any secular value in giving anything to religious institutions? What is the return on our tax investment? We lose revenue through near-total tax exemptions and tax-deductible donations. We lose when churches get credit for doing good works that are funded by the taxpayers. Secular charities do as much or more without presenting us with problems about state-church separation, use of government funding for proselytizing, freeing up church money to influence elections and public policies, setting up programs and projects that undermine scientific knowledge and education, and setting off culture wars. I know one politician who, at a political meeting I attended (not open to the public) said that, when social services are needed the government should provide them and not give funds to churches to do them. He was right, but of course he doesn't dare say this publicly.

And what is the value of having government help fund religious theme parks? A few low-level jobs might be created, but other businesses create jobs too, and with less damage to the intellectual development of children—and they pay taxes. Given these handouts of indefensible subsidies, grants and giveaways, and the lack of social responsibility in using them, could it not arguably be claimed that religion is this nation's ultimate welfare cheat?

11

To the Barricades:
Passionate Intensity, Political Strategy

"It is the role of unbelievers to force religions to be benign."
— Martin Marty, Lutheran theologian, keynote speech,
Religion in Public Life symposium, Minneapolis MN, April 28, 1998

It's said that there are three kinds of people in the world: A small group that makes things happen, a larger group that watches things happen, and the vast majority that has no idea what's happening.

In July of 2017 I spent 11 hours as a delegate at the Minneapolis Democratic party convention for endorsing candidates for mayor and other city functions. (We had a serious brains-falling-out situation in foolishly accommodating some religious beliefs but that's for the next chapter.) On hand was the small group that makes things happen (party leaders, public officials, candidates and their campaign committees) and the larger group that watches things happen (1,200 convention delegates elected at precinct caucuses). Outside the convention hall was the vast majority that had no idea what was happening and still doesn't and probably never will because they don't care about politics.

There were several candidates for mayor but no one got the 60% needed for endorsement so they all went on to the general election. The newspaper (*Star Tribune*, July 11 and ever since and as always) had writers referring to convention delegates as "insiders" or "elitists" as though that is something pernicious and undemocratic. News reports and columnists suggested that the decision about who will be mayor would be made more democratically at the November election. That's when some percentage of the vast majority that has no idea what's happening shows up to vote, although not particularly knowledgeably, as anyone who (like me) has done voter surveys can tell you.

All that aside, the most interesting thing about the convention was the involvement by the Anti-Trump Resisters. More about that when I get to the mechanics of political party activism.

This may be the most useful chapter in this book, assuming there are enough Trump resisters with enough passionate intensity to take the simple action necessary to be politically effective. The other chapters describe the problem with allowing religion to be involved in public life; this one tells you how to fix it. Its purpose is to put some of the millions of Trump resisters who have been marching in the streets into the group that makes things happen and to put the rest of them into the group that doesn't just watch the first group but helps them with a little, also simple, civic action.

You are not likely to find this information anywhere else. No other writers I know of show an understanding of what to do about the Trump administration beyond public protests, and emails and phone calls to legislators. A typical example is the December 2017 issue of *Church & State*, the newsletter of Americans United for Separation of Church and State (AU). It has an article titled "Empowering Activists" about ways to oppose Trump's anti-state-church-separation agenda. It's about lobbying and sending emails and taking legal action. Not a word about the political party activism that works and has been massively proven to work, which is the focus of this chapter.

Of course, organizations like AU need to appear non-partisan, so to suggest getting closely involved in party politics runs counter to that. It also runs counter to the social taboo against criticizing a religious belief, however disastrous its effect is on individuals and society.

Once again we are dealing with a problem that is serious but cannot be discussed openly. Separation of church and state is about keeping government out of religion and religion out of government. The two can never mix because the secular is reality-based while the sacred is fantasy-based. Each has its own sphere of operation and unless public safety is involved, they should stay in it.

There is nothing wrong with AU's outside-looking-in activism (although its legal action is risky, given the makeup of the increasingly right-leaning judiciary). All those things help, but it's downstream stuff that doesn't deal with the upstream source of our problem. It amounts to political begging for mercy from people who seem to like nothing better than imposing more misery. We have been thrown into a dank social/political hole. We need a political shovel to dig us out and it's called political party activism.

This is about being the insiders and elitists and controlling the party and its philosophy and selecting and electing the candidates who will put progressive policies into law. The religious right did that in their takeover of the Republican party, so it's not like we're inventing the wheel. You can't say it can't be done when it's already been done so well. It can be done again, not just in the Democratic party but in pulling the Republican party out of the fundamentalist muck it's in so it can get back to being rationally secular.

My focus is on the Democratic party, but that's not because I know so much about it or favor it—it's because you need the resources of a large and influential political organization if you want to change the political landscape. The Democratic party is all we have. The religious right has taken over the Republican party and the "third parties" are too small to be effective. You work with what you have, not what you wish you had. Besides, most of the Anti-Trump Resisters were supporters of Bernie Sanders, so the basic progressive political agenda is about the same, meaning the Resisters should find a lot of support among the Democratic party activists.

The strategy I will describe is direct, simple and effective. It consists of getting some of those millions of marchers to do something useful upstream where it counts. We have seen that there are millions of liberal progressives in this country. All we need is for some of them to engage in the same direct involvement I've had and we will stop Trump from unraveling our civilization. Doing this requires taking over the Democratic party because it is the only political party large enough and with a national structure and fundraising and organizational resources to be effective. After 50 years of close involvement, I know how it works.

Frankly, the Democratic party is a philosophical disaster. Ever since the religious right took over the Republican party, the Dems have been a roll-over-and-play-dead bystander to the Republican assaults on our civil rights and liberties. Comedian Bill Maher regularly lampoons the Dems for being spineless wimps and he is right.

The Republican party has become a religious right extremist party. To counter its policies often requires questioning the party's religious values and that is taboo. (You get called "godless" if you do that—the ultimate political-career-killing slur. More about that in the next chapter.) So the Democratic party seeks to be "nice." It seeks to be "fair." It hasn't figured out that those concepts mean nothing to the religious-right-controlled Republican party. I suspect it doesn't want to figure it out because that might require taking opposing action and it has no idea how to wage a fight like that. . . . No, there is no endnote to document this. I speak from personal experience, lots of it, some of which I include in this book. I write this in one more of my many bursts of hope that have never been as fruitful as I would have liked because there were never enough like-minded people willing to do what was needed to pull it off. I'm still waiting for the 70 years of marching for women's right to vote to pay off in women voting in numbers that produce significant social improvement (but we'll see how the "Me Too" uprising against sexual harassment turns out).

That slender "gender gap" percent we get is just a ripple from the affected 50% of the population when we need a tidal wave. There were women voting for the crotch-groping misogynistic Trump who said that was an expression of their feminism. Somehow it showed how liberated they were. They must feel that a slave mind is a terrible thing to waste by not using their hard-won right to vote to maintain their slave status.

Maybe this time it will be different. (Yes, I know that's the definition of insanity.) I have seen these mass marches before, sure that they would change things and the promise of peace and social justice would be fulfilled. It wasn't. The labor union marchers of the early 20th century became God-and-Country jingoists for Sen. Joseph McCarthy's 1950s witch-hunts. The anti-Vietnam War marchers grew up to vote for Reagan and the Bushes. The social change rallies and marches for Howard Dean in his impressive run for President in 2004 fizzled in a low turnout at caucuses and primaries.

Will the Resister marchers hang in there this time and finally do what's needed to achieve a culture in which social justice is a basic unquestioned value? "Hope springs eternal," as they say. It's also true that, "Where there is no hope the people perish." But where is the saying that celebrates the achievement of a hopeful vision? It's always, as I said a few years ago when one more hopeful vision failed, "How can we lose when we're so sincere?" So we try again.

Unlike other commentators, I've been closely involved in the political system for decades. I've held positions in the Minnesota Democratic party at every level from the precinct caucus to the state committees. I saw how this culture war got started and how its authoritarian hordes have been running off with our rights ever since. I've been doing my best to stop it. This war has been going on for a long time and for the most part we have been losing. It may be a long time before it ends, but it will, and perhaps not well if we don't understand it and how to fight it.

The good news is that something like a stiffened spine seems to be showing up within the political left, whose idea of how to fight for their values is normally to be nice and accommodating. So there's hope. People who were decent and rational enough to be immune to Trump's carney hustle realize the damage he is doing and seem ready to take action— but what they're proposing is not the most effective. I'm not discounting the impressive organizing and marches. Millions of women marched for their rights and the rights of minorities; millions marched in defense of science. (And isn't it a sign of how bad things are when we have to march for facts?) There is a massive resistance movement forming to counter what Noam Chomsky has called a "race to the precipice" as the Trump administration unravels civilization with his backtracking on civil rights, anti-science delusions, climate change denial, and reverse Robin Hood tax and social policies.

All well and good, but what is the Resistance telling us to do about this? March and picket, call and email legislators, have a lobby day at the Capitol and send money to the groups telling us to do those things. It all helps, especially to raise public awareness. Attending pubic forums is especially useful in getting candidates to state their positions on the civil rights and liberties Trump has been trashing. The only bad, truly deplorable, suggestion for action I've heard (and I've head it way too often) is that we should try to understand the Trump supporters and see value in their complaints.

No, you don't do that! Never! Don't back down or compromise humanitarian values! Stick up for them forcefully! Don't backtrack on civil rights and liberties, and don't waste your time trying to change minds that can't be changed. Reason doesn't work with them, so go full-on against their moral decay! Trump's supporters are too deep into a 1950s God-and-Country racist, sexist, homophobic ideology to understand or accept reality. There is not even a moral sense to appeal to. How is it possible to vote for Trump after listening to his rants and still claim to have a working moral compass? You can't change Trump's supporters by catering to them because they have no sense even of their own secular interests, whether it's about jobs or healthcare or public schools or the safety net or anything else needed for a humane civilization.

I know Trump supporters who could not exist without the government-provided food, shelter and healthcare they rely on. Yet they rant against that and are sure that, without it, there would be help available. Maybe kindly private citizens would be there. Maybe God would provide. (Just like before we had these programs? Yeah, I remember how *that* works.) Listen to them rant against government-run healthcare while they scream "Keep the government's hands off my Medicare!" They rant about Obamacare but are fine with the Affordable Care Act and don't know it's the same thing. Listen to the rants about manufacturing jobs going overseas from those who are happy to buy everything made in China. They complain about small businesses being driven out of rural towns by big-box retailers, but who drove them out? They did by abandoning mom-and-pop stores to save a few pennies at Walmart.

Here's an account of how this happens from Jim Witt, the former owner of Borg Drug in Ashby, Minnesota. It's from a letter written on January 24, 2007, to his customers, of whom I was one. (I got my meds from him by mail to help keep him in business.) He notes the negative role of pharmaceutical companies and Republican policies in hindering small businesses while enhancing the ability of large corporations to dominate the market. As for the role played by his customers in putting him out of business, he says:

> ". . . Surprisingly, the third reason I decided to sell my drug store was the lack of support from the local community. The local newspaper did not even mention that we were on the CBS

National News [it had reported on Borg Drug's fight for lower-cost drugs]. I asked local customers to make a few changes to make low prices possible and so we could help other customers across the country save money. I asked that local customers call us with their refill orders at least one day in advance.

This small inconvenience allowed us to order the needed medications to be delivered the following day and keep our inventory cost and prices low. We also cut back our store hours to cut down on overhead expenses and to allow employees to have more time off to spend with their families. I even sold the giftware inventory to someone else so I could concentrate on the medication dispensing aspect of the pharmacy business. I let the giftware buyer use my floor space rent fee, paid for all utilities and most supplies, and let her use my clerk during pharmacy hours.

Living in a small town is supposed to foster traditional family values. The changes I asked my local customers to make were met with resistance. It was much more common to hear complaints from local customers about our services than it was to hear positive feedback about what we were trying to do. Several customers including other local business owners even changed pharmacies. I thought all people from Ashby would be proud of Borg Drug but this does not seem to be the case. . . ."

Four Steps: Show Up, Sit Down, Raise Your Hand, Take Over

What can the millions of Resisters do to bring about a socially progressive society? Lots of things and it does not include a recent "brains falling out" proposal by aggressively liberal Resisters in Minnesota. They suggested that municipal governing bodies "co-govern" with various issue-oriented Resister groups. In other words, elected bodies such as the city council would have to ask Resister groups for permission to make an official decision.

We don't need that. We already have "co-governing" in the Republican party (and sometimes in the Democratic party) where legislators check with religious leaders about what bills they should propose, support or reject. It evidently hasn't occurred to the Resisters that (as I will explain) they could *be* the governing body—the city council, the school board, the park board, the law enforcement agencies, the county commissioners, the legislators.

Please, all you millions of marching Resisters—*learn how the political system works!* If you want progressive policies, you need progressive laws. Only elected officials make laws and they are voted into office to do that. But they need to be on the ballot and they get there by being endorsed by a political party or, absent that, by winning in a primary election. Almost no one realizes the importance of party involvement in the endorsement and election process or they dismiss it as some "establishment" thing political parties use to circumvent the will of the people. But it's the key to success.

The power of party support is profound! Only a routine apathy is keeping that power dormant in the Democratic party. Not so with the Republican party—the GOP, aka God's Own Party. It has been religious right litmus-tested from top to bottom. No sign of apathy there. Most politically involved people on the left don't realize the power is there and don't use it to get solid commitments from candidates as a condition of endorsement—or general support when there is no endorsement and a primary election with several equally good candidates. I've seen endorsements granted automatically with no interest in whether the candidate's views aligned with the party platform.

Most voters don't know much about the candidates so they vote for the candidates endorsed by whatever party they have a habit of supporting. Normally it's a small number of political party activists who decide which candidates to endorse. They are not shills for Wall Street or wealthy fat cats or techie-class professionals or otherwise influential types. They are ordinary people—you, your neighbors, me—and going forward it could be a lot of those millions of marchers. What the rest of those millions of marchers who don't get that closely involved can do is outvote the Trump hordes when the candidates' names appear on the ballot. What was voted in in 2016 can be voted out in 2018 or 2020 and beyond, as long as it takes.

Although you shouldn't ignore the rural areas (there *are* some good people there and you might get some surprisingly good results) you should focus on organizing the metro areas where the liberal vote lies. The heavily populated liberal metro areas in a state can—if organized—out-vote all the sparsely populated rural areas combined. Also, in any area where the religious right dominates the political system, you can take the political parties away from them by outnumbering them in caucuses and primaries and on political party committees. Do that and you can control who your candidates are and what they stand for.

Here's where the four-step strategy kicks in: Whenever a political party is organizing as an election season begins, find out where the meetings are and **(1)** show up, **(2)** sit down, **(3)** raise your hand when there's a call for delegates, committee members or whatever, and then, when you have enough progressives on your side, **(4)** take over by voting for whatever advances a progressive agenda.

Critical Mass: Out of the Streets, Into the Precinct

Significant political change comes only when a critical mass of citizens becomes activated. This happened in the 1970s when the U.S. Catholic bishops set up their Plan for Pro-Life Activities after *Roe v. Wade*. The church's monolithic structure enabled them to organize nationwide down to the smallest rural parish. It was most successful with the Republican party. This "out of the pew and into the precinct" strategy showed how easy it is to take over a political party because so few people care about party politics.

The Resisters and the Democratic party's liberal base can use the same strategy, but this time it's "out of the streets and onto Facebook and into the precinct." The Resisters have social media now to create the critical mass needed to counter the monolithic power of the Catholic bishops. The resistance leaders need to get this critical mass aligned with the power and resources of a national political party. Right now, that's the Democratic party and it is already set up. Its platform is as social justice oriented as any Resister could want. It just needs a Congress where the majority consists of Resisters committed to implementing it. Political parties exist in every state. All are focused on getting their candidates elected, even though, in the Democratic party, they never seem to know why. They let their candidates create their own agenda, which may be at serious odds with the party platform in some respects, not that anyone seems to care.

Here's an example: When Bill Clinton was preparing for his presidency, his transition team set up a platform committee to establish his agenda. I was the delegate from Minnesota, tasked with bringing Paul Wellstone's single payer healthcare proposal to Washington D.C. for the hearings. Delegates from every state were there, each presenting their state's top proposals. A Clinton representative heard each one and then said whether the Clinton administration accepted or rejected it. My turn came and I introduced the single payer proposal (essentially the same as what Hillary Clinton had been fighting for). The Clinton rep said, "The Clinton administration rejects that." Somewhere back down the line of political positions Bill had been endorsed for, single payer should have been brought up as a condition of endorsement. Obviously it wasn't.

Political parties endorse candidates for school boards, park boards, mayors, city councils, governors, state representatives and senators, U.S. representatives and senators, attorneys general, sheriffs, county commissioners and many other positions needed to keep a civilization intact. They make and enforce the laws and approve nominations for the state and federal judiciary and Supreme Court justices. You want them on your side. You need to replace any religious right politicians in the political parties with others who are secular minded, science minded, and humane minded. A fair number of secularists may be hiding out in the Republican party, hoping for a way to bring their party back from hell. If you find them, work with them. It's all to the good if they can turn a few religious right Republican districts into moderate Republican districts whose legislators can help put some secular sanity into government.

What It Takes to Gain Political Power

First, get organized by state. You can't do it like the Catholic Church did after *Roe v. Wade* because we aren't gathering in a church every Sunday morning to hear hysterical rants about how abortion murders babies. But this time we have social media. USE IT! Start politically oriented Resister meetups aimed at political party involvement. Get a plan of action going, such as seeing how many Resisters can get elected to a party position and have them all report back. Aim to increase your party position numbers with every election cycle.

If you have politically savvy friends whose views you agree with, ask how to get involved and then follow them around to meetings and events and do what they do. At some point you'll find yourself on a committee or a delegate to something and you'll be in and involved. If you're on your own with no knowledgeable guide, just go to your state political party's web site. It will tell you how to connect with them. It varies from state to state. Read the party platform and constitution. Find out what they're doing, where they meet, how they function politically (precinct caucuses, primaries, district meetings, etc.). If what they are doing conforms close enough to your political views, then show up at whatever events are available, sit down, and get involved. It might help to bring a friend or two along for company to ease that "fish out of water" feeling, but it's not necessary. If they're electing delegates or committee members for something and they ask who's interested, raise your hand. Doesn't matter if you don't know what it's all about; you'll find out soon enough. You will be working the four-step strategy. Caveat: If the party offers a lot of bureaucratic stuff about its organizational structure, *don't read it*. (In Minnesota the Dems have a 40-page mind-numbing bureaucratic horror certain to discourage participation.) Ignore all of that. Just show up, sit down, and raise your hand.

I did that some 50 years ago at my first precinct caucus. I went because I was opposed to the Vietnam War and favored Gene McCarthy for president. Someone said I could support him by going to the precinct caucus (whatever that was). So I went. Someone running the show asked who wanted to be a delegate. Delegate for what? No matter. I raised my hand. I got to be a delegate because there were more slots available then people available and willing to fill them. I went to the district convention where there were further elections for something or other. (If you don't get a delegate spot, go for election as an alternate. They take the place of the many delegates who were elected but don't bother to show up.)

I went along with all this, assuming it would eventually make sense. I started getting phone calls from political activists looking for McCarthy supporters. They were having meetings. I went and found a whole world of political action opening up. I was hooked. I got to vote for anti-Vietnam war delegates to the famously contentious 1968 Democratic National Convention. I got to be a delegate to endorsing conventions. I voted to endorse anti-Vietnam War candidates. They went on the ballot. I helped put them there!

Later it was other issues such as women's rights and gay rights and getting religion out of government. I joined the Minnesota Democratic party's feminist caucus. Our board consisted of about 50 members from around the state. We had board meetings before the election season started and everyone was urged to attend the precinct caucuses and get elected to a party position. We met afterwards to compare notes. Almost everyone had a position. Some even ran for political office. I got on our state platform commission. We did this every election season, getting one party position after another and sometimes getting a board member elected to public office.

After a few years the entire governing structure of the Democratic party at the state level was made up of feminist caucus members. Aren't there 50 Resisters in every state who could do the same? Of course we had supporters, but so would 50 Resisters. Unfortunately, once people get to be in important leadership positions, the fire sometimes seems to go out. Maybe it's just the nature of politics. Maybe it's human nature to want to keep a leadership position and not jeopardize it by standing up for a social justice principle against those who think otherwise. Maybe the Resisters who do this today will be committed enough to keep the fire alive.

Some always try to do that. This book is dedicated to the late Sue Rockne, a member of our feminist caucus. As a delegate to the Democratic National Committee (DNC) she stood up for women's rights against Minnesota's Democratic governor, Rudy Perpich, who opposed abortion rights. Perpich had won election in 1982 against Republican Wheelock Whitney, a moderate who supported women's rights. I voted for him—pasted his bumper sticker over Perpich's on my car among my array of Democratic stickers.

Sue was challenged at a state central committee meeting for refusing to support Perpich. She held to her principles with integrity and conviction and so she lost her position on the DNC. If only there were more like her. If only we could put more people on committees who would support people like Sue Rockne. We need principled activists in those lower level committees to keep the fire going in the upper levels of leadership.

Example: A few years ago we had a precinct caucus attended by only 18 people. When platform resolutions were offered, an attendee proposed one calling for stronger support for the Bill of Rights. Another objected that if the Bill of Rights allowed women to have abortions, he was opposed to it. The vote was 4 in favor, 14 opposed. That precinct elected delegates to party committees where rules and agendas are set, and to district conventions where candidates for public office are endorsed. How do you think the 14 opponents of the Bill of Rights voted? How would they vote if today they were Resisters? The Bill of Rights would have strong support. Lower party levels put people on the upper party levels. So show up!

Things That Help, Things That Don't

There's nothing sacred about political parties. The Democratic party once supported slavery but found its soul when it became the champion of civil rights. The Republican party once supported abortion rights and civil rights but lost its soul when it became the political arm of the religious right. Political parties are whatever their more or less active members make them, and the leaders generally go along with whatever that is. It isn't much in the Democratic party these days because there never seems to be a particular agenda beyond organizing meetings, fundraisers and get-out-the-vote campaigns. They are a platform for the politically ambitious, a vehicle for promoting an agenda (pernicious or positive), and a faint hope for those who want a better world. They are an open door that can't be locked.

What would happen if a substantial number of those millions of marchers turned up at their party committee meetings or precinct caucuses or primary elections? A lot depends on your district and the level of political heat therein. In my district in north Minneapolis, we barely had enough attendees at our last precinct caucus to fill the delegate slots for the next-level convention. At the same time in south Minneapolis, hundreds of people turned out, fistfights broke out, police were called, and the precinct caucus was moved to a nearby city park to accommodate the attendees.

Why the difference? My district is well settled and politically it's the same-old, same-old. In the other district hundreds of immigrants who are now citizens had moved in, all eager (well, maybe overly eager) to experience the political democracy that did not exist in the dysfunctional terrorist-controlled nation they came from. Some things are more politically motivating than others—especially one's ethnic background. We get a lot of identity politics.

Fair enough, except for primary elections when the endorsed incumbent with a solid progressive record gets challenged by a newcomer whose credentials consist almost entirely of an ethnic background that matches that of the new voters. The newcomer gets elected because so few people vote, thinking the endorsed candidate is a shoo-in, while the challenger's supporters show up *en masse*. We lose excellent legislators this way (recently state reps Phyllis Kahn and Joe Mullery, and Minneapolis council member Barb Johnson, to give well-earned credit where it's due).

But Resisters can also win this way. What this tells us is that the political door is indeed wide open. If the Resisters want to walk in, sit down, raise their hands, take over, elect their delegates to endorsing conventions and party committees or turn out *en masse* for primaries and get their people in office, there is nothing stopping them. Find out from the party's data bank how many attended recent caucuses or primaries or were delegates to conventions. Then send in at least twice as many Resisters the next time around and the time after that as long as it takes. Just vote yourselves into party positions where you can set the agenda and the rules and endorse candidates who share your views on issues. If you are in a right-wing district, keep chipping away at the ideological makeup of the party structure until you gain control. That can be a bit tedious but not difficult. All it takes is a willingness to be an involved citizen. And it works!

I watched this grassroots involvement work disastrously when the very involved religious right steamrollered over the once-respectable Republican party. I watched it work successfully when I and other progressives organized and saved the Democratic party from the same fate. One of my fondest memories is of seeing the state leader of the "pro-lifers" get up at a state convention and announce that they were leaving the party because they were not welcome. Good riddance! Some Democrats who are so open minded their brains fall out are horrified by that and say we should be a "big tent."

Really? A tent doesn't move! Big tents are OK when what's going on in them operates along a fairly reasonable political spectrum. It used to be said that there wasn't a dime's worth of difference between the Democratic and Republican parties and that was true to some extent. Although the Republicans favored business interests and the Democrats favored working class interests, both operated within morally oriented political boundaries that maintained a civilized society. The religious right ended that in the 1970s with its morally depraved inhumane dogma-driven anti-abortion, homophobic agenda and we've had a dysfunctional political system ever since.

The scourge of apathy destroyed the moral integrity of the Republican party. I was working at the time and my Republican co-workers were appalled at the controversy over abortion at precinct caucuses. But what did they do? They stayed out of party affairs. Apparently this attitude prevailed throughout the party nationwide. I remember reading news reports that moderate Republican voters were protesting the religious right takeover by refusing to be involved or donate to the party. So how did that work for them? They left the door to the candy store not just unlocked but wide open and the religious right walked in with their racist, creationist, anti-abortion, homophobic, anti-science, Christian nation dogmas and a political agenda to turn those views into legislation nationwide.

They had no problem putting their people into party positions from which they could endorse candidates for political offices from city council to school board to governor to U.S. senator. As for the overwhelming religion-based agenda, what I heard from my Republican associates was that the Supreme Court would protect us from any religious overreaching. So, looking just at the increasing restrictions on abortion and the *Hobby Lobby* court ruling, and knowing there's more of that to come, how has that been working out?

On the Democratic side it was different. The party's less-affluent base was more vulnerable to the religious right's socially restrictive policies. In Minnesota our feminist caucus—founded by Koryn Horbal, Yvette Oldendorf, Jeri Rasmussen, Peggy Specktor, Cynthia Kittlinski and Mary Pattock—organized statewide, door knocked, lit dropped, phoned and worked on campaign committees to get rid of religious right politicians and replace them with civilized candidates. I got on the state platform commission and we maneuvered that document into an "ongoing" version difficult for future state conventions to change. We made it so-cially progressive from beginning to end, even to requiring churches to pay their far share of taxes.

One problem was the industrial unions (the service unions were and have been OK). While we feminists included support for labor unions among our requirements for endorsement, the industrial labor unions generally did not do the same for us. We had one especially conten-tious time when a labor union endorsed a misogynistic candidate for the state senate (because he was "good on labor issues") to challenge Don Betzold, our party endorsed pro-union, pro-women's rights candidate, in two primary elections. The labor union's candidate won in the first primary but Betzold won the next primary in 1992 and stayed in office until the Republican steamroller of 2010 unseated him along with other progressive legislators—no thanks again to those voters who stay home in the always-low-turnout off-year elections.

There was also the time during my labor union activist days in the late 1960s when I (an elected union official) opposed the Vietnam War. At a meeting, union members objected that I was taking away their war-related manufacturing jobs. I said that if keeping their jobs meant a hundred of our guys coming home in body bags every week, they could stand in the unemployment line until hell froze over. (I lost the next election.) Such instances of misogyny and God-and-Country jingoism may help explain the white male blue-collar support for Trump, and the charge that the Democratic party has not been supportive of organized labor. Maybe it's the other way around.

A couple of caveats. A heavily gerrymandered voter repression state can be a roadblock to Resister goals. We can't overcome that until we get a president and Congress willing to get rid of those roadblocks. Also, this strategy applies only at the local and state levels. At the level of U.S. President, a lot of money and influence goes into creating the party's candidate. You need impressive Resister donations to compete. At the time Bill Clinton began seeking the party nomination there were six or seven others competing with him. Bill was at the bottom of my list of preferences (my first choice was the progressive Tom Harkin) but one by one the others were priced out of the running. (Personal note on the 2016 election: I supported Hillary Clinton based on what she said she wanted to do and what she had done and worked for, *not* for anything Bill did or didn't do.)

What It's Like to Be One of the Few People

Here are some instances that show the direct power you have as one of the few people who show up—and also speak up as needed.

1. I was at my congressional district endorsing convention a few years back. Our congressman, Martin Sabo, had been in office for several terms and was a shoo-in for reelection. Legislatively he was doing a good job, but he had reportedly become arrogant and dismissive of constituents who visited his office to discuss their concerns. It was said that he put his feet on his desk and blew cigar smoke in their faces. At our convention, several people challenged him for endorsement. We went to six ballots, one especially charismatic woman closing in on his slight lead, but without him reaching the 60% for endorsement. So finally Sabo went to the microphone, said he realized how poorly he had behaved, apologized sincerely, said it would never happen again, finally got endorsed, and did change his ways. If he had lost the endorsement he could have easily lost the election with his shoo-in status so badly damaged. This U.S. congressman was beholden to a small group of ordinary citizens for the continuation of his political career.

If you are helping to endorse a candidate, you have more power than any politician-buying corporate lobbyist. Why? Because the candidates they seek to "buy" have to come back to their district for that all-important endorsement. They might not get it if their constituents see them as voting for, say, more coal mining and in the pocket of the fossil fuel industry. If you're not sure how a candidate stands on various issues, ask her or him and insist on a straight answer. Publicize it so it's common knowledge. Questions should be phrased so the religious underpinning is understood where there is one because that is not always recognized. "Culture" is often used to justify a position to sidestep its basis in religious dogma. Insist that candidates' position statements include the reasons— ethical and/or pragmatic—why they take that position. Do not settle for vague answers such as, "I'd have to see the specific legislation" or "I'd be guided by my ethical principles." A question to ask for religion-based issues is, "Do you see any reason for the government to be involved in these matters, and why?"

2. We had a state representative who, although identifying himself as a progressive Democrat, always voted for anti-abortion legislation because, he said, if he didn't, the anti-abortion people would give him a hard time, while the abortion rights people didn't bother him. So I rounded up two abortion rights people from every precinct in the district for a total of 18 and arranged a meeting with him at his house. We expressed our concerns with how he was voting. He said he didn't like feeling threatened and would make no commitments. However, at the next election cycle, he decided not to run again and we endorsed and elected a progressive Democrat.

3. At this writing we have had another mass shooting, this time in Las Vegas. Commentators ask why legislators refuse to pass gun control legislation such as background checks that the great majority of citizens favor. Here's why: We had a progressive Democrat in office—Rep. Phil Carruthers—who tarnished his great record by voting one time for an NRA gun rights bill. At a district committee meeting we asked him to explain himself. He said he would have faced a primary challenge from the gun rights people and would very likely have lost because so few people vote in primaries and he would no longer be able to achieve the otherwise good legislation we wanted. We understood. Primaries are a death trap for progressive candidates. As William Butler Yeats noted in *The Second Coming*: "The best lack all conviction while the worst are full of passionate intensity." The "worst" always show up. We lose excellent politicians to the apathy of the "best." Those gun control surveys should ask respondents who favor gun control if they voted in the primary. After the next mass shooting, don't blame legislators for not passing gun control legislation, blame voters who ignore primary elections and leave excellent candidates at the mercy of the gun-obsessed.

4. I watched how the religious right took over the once-honorable Republican party in the 70s and 80s following the *Roe v. Wade* ruling. In Minnesota our few people trying to keep the state from becoming a theocracy found enough passionate intensity to finally prevail. For example: In the district I lived in at the time, with 2/3rds of the party structure anti-abortion, I called NOW and NARAL for any abortion rights names they had for my district. They had one. I called him and asked if he knew any others. He gave me a couple of names. I called them and asked if they knew any others, and so on. Along the way I found activists to help with this project. At every precinct caucus we called the abortion rights supporters and year by year our numbers increased. After 10 or 12 years the abortion rights constituency became 100% of the party activists and all of our legislators became supportive of abortion rights (there was only one among 21 district politicians when I started), The anti-abortion people left to join the Republicans. In addition, statewide, we improved the party platform to support abortion rights, gay rights, minority rights, reality based sex education, and teaching evolution in public schools. This took place with the public unaware of what was happening. They weren't aware of how the "friends of the fetus" took over and they weren't aware of how the forces of civilization fought back. It was just the few people willing to be involved who supplied the "passionate intensity" that progressives often find so hard to call up for fear of not being "nice."

5. Then there are the "civic religion" things, like the Pledge of Allegiance recited sometimes at city council meetings and political conventions. The insertion of "under God" is irritating. It was put there during the Cold War anti-communist witch hunt era to discriminate against atheists as "godless commies." As the congressional representative said in introducing the "under God" bill, "an atheistic American is a contradiction in terms." And as one of my old Catholic instruction books from the 1930s says, "The only reason one would be an atheist is to feel free to live a depraved life." This assumed moral depravity is an embedded social notion that preserves the pledge as a religious version of Jim Crow bigotry. The inserted phrase could just as well be "white and Christian" because that meant exactly the same as "under God" in the 1950s.

At Democratic party events I have sometimes managed to keep the pledge off the agenda. At our March 2017 ward convention for endorsing a city council member, it was back on and I decided to object. Our district chair agrees with me but likes to work behind the scenes. I went to the microphone and asked the co-chair if I could make a statement. OK. So I called attention to the party's Affirmative Action statement, then noted the Pledge and its Cold War bigotry against non-religious citizens. I said the convention should be aware of what they were about to do—"use religion as a club by reciting a patriotic pledge that marginalizes half the people in this room." The supportive applause showed that "half the people" was an underestimate. My district chair, also co-chair of the convention, went to the microphone, said "Perhaps we could sing the "Star Spangled

Banner" instead" and called on two young women to lead us in the song. Then the other co-chair noted how appropriate the song was, since it was written during the War of 1812 when "a foreign power had taken over the White House." Laughter and applause followed as everyone got the Trump connection. Several politicians were there seeking support for endorsement. They certainly noticed the pro-secular sentiment. Two of them came over to thank me and agreed with me. (There was no endorsement because no candidate reached the 60% threshold so they all went on to the general election.)

An Impressive Start: Resisters Get Politically Involved

Here are examples of how political involvement can work for Anti-Trump Resisters from the "inside" of politics where it all starts as well as from the "outside" of politics where it all ends in an election.

1. At the Minneapolis city convention there were several candidates for mayor with no one getting the 60% needed for endorsement so the winner was determined at the general election. All of them had a progressive agenda and organized their supporters through social media from the Resistance movement. The supporters went to the precinct caucuses, got elected delegates and showed up at the convention. If those politicians can keep their supporters organized they could fill many party and elected positions. All they have to do is show up, sit down, raise their hands and take over.

2. The Dems finally got their act together in Alabama in 2017, when their U.S. Senate candidate Doug Jones narrowly defeated Roy Moore (religious-right former judge with a record of moral and ethical depravity). Deep red Alabama had not elected a Democratic senator in 25 years. According to NPR news reports, Democratic party activists got well over 90% of blacks and over 50% of all women to vote for Jones, outvoting the 80% of white evangelicals who voted for Moore. Jones's record of opposition to the KKK apparently was a big motivator for the black demographic. Jones won because the issues and Moore's sleazy record motivated a critical mass of citizens to overcome their usual apathy and get out to vote. Democracy is always up to the citizens and we get the government we deserve.

12

RELIGION IN PUBLIC LIFE?
WHAT COULD POSSIBLY GO WRONG?

". . . Things fall apart; the centre cannot hold. Mere anarchy is
loosed upon the world, . . . The best lack all conviction while
the worst are full of passionate intensity. . . . And what rough
beast, its hour come 'round at last, slouches towards Bethlehem
to be born?" — William Butler Yeats, "The Second Coming"

The rough beast is in the White House—clumsy, ignorant and flailing about, dragging in a retinue of opportunistic followers seeking to use this ignorant beast to advance their own authoritarian theocratic agenda. The rough beast's erratic behavior makes it impossible to predict the ultimate effect on our civilization, but it can't be good.

The only thing we know, but haven't had the social courage to deal with publicly, is that we are in a head-on clash of cultures—one liberal-secular, and one authoritarian-sacred. We have been working toward this confrontation since the Enlightenment period of the 17th and 18th centuries. That opened many minds but very few mouths, so a useful public examination of these deeply antagonistic worldviews has never happened.

And, yes, they are deeply antagonistic despite imaginative efforts to see a complementary aspect. The most noted advocate for this idea was Stephan Jay Gould (1941-2002) a paleontologist, evolutionary biologist and science writer, who called the two views "non-overlapping magisteria" (teaching authority). This was a typically liberal effort to resolve the conflict between science and religion after Pope John Paul II said in a 1996 address to the Pontifical Academy of Science that "truth cannot contradict truth."

Of course it can't, but since when is religious "truth" anything but wishful thinking maintained by a self-proclaimed "teaching authority" with no verifiable credentials whatsoever? As for the pope saying science deals with facts while religion deals with "values," look at history and read the previous chapters in this book. Even Gould's grandiose terminology can't make the reality based facts of science and the myth based irrational "values" of religion equally valid. You can't make a silk purse out of a sow's ear. Although the pope and the accommodating liberals may see equal validity by calling it non-overlapping magisteria, the sow's ear of religion does not have the equal validity of the silk purse of science.

The advocates for the sacred don't hesitate to fight ferociously to maintain their centuries-long hold on the culture. As for the advocates for the secular (which includes the decent, liberal, un-dogmatic religious left), they typically run scared. They think we have to be nice, never offend the religious right, accommodate their demands, and turn the other cheek. When have we ever made any progress with that strategy? It's time we stopped avoiding the secular vs. sacred issue and brought it out into the open.

Here's what one of our supporters, Tama Matheson, a London-based playwright, says in "Childish Things," an essay she has been preparing for publication (excerpt included here with her permission):

> . . . We have no obligation to understand religion, no duty to re-spect it, no moral imperative to defer to, or esteem, the credulity of its adherents. Religion, as a way of approaching the world (and by this I mean all religions), deserves no privileged status in the realm of ideas, no asylum from the assault of reasoned and incisive criticism. The notion, or feeling, that religion should be somehow outside the jurisdiction of rational appraisal, is itself a piece of superstition, foisted upon us over many centuries by religious demagogues. Unfortunately, the public has so deeply drunk of this intellectual barbiturate that even the most rational thinkers now hold it somehow wrong or unfair to question peo-ple's beliefs. This is an outrage to liberal values. No ideology, in a free society, should be immune to criticism—especially not a belief system that presumes to tell us how to conduct our lives. Any belief system that *does* do so should be scrutinized even more minutely precisely because of its moralistic presumption.

The First Question to Ask: Do We Need Religion?

It appears that the more advanced and democratic a civilization be-comes, the less religious it is. The "Golden Age" of Christianity in Europe

gave us the Dark Ages—a time of little or no intellectual or scientific progress. We are still trying to recover from that, with the northern European
countries recovering the fastest. For example, according to a report from
a 2016 census in the Netherlands, fewer than a third of Dutch people
have a religious faith and nearly one in four describe themselves as atheists. The trend towards secularization also saw a decline in the number
of people describing themselves as spiritual, which dropped from 40%
10 years ago to 31%. The number who believed in the existence of a
higher power fell from 36% to 28% over the same period. Overall 25%
of people identified themselves as Christian, while 5% were Muslim and
2% belonged to another faith group.

The survey also found support for the separation of church and state,
with a majority saying that politics and education should not be influenced by religion. Within the Christian group the survey also found a
trend towards more secular beliefs. Just 13% of Catholics believe in
heaven and fewer than half believe Jesus is the son of God. The trend
was less pronounced among Protestant congregations. (Around 2,100
people were canvassed for the "God in Nederland" survey, carried out
every 10 years since 1996.)

Much the same thing is happening throughout the northern European
democracies. In Britain, the UK web site rt.com posted an article on
Dec. 2, 2017, titled "In God we trust? Brits are losing faith in the clergy."
It noted a survey showing that the number of believers was 85% in 1983
but now the non-religious are at 48.6%, outnumbering the Christians,
who have dropped to 43%. Less encouraging is that the number of the
far less progressive Hindus and Muslims has quadrupled, due largely
to immigration.

Opening the Can of Worms

Why the drop-off in religiosity? The best guess is that talking openly
about religion is more acceptable there. But what is it about religion that
we dare not question it publicly? The answer, of course, is that religious
beliefs do not lend themselves to questioning because they are too
ludicrous once they get beyond the basic civic values about not killing,
stealing or bearing false witness. Those are *not* religious values *per se*,
even though religions borrow them. They are just simple necessities for
a civilization to function.

Religious beliefs are a can of ideological worms that defies rational compre-
hension. Rational arguments never work for religion. If they did, we wouldn't
have religion. But before we take a look at what's there, if anything, I need to
say something about religion in general. I am using "religion" in its traditional
deity-based meaning, not as in "baseball is my religion" or to describe a
humanistic secular worldview. I am all for freedom of belief as long as you
are not hurting anyone. Just don't try to foist that stuff on everyone through
laws, even though religions generally demand that. Many people also
believe in astrology and other woo-woo stuff. But again, as long as they
keep it out of law and public policy they can believe in whatever wacky stuff
turns them on. The human brain is a cobbled up mess so we have to shrug
off some of its effluvia. (I'm waiting for gene editing to fix this.) Meanwhile,
don't use your mystical beliefs to hurt innocent people, especially children.
Don't seek government support to promote them. Don't ask the taxpayers
to subsidize them. Don't bring them into secular events.

Religious doctrines and rituals have no public value. They are your
private guilty pleasure or hair shirt or chastity belt or security blanket.
When brought into the public sphere they are, by their nature, divisive.
When they are imposed on citizens by law they cause nothing but social
and personal misery.

What do religions teach or do that is deserving of respect?

. . . Oh, they believe in feeding the hungry and sheltering the homeless.
Yeah, but almost everyone believes that, with or without religion, because it's part of our human nature to generally look out for each other.
But how much would religions do if government wasn't paying them to
do it? About as much as they did before there was government funding—almost nothing.

. . . Oh, they are all about morality and we need them to tell us what is
moral. Really? Like we would have no idea how to treat our fellow humans without their guidance? Read the history of religion, and the atrocities going on today in the Middle East, and the ranting of the religious
right in this country, and this entire book, then let's talk about religion and
morality. Has anyone who believes religion has social value ever looked
at a religion closely? . . . At how it was founded? . . At what it teaches and
why? . . . At what its social and political impact on civilization has been?

Read the biblical account of Moses getting the Ten Commandments. Notice how he interprets the volcano's rumbling as the voice of Yahweh. Notice how he makes sure that only he can approach Yahweh and talk with him. Notice the theatrics with the golden calf that strike fear in the Hebrews to control them. Notice how the instructions following the Ten Commandments require the Hebrews to set up lavish living arrangements and provide worldly goodies for Moses, his brother Aaron and family members. Notice what a fine prototype this is for today's televangelists with their mansions, private jets and the sumptuous living they achieve by convincing gullible followers that they bring a message of prosperity and salvation from "God." Notice how they always want you to send money.

The Catholic Church is the Roman Empire reborn as a political powerhouse and made sacred and untouchable with a global monolithic structure, an "infallible" pope, an "infallible" Syllabus of Errors that denies every civil liberty we value, and nonsensical doctrines presented with the most outrageous chutzpah imaginable.

For example, what are we to make of the public respect given the Eucharist, the doctrine of transubstantiation where a baked flour-and-water wafer—library paste—is claimed to be transformed into the "body and blood, soul and divinity of our Lord and Savior Jesus Christ" by magic words uttered by a priest? But then, this religion also claims a cluster of undifferentiated cells the size of the period at the end of this sentence is a "person" and our laws must reflect and humor that insanity.

With all this, it's good to remember the words of Pope Leo X in the Middle Ages: "What profit has not that Fable of Christ brought us?" (quoted by Joseph Wheless in *Forgery in Christianity*). Church apologists dismiss this as just a flippant remark by one pope. Nice try, but Leo knew his church's history as well as all credible historians do. "Fable" is exactly what it is and "profit" is exactly what it brought. Leo's comment has the self-satisfied flippancy that comes from such knowledge. Let's also consider Christianity's history of religious wars and persecutions and crusades and inquisitions and witch hunts and burnings at the stake and the whole series of outrageously criminal popes in the Middle Ages.

Protestantism is a spinoff of the Catholic Church, all wrapped up in as many and varied interpretations of the Bible as possible. The belief spectrum runs from barbaric "God Hates Fags" biblical fundamentalism to a social justice liberalism that is about the same as reality based atheism but glossed over with enough god-belief to generate social fawning and government perks. The Protestant and Catholic churches never fought for social justice. As religious historian William Sierichs Jr. says, those that did (now called the religious left) had to abandon their traditional beliefs so they could be moral.

Have we found any social values yet in these religions that might justify their intrusion into public life? Consider this:

The Protestant Christian right has been organizing to take power for de-cades. It has a vast network of schools, colleges, law schools, and radio and TV stations (Fox News). It is embedded culturally mostly in Red states where fundamentalist views have long been accepted and openly pro-moted. Anti-democratic, barbaric quotations from religious right spokes-persons have appeared even in some mainstream media outlets. All the big names are well known: Jerry Falwell, Pat Robertson, Pat Buchanan, Randall Terry, etc. (Most are Catholics, part of the Catholic-Protestant anti-abortion coalition.) Here's one by Gary North, quoted in *Christianity and Civilization*, Spring 1982. Notice how timely it still is:

> So let us be blunt: we must use the doctrine of religious liberty to gain independence for Christian schools until we train up a generation of people who know there is no religious neutrality, no neutral law, no neutral education, and no neutral civil gov-ernment. Then they will get busy in constructing a Bible-based social, political and religious order which finally denies the reli-gious liberty of the enemies of God.

This right wing Christian power mongering and money-grubbing can apply to all supernatural religions everywhere in both red and blue states, given how accommodating our social, political and judicial systems are to them. We don't have religious wars in this country because religions have found there is plenty of room at the government trough for all of them and their shared goal to impose their racist/sexist/homophobic views on all of us.

Many fire-and-brimstone Bible thumpers are actually Catholic. But all extremists are alike in their worldviews, mainly in their obsession with controlling women's sexuality and reproductive functions. Here's an assessment of one of their leaders by an atheist colleague, Sally Chizek, in a letter to the *San Antonio Express-News* but not published. It's an open letter to Dan Patrick, the Lt. Governor. (Sally says some facts are taken from the magazine, *The Public Eye*):

Just when I thought it was safe to go into the water ... Dan Patrick, Lt. Governor of Texas, you're a Christian Reconstructionist? It sounds like it when you said that elected officials must look to Scripture when they make policy, "because every problem we have in America has a solution in the Bible." Really?

Let me give you a little background: In the 1970's, R. J. Rushdoony (4-25-16 - 2-8-2001), a Calvinist theologian, gave birth to Dominionism stemming from God telling Adam and Eve to have dominion over Earth and animals. Christian Reconstructionists believe in Biblical law (including stoning as punishment for adults and children) and seek to replace secular government and the Constitution with a system of Old Testament laws. They believe Christians need to regain control over political and cultural institutions. According to author Frederick Clarkson, Reconstructionists believe government, law, sciences, economics, business, education, medicine, art, etc., must agree with the Bible. If not, they would be dismantled and "Reconstructed." They believe moral choices and interpretations of Biblical Law should take dominance in all areas of society throughout the world. Approved methods of capital punishment, which are central to God's Judgment, are stoning, hanging and burning. It will apply to abandonment of faith, heresy, blasphemy, witchcraft, astrology, adultery, sodomy, homosexuality, incest, striking one's parents, incorrigible juvenile delinquency, and in the case of women, unchaste before marriage.

The Reconstructed "Kingdom" will have minimal national government, and its main function will be defense by the armed forces. The church will be responsible for health, education and welfare. Deregulated corporate businesses and unfettered capitalism will enrich true believers and help the church.

Lying is an integral part of this "might makes right" philosophy as the end justifies the means. Does this sound familiar? When Rushdoony died, I thought the movement had died off. Was I ever wrong! Standing between us and Reconstruction is the Constitution with its strict separation of church and state.

We have to be vigilant about changing our democratic ways to those advocated by a 2,000-year-old book that, while it may contain some good advice, speaks of horrors and behaviors that we would not tolerate in this day and time. We must govern with the best thinking people we can elect for the benefit of the many.

Is Sally's concern about a possible Reconstructionist takeover exaggerated? We will see. Liberties are usually lost incrementally, affecting only the marginal segments of the population at first so no concern arises at the time. Note this: We have the Supreme Court interpreting religious liberty as the right of employers to impose their religious beliefs on employees by denying benefits that run counter to those beliefs. We have gerrymandering and voting restrictions that disenfranchise large numbers of citizens and skew a district's demographics for political advantage. Laws are proposed by religious right-dominated legislatures to prevent a state's liberal-dominated cities from protecting various civil rights and workers rights of their residents. All incremental losses. All affecting marginal populations.

So much for the Judeo-Christian religions. How about Mormonism? Very influential in some states. This is an ambitious mission-oriented church founded by Joseph Smith, a con artist with an arrest record as a swindler. He sold his followers on the idea that the angel Moroni brought him golden tablets from heaven, written in Egyptian hieroglyphics, that Smith supposedly translated into the *Book of Mormon* by viewing a seer stone he put in his hat and then talking through his hat. Smith's story was supported by his drinking buddies/relatives. The golden tablets would have been better evidence but Moroni took them back to heaven, leaving Smith with just those buddies to back up his story, so they will have to do. They are mentioned in the intro to the *Book of Mormon*, but with nothing about drinking (that's just my guess, but a safe one, all things considered).

How about Christian Science? Mary Baker Eddy founded it as a spinoff of a mind-over-matter carnival act after her partner in the act died.

Her "sacred book" is *Science and Health with Key to the Scriptures.* It teaches that disease does not exist and can come into existence only if you believe it exists. You fend off this belief with prayer. A lot of kids have died from an overdose of this prayer.

In recent decades the religious conflicts in the Middle East have exposed us to the religion of Islam and its beheadings and stonings and terrorist bombings. Here we have religious beliefs tethered politically to immigration policies and terrorism. Muslim immigrants insist that Islam is a religion of peace. All religions say that, even when their scriptures say otherwise. The Bible is a catalog of religion inspired and even mandated horrors. So is the Koran. I have a pamphlet that quotes several passages written by Islam's founder Mohammad (ca. 570-632 CE) that advocate violence against non-Muslims and, of course, against women. Nothing new there.

Some people worry that Muslims will bring Sharia law with them and try to impose it here in ways that could have a negative effect on all of us. Sharia law is for Muslims what Canon law is for Christians, specifically Catholics. These are religious laws and neither should be allowed to have any civil application or be involved in any way in our public life and government policies. Yet, as this book shows, here in the United States we have been living under Canon law since the first Europeans came here. It's at least as bad as Sharia law but we can't even talk about it, much less get rid of it.

Other than that, Islam presents a problem with its religious practices even when its atrocities are abandoned. We have managed to work through the Christian Bible-based Blue Laws and Jim Crow Laws by gradually ignoring or outlawing them. Now we have the Muslims. Because of their religious beliefs they are not allowed to be around dogs, eat or handle pork, or drink or handle liquor. They are required to pray for 15 minutes several exact times a day and do foot-washing rituals. There is something about beards and hair too. Their misogyny and those chastity-protecting burqas and hijabs are deplorable. They tend to have large families, presenting the threat of a political takeover by population growth in a couple of genera-tions. If religious beliefs hold up with the numerical increase, the problem is obvious. Let's hope the younger generation becomes more rational.

Some of these practices have been or are being negotiated away out of sheer practical necessity, but none are necessary in any real-world sense.

I was once a Catholic. I did not eat meat on Friday because I was told I would go to Hell if I did. I wore a head covering in church because I was told I had to show submission to "God." Then the beliefs got changed but nothing in reality changed. In real-world terms it didn't matter if I ate meat on Friday or not or if I wore a head covering in church or not. Muslims have these rigid prayer times. I've heard Muslims say they don't always adhere to them. For Catholics, missing mass on Sunday is a mortal sin, yet many Catholics miss mass and don't seem to worry about going to hell.

Does anything in the real world change if a Muslim abandons the religious rituals? Is there any reason Muslims can't adjust to our secular ways instead of trying to get us to accommodate theirs? It can't be that hard. A few years ago I read a book, *Princess: A True Story of Life Behind the Veil in Saudi Arabia* by Jean Sasson. The princess was one of the many wives of a prince who was one of the Saudi king's sons. She described what her life was like. There was a big difference between public and private behavior for women as well as men. In public it was very Muslim: burqas and submission and male chaperones and restrictions. In private it was very western and hedonistic with high-end living, cocktail hours, designer clothing, sexy lingerie and shopping trips to Paris . . . But also there was that endemic misogyny. One of the princess's close female relatives, accused of adultery in the midst of this schizophrenic lifestyle, was drowned by family members in a religious punishment ritual.

Why can't Muslims adjust their beliefs to reverse this arrangement? Why not live a secular western lifestyle in public and a religious burqa burdened lifestyle in private where religion belongs? (Just don't drown anyone.) If Catholics can deal with the threat of hellfire for missing mass on Sunday, Muslims can deal with missing prayer times if they have better things to do.

So there it is—the basic irrationality of all religions, and we are supposed to respect them? Religion is just brainwashing with a sideline of tax fraud, courtesy of religion-coddling legislatures and courts.

Accommodation: The Placate-and-Coddle Approach

Nothing about religion deserves the respect and public accommodation it gets. The assumption is that religion is a cultural necessity and is all about peace and love. It's really about the sacred vs. secular political struggle for cultural control. As for peace and love, what religion does—as I've heard it said—is provide solace for the turmoil it creates, 9/11 being the example that stands for all time as the ultimate faith-based initiative. The Republican party makes religiosity a foundational element in its platform. There is not a word about accommodating any part of a secular worldview. The closest it comes to social justice is to assure us that if conservative religious beliefs are enforced and business taxes, regulations, environmental restrictions and worker protections are reduced, all will be well.

For the Democratic party, its platform mentions religion only off-handedly as doing good work (so the party can't be accused of being entirely godless). It's part of the progressive worldview that wants to play nice. It says a lot about social issues, with a detailed agenda for fixing the nation's many problems, if only the wealthy would pay their fair share of the cost. It would be *really* nice if it said the cost could be covered by taking religion off the welfare rolls instead of giving it all those accommodating tax exemptions and paying them to do that "good work" the platform mentions.

I don't remember the Democratic party ever mentioning a god or religion until the Republican party got taken over by the religious right and started emphasizing that to attract "values" voters. It seems to have started with the national Republican party convention in 1988. I was watching it on TV when the Catholic conservative commentator William Buckley Jr. came on with a speech that included denouncing the Democratic party as "godless" for not including "God" in its platform. I of course cheered that remark but news reports soon followed about how the party's leaders thought they should counter that "godless" charge by getting more religious.

Sure enough, the party started running scared instead of countering the "godless" charge with a strong moral message that respected religious privacy and denounced religious bullying. In no time at all we were getting the "under God" pledge of allegiance and even invocations at party events. The party was running from its secular values, thus shooting itself in the foot, which became increasingly obvious at election time. Here are some examples of how the placate-and-coddle approach to religion has worked—or not. They are instructive on several levels.

1. At a committee meeting in my congressional district we tried to accommodate religion in scheduling a political event. Couldn't do it on Sunday

because that was important to Christians. Couldn't do it on Saturday because it was important to Orthodox Jews. Couldn't do it on Friday because there was something special about that for Muslims. OK, how about Thursday? A woman in front got up and said we couldn't do it then because Thursday was sacred to the Wiccans. When the laughter died down we decided that religious events would have to be ignored. After that, the only scheduling conflict we made sure to avoid was an NFL football day.

2. There was one time our congressional district decided it was important to accommodate the Orthodox Jews in scheduling an endorsing convention since they couldn't do anything on the Sabbath (Saturday) until sundown. The convention had to be held on a Saturday, so we convened it at 7 p.m. and were there until 3:30 a.m., bleary eyed and marginally functioning. We never did that again.

3. I was talking with Mike Hatch, a former state Democratic party chair, asking his opinion on state-church separation. He answered by telling this story: When he was chair, some Christians asked to have an invocation at the next state central committee meeting. He said OK. When the meeting convened, several Native Americans came on stage, did a chanting and drumming routine, and the meeting proceeded. After the meeting, the Christians asked Mike why there wasn't the promised invocation. Mike said (about the Native Americans), "That was it." Mike made his point and it was a good one. He said the Christians walked away and never asked for an invocation again. For some believers it's either their beliefs or nothing.

4. We need more political leaders who can separate religion from politics. We didn't have it at another Democratic party event, the annual Humphrey Day Dinner honoring out former U.S. Senator/Vice President/ civil rights advocate,. The chair, Todd Otis, had included a religious invocation. Everyone at my table looked at me with big grins. Yes, I was upset and they obviously enjoyed the idea of me doing something about that. I did but it wasn't easy. All year long I talked with Todd and state executive committee members about getting rid of invocations. Todd was for them (whether for political or personal religious reasons I don't know). One committee member left the room when I brought up the topic because she represented our Iron Range and its large number of religious conservatives. She was afraid to even be present at a discussion where anything religious might be questioned. The committee couldn't decide what to do but I had an ally in Bert Black, a district chair. He was a secular Jew and knew a rabbi who might help. The rabbi wrote an opinion piece for the *American Jewish World* objecting strongly to that invocation as divisive. (Secular atheistic Jews have political clout that non-church-connected atheists can only dream of.)

Todd gave up on the invocation but seemed worried that people would be upset with him for that. At the next dinner the event opened with just a tribute to Hubert Humphrey. After the dinner I stood with Todd as people came by congratulating him for that wonderful tribute. Not one person said anything about an invocation. As I pointed out to Todd, no one cared and no one missed it. It has always been clear that we don't need religion at Democratic party political events. Accommodation just generates unnecessary problems.

5. What are we to think of the progressive Sen. Bernie Sanders? On April 20, 2017, the National Public Radio (NPR) online newsletter reported that Sanders was campaigning at a rally for Omaha mayoral candidate Heath Mello, an anti-abortion Democrat who has not just passively supported anti-abortion legislation but has authored restrictive bills. The rally, part of a series of "fight back" events against the Trump agenda, had the support of the Democratic National Committee (DNC) and its chair Tom Perez. Sanders justified his sell-out of women because Nebraska is a conservative state so Democrats have to be conservative to get a progressive Congress. Good luck making sense of that. The NPR report said NARAL president Hyse Hogue called the DNC-Sanders action "politically stupid" and said the "fight back" tour looked more like "a throw back tour for women and our rights." I have heard atheists defend Sanders because "He's good on other issues." So was Hitler. I heard he loved dogs and built great highways.

With what other group is it OK to not just take away their civil rights and liberties but their bodily autonomy as well? Don't some of those millions of marchers live in Nebraska? Couldn't the DNC and Sanders send them into the state's political parties and take them over? (Read Chapter 11 again. The population is less than 2 million and they have a unicameral legislature so the takeover numbers needed is doable.) I understand that

Sanders backed off from his support for Mello due to abortion rights pressure but it is disconcerting that he had been so willing to throw women under the bus.

6. Just as bad was the news report that some DNC staff people got the bright idea to undermine Sanders' election campaign by outing him as an atheist. Sanders evidently believed that being an atheist is a political kiss of death (but so would being a socialist in the hands of the Fox News propaganda machine if Sanders had won the nomination) so he defended himself by saying he is a secular Jew. That means he likes the cultural stuff but not the god stuff. That makes him an atheist because he has no god beliefs.

7. So let's hear from an atheist leader, David Silverman, president of American Atheists. He should have some good ideas for fighting the religious right. Or not. In March of 2014 Silverman went to the Conservative Political Action Conference (CPAC) where Sarah Palin was the keynote speaker to let the generally atheistic libertarian contingent of the political far right know they are welcome in his organization. After all, he said, "There are secular reasons to oppose abortion" and he was there to seek common ground. (No, David, there are NO secular reasons to oppose abortion and your "common ground" is a fetid sexist swamp and your moral compass is badly in need of adjustment.)

8. Then there is the rush to welcome the Middle Eastern immigrants. Fine, but why include their religion? In my liberal city, Minneapolis, some of our politicians can't seem to separate national ancestry from the Islamic religion. Our mayor Betsy Hodges (now former mayor—she lost the November 2017 election) gave her State of the City address in May of 2017 in a mosque. It was an official gesture of inclusion for a religion—a violation of the First Amendment, since religion is a private matter in which government should have no involvement.

Earlier she met with some Muslim women and got cozy with them by wearing that ridiculous hijab. As a matter only of good political sense it is seriously wrong to join in other's religious beliefs. Would she help the Santarians do their chicken-sacrificing ritual? One council member called me to ask what I thought of all this. I said secular events should be held in secular venues and religious events should be held in religious venues and mixing them up is inappropriate. She agreed, but we will probably see more of this. It's fine to welcome new citizens into our public life, but keep it entirely secular. Don't include religion—it is inherently divisive and functionally useless.

9. At the national level the Catholic Church has a "Red Mass" especially for incoming politicians—executive, legislative and judiciary members. Politicians feel obligated to attend. The sermon is usually political and favoring Catholic positions such as anti-abortion. I don't know how anything can get more politically shoot-yourself-in-the-foot immoral, disgustingly groveling, and unconstitutional than for any politician to attend this mass.

10. Then there was the Convention from Hell. On July 8, 2017, I was a delegate at our Minneapolis Democratic party endorsing convention. We were endorsing for mayor, park board and other positions. I have been going to these things for 50 years and this was the worst. Poorly run, dragged on for 11 hours, and sucked up to religion outrageously. On the plus side, the Anti-Trump Resisters had been organized and showed up in large numbers. On the minus side, these newbies were so clueless about issues that their ignorance and lack of common sense defined the liberal brains-falling-out *modus operandi* for all to see.

The pledge of allegiance was on the agenda. I tried to stop it but the convention chair got it going before I could get to a microphone. I wasn't involved in setting up this convention so I didn't know that someone had slipped in a Rule 15 that required us to recess at certain exact times of the day for exactly 15 minutes each time so the Muslims could go out for prayer time. There were three of those breaks over the course of the day and they dragged on for half an hour, not 15 minutes. We could do absolutely no business during that time! It was so unnecessary! We elect convention alternates to take the place of delegates who don't show up or have to leave the floor. Couldn't the Muslims elect alternates to take their place at prayer times? I was horrified and tried to take out some of the Islamic submission crap. I offered an amendment to at least delete the word "prayer" so people could use the recess for whatever they wanted. I said we should not be giving prayer instructions. No dice. The Muslims talked about how precious that prayer stuff was and my motion was voted down with only 1/3 support.

Then there was the challenge long-time activist Flo Castner raised to not allow an alternate to be registered. She gave solid evidence that the man was a very far right Republican. Flo said we were the Democratic party and should not allow hard core Republicans to be active participants in our convention. But one woman got up and said we should not have any litmus test. We should be a big tent and welcome everyone! And the Jews should welcome Holocaust camp guards to a Jewish event? And the black community should welcome the KKK? Flo's motion went down the same as mine.

This is what I mean by some liberals being so open-minded their brains fall out. We had brains falling out all over the place that day. I took this up at our senate district meeting but got nowhere. Very few people showed up. Apathy reigned and no one wanted to stand up for anything that might be contrary to the wishes of Muslims or any religion for that matter. The party can't do a simple thing like eliminating the pledge of allegiance (which no one would notice) out of respect for their largest constituency—the non-religious—but they can screw up an entire convention to keep the Muslims happy. Now tell me how inviting religion into these very secular events does anything but cause trouble.

11. I don't know how this one can be beat for running scared. I once got a fundraising mailing (it's saved in my yellow-for-cowardice file folder) from Planned Parenthood. The message began, "They call you 'anti-family.' They call you 'promoters of promiscuity.' They are the zealots who oppose family planning and you and I can't afford to lose to them." "They" are never identified. "They" are "some people." "They" are said to have a global reach that is frightening. "They" are "anti-choice forces" that parade around the world opposing family planning and causing the deaths of millions of women. The Pro-Life Society of Zambia, we learn, is "funded by a U.S.-based anti-choice group." We also learn that "they" are obstructing family planning in Honduras where women's needs are critical. Finally we are told, "We must be as well organized, as sophisticated, and well funded as the aggressive anti-choice elements." . . . whoever they are.

A global threat, well organized, sophisticated, causing the suffering and death of millions of women! An enemy we cannot afford to lose to, yet we dare not name that enemy, for fear of—what? Being called a bigot . . . and slimy . . . and anti-Catholic or anti-religion, while "they" continue their dirty work, safe from exposure, protected by today's timid feminists, pandering politicians, and apathetic media.

Background: I was called bigoted and slimy and anti-Catholic in an Oct. 30, 1993, *Minneapolis Star Tribune* op-ed piece, "Another campaign brings out bigots," by Denis Wadley, a Catholic high school English teacher, for noting in our Feminist Caucus newsletter that we could not support a particular candidate (a Catholic) for public office because, when allowing himself to be screened by us, "he said he would use his power as an elected official to oppose abortion rights because of his church's teaching." It was all about state-church separation. At a Caucus board meeting one member berated me for "offending the pro-lifers." No board member present at that time supported me (although others did later). Were they that fearful of criticism from Catholic sources? It seemed so.

Does the religious right hesitate to name and shame and blame Planned Parenthood? No. They go for the jugular, with lies and even fraudulent videos. The attacks are endless. Yet Planned Parenthood adopts a pitiful "Please, sir, don't hit me." posture, pleading that only 3% of its work involves abortions when it should be speaking proudly about helping women who need that service. No battle is won from a kneeling position.

12. Then there are the accommodations that liberals favor and are proud of and see as victories of the secular over the sacred. In fact, they are defeats of the worst kind. These are the "equal treatment" issues where the non-religious get administrative decisions and court rulings that allow them to participate along with religious groups in invocations, monument installations, memorials and other such government related events. They happily get to take turns, to have exhibit space, to make opposing "free speech" statements, and so on. Very democratic. Very inclusive. Very ineffective.

Probably at least 90% of these events feature the religious point of view because it's the majority view. The non-religious get their turn at invocations maybe one out of 20 times because the other 19 are the religious groups taking their turn. The Knights of Columbus will put up the Ten Commandments on government property all over the country while American Atheists gets an opposing monument in a couple of locations because they don't have the resources for more. In October, 2017, the Freedom From Religion Foundation

(FFRF) won a lawsuit in federal court allowing it to put up a Winter Solstice and Bill of Rights Day display along with the Christians' nativity scene at the Capitol in Texas. The religious majority prevails again.

Crosses as veterans' memorials and nativity scenes and Ten Commandments massively outnumber the few secular installations be-cause the Christian viewpoint massively outnumbers the non-religious viewpoint. But the secularists argued for equal rights, for a "place at the table," and the courts gave it to them. For all practical purposes, it's like being put at the kids' side table where they won't interfere with the grownups at the banquet table.

What atheists have done is establish court precedents that allow the many-in-number religions to use government functions for propaganda while the few-in-number secularists end up looking like kids running a lemonade stand. This is not to say legal challenges shouldn't be made. However, the goal should not be to have a "place at the table," but to have no need for an anti-religious presence because religious beliefs are no longer allowed to intrude in public life.

Accommodating the Ultimate Abuse

After every mass shooting or natural disaster the media show photos of people gathering in churches, lighting candles, weeping and consoling each other. How sad, pathetic and dehumanizing to be seeking comfort from a god they all believe to be all powerful, all good, all knowing, etc., and yet did nothing to stop that tragedy or any other tragedy from hap-pening. Not even the 2012 Sandy Hook elementary school slaughter of those innocent, trusting little kids—20 of them and six of their teachers. The church gatherings are like battered women who keep returning to their abuser, saying how much they still love him, begging forgiveness for whatever they imagine might have brought on the abuse. Of all the ways people have of accommodating religious beliefs and elevating the social prestige of religion, this is the most incomprehensible.

When these tragedies happen, churches and their useless gods should be ignored. People should gather instead in park buildings and civic centers and libraries and schools to weep and console each other and memorial-ize those who were loved so much and now are lost forever. The joys and sorrows of life are best shared with fellow humans. We need to look at each other and not up at crosses, statuary and other mythological detritus, the belief in which, too often, directly or indirectly, brought on the tragedy. None of those people praying to their god for solace would—if they were God—ever allow such tragedies to happen. They are too humane and decent for that. They worship a god that is not nearly as moral as they are.

An Inexcusable Accommodation

Go back and read the chapter on healthcare about faith healing. There is an example of the worst kind of religious accommodation. There is no excuse for it. This could be low-hanging fruit for progressives. Those atrocious laws have to go! A good Resister project might be for those marchers to descend on state legislatures and demand repeal of the child sacrifice laws. All it takes is putting the repeal bill on the Consent calendar for automatic repeal without discussion. No one would care, probably not even Minnesota's Sen. John Marty, who is Resister-sympathetic if not full-on supportive and needs to make up for his earlier brains-falling-out support for faith healing. The faith healing constituency is too small to be politically threatening so there would be no legislative exposure to the "third rail" of religion. Go for it!

Stopping the Accommodating

Can we please stop this nonsense? This book has suggestions for political action so here are a few more along with other things you can try to help keep religion out of public life. Some will work; others may or may not work.

1. Don't fight the Ten Commandments on First Amendment grounds or ask to put up your own version. Read those things! They are barbaric! The first version even requires you to sacrifice your firstborn son to Yahweh. (The second version allows you to sacrifice a pigeon instead, but there are other revisions like forbidding you to boil a baby goat in its mother's milk.) Oppose the Commandments because such barbaric and primitive non-sense does not belong on public property. They are an insult to the public's intelligence. If this gets people to actually read the Commandments they will probably not agree publicly for fear of poking the sacred cow, but will find a politically palatable way to just not deal with the issue.

2. Don't ask to take a turn at giving a city council invocation. You will be outnumbered by the religious turn-takers. You will emphasize your insignificance and your lack of political clout. Get to know your council members personally. Donate to their election campaign. Get on their election committee. Get like-minded friends to do the same with other council members. Then ask that the invocations be left off the agenda and see how much more willing they are to do that. Run for election yourself and/ or get better candidates to run for council. Require the council to show any identifiable value in the time-wasting prayers. Move to have a section of the Constitution read instead—by you, with you picking the parts to read. If you can't do any of this, look for like-minded but more outgoing people to do it for you. You can get more ideas from watching your own city council.

3. Try to outsmart the pushy religionists. The 9/11 memorial in New York City offered a good chance to do that but the atheists didn't take it. Someone (a priest I believe) had found a cross-shaped section of iron girders in the fallen towers and declared it a sign from God or at least a symbol of–what? God's love and protection? Yeah, why not? So there was a campaign to install this piece of debris along with a religious statement. The atheists objected on constitutional grounds and the court ruled against them. I had told them they could never win on legal grounds so why not set up their own debris symbol. (Since there is only one 9/11, they wouldn't be outnumbered.) I said find something circular like a barrel rim and say it's a zero to represent the sum total of all the gods in the universe and put a nice sign on it about what religion hath wrought. Well no, the atheists stuck with the lawsuit and lost and set yet another precedent for religious accommodation.

4. If the religious stuff is at your social activities, like your sewing circle or bowling league, SPEAK UP! Object politely that you want to avoid any divisiveness. They're your friends so they will want to accommodate you. After I let my neighborhood association know I am an atheist, they called me the following December to make sure they didn't do any offensive holiday stuff. I said I was OK with wreaths and we got along fine.

5. For accommodations going on in your political party, read the "Barricades" chapter, get involved, locate like-minded activists, and take over.

6. It's OK to sneer at burqas and hijabs. It shouldn't take more than one generation of young Middle Eastern women born in America to abandon them. The main problem with these wearable tents and head coverings is their religious connection. As such they do not deserve respect. They are blatant symbols of a misogynistic culture. They are designed to protect the chastity of Islamic women. They are sexist. Since the need to protect Islamic women's chastity is due to the need to control some Islamic men's horny tendencies, why not just put chastity belts on the men? The hijab is insulting. It is actually a way for a woman to show she is not a prostitute. In biblical times (where this stuff comes from) prostitutes uncovered their hair to show they were open for business. So what's going on with these Muslim women today that they need to show they are not prostitutes? Ask them. It's a custom they can't get out of without rocking the cultural boat. Why else would they decorate these coverings and do everything possible to make them look more like what they are not if they thought being ridiculously covered up for no practical reason was so great?

A Fatal Accommodation in the Middle East?

I haven't said much in this book about the international problems created by allowing religion into public life. The ongoing news from the Middle East has made them obvious. The United States government seems to have tried, through the United Nations, to keep the peace (such as it seldom is) as much as possible—except for women's rights, of course. We get a Republican president and the birth control and abortion restrictions go on; we get a Democratic president and they go off. Back and forth.

Trump, having promised to fulfill the religious right's heart's desire, has the restrictions back on. The result of this accommodation is that many women in the misogynistic countries the U.S. deals with will suffer abuse, pain, injury and even death because access to contraceptives and abortion has been cut off, but the religious right has never shown any concern about that.

Then there's climate change denial—another accommodation of the religious right belief that Earth is in God's hands, so all will be well—and so will the bottom line of the fossil fuel industry. The larger social effect of overpopulation has yet to hit home even though it exacerbates climate change and makes it harder to adjust to it. Unlike our ancestors, we can't just pack up and leave a deteriorating environment for a better one. Those better ones that once had plenty of room in a less-populated Earth are now overcrowded.

The reproductive rights restrictions and climate change denial are bad enough, but now (at this writing) Trump, so ignorant of religious right beliefs, is setting us up for a horrendous disaster. He has declared Jerusalem the capital of Israel. This city is foundational to Christians, Jews and Muslims. They all want it and the only solution is to share it, which will not happen until a settlement is reached on who controls what part of the geography.

The religious right sees the decision as setting the stage for the Battle of Armageddon and the End Times when Jesus returns for the Final Judgment. With the Middle East being so unstable, and with nuclear warheads available all around (some in seriously unstable hands) this doesn't look good. Fortunately, not every believer is buying this End Times stuff. According to an article by Noah Landau in the Israeli news-paper *Haaretz*, Christians and Jews alike are urging Trump to reconsider his decision.

An Endemic Problem: Male Sexual Aggression

Here is a religion-enhanced (though biologically based) behavior that has been going on since forever and it's well past time to stop it.

At this writing, we are into what the media call a possible watershed cultural event. The sexual groping, ogling and outright assaults that men have inflicted on women for millennia, affecting their jobs, self-esteem and sometimes their safety, have suddenly become the *cause du jour.* Women by the hundreds have been speaking up and naming names, motivated by the crude sexist behavior of Donald Trump, of which he bragged about and for which he was excused and admired by too many voters to the extent of electing him president. Enough may finally have become enough, but we shall see. Politicians, celebrities and corporate leaders are being outed almost daily by women for past, long past, and present horny behavior.

There are calls for the resignation of sexually aggressive politicians, Republican and Democratic, and some are leaving office. At this writing, Sen. Al Franken is the latest to announce that he is resigning as one of Minnesota's senators in the fallout from a number of accusations of sexual impropriety. This is not good news for us Minnesota liberals because Franken has been a heroic supporter of women's rights. But guys are guys and the connection between their brain and genitalia is not always operational.

Beyond that, a lot of politics is at work here. It appears that the Dems are setting up the party as having the integrity to hold their own to account while the Republicans supported a crotch-grabbing dirty old man for president and a child molester for governor of Alabama. We'll see how that goes but don't bet on it going well.

As for the reaction at my local atheist Happy Hour, one man said that if the truth were known about all the politicians in Congress, the place would be almost emptied by the resignations. One woman said the problem with men is that they think they are god's gift to women. One of the men disagreed and said, no, men think women are god's gift to men. He got that right. The evolutionary imperative to reproduce has men seeing women as their rightful property. So "copping a feel" (or worse) is just exercising that right.

Consider astronaut John Glenn. He admired women's abilities, as shown in the movie *Hidden Figures* where he refused to take off in the spacecraft until the black woman math expert verified the trajectory calculations. He insisted on her because of her skills. Yet, later, when NASA began allowing women to be astronauts, Glenn (as I read in a news report) referred to them as "90 pounds of recreational equipment." It seem men cannot stop seeing women primarily as god's gift to them for their comfort and sexual pleasure.

Efforts have begun everywhere to develop rules of conduct. I expect such social controls will be more effective with liberals like Sen. Al Franken than with religious-right zealots like Roy Moore. Liberals tend to see value in equitable treatment and respect for women's rights, so there's something to work with. Religious-right zealots see women from a biblical perspective that has them subservient. We see this in their legislative proposals that inflict as many restrictions as possible on women's reproductive rights from contraception to pregnancy to childbirth to childcare (read Ch.5 again).

But why not go to the Bible for ways to control fundamentalist men's sexual urges? Doesn't Jesus say that a man who lusts after a woman should pluck out his eyeball? (Matthew 5-27:30, Gideon Bible) The Bible does a lot of warning against lust. (See https://christiananswers.net/q-eden/lust. html for an entertaining list.) Apparently, this lust thing is very strong, but there should be better ways to control it than removing a guy's eyeball.

One of the problems in finding a solution is that the possibility exists that some women might falsely accuse a guy of sexual harassment to get even with him for something. Yes, this is likely to happen, al-though probably not often. On the other hand, there are no innocent men out there. Even if they have never made a crude move toward a woman, they have witnessed other men doing it and listened to them laugh and brag about it and seen how women's work and skills have been demeaned and underpaid. But how many of them come to women's defense? The liberal men do on economic issues, but not so much or at all on the grope-and-grab issues. I will leave it to the men to figure out why. Since they are the problem, they should have a good understanding of their primal drive to grope and grab and what to do about it now that we are past our cave dwelling phase.

Meanwhile, for starters, everyone has to speak up. *Everyone!* . . . the women who are harassed and the men who stand by and watch it happen. Women should spread the word to other women about certain men's behavior to establish a pattern and ensure the woman's credibility when she makes an accusation. Men should report instances of sexual aggression when they see it to establish their reputation for supporting women and thus deter false accusations against them.

One thing political parties might do in screening candidates for any of-fice is to ask how they will help eliminate sexual harassment. All of them will say they will never do that themselves, but they also need to affirm that they will report any and every instance of sexual harassment they observe in others. The guys need some skin of their own in this game and this might do it.

A major part of the problem is the imbalance of power between men and women so why not affirmatively put women in the majority of power positions in as many fields as possible? It's easy enough in politics, so that is a good place to start because that's where laws are made. So make them.

Acknowledgments:
The Ultimate Endnote

This is longer than most acknowledgments but so many people helped in so many ways that as many as possible deserve public recognition. The combination of inspiration, expertise, practical support, contribution of ideas and materials and resources was extensive. So I don't care how long this is.

Right up front I want to recognize three irreplaceable people who looked forward to reading an earlier version of my book. They cheered me on and up, and would have loved this follow-up edition that takes on the Trump fiasco. But they were taken away in death. They have remained, and always will be, a constant inspiration.

One was my dear Quaker friend and long-time political colleague, D Perry Kidder, a sensitive, lyrical writer of short stories and memoirs. We occasionally attended each other's Quaker/atheist events and she had agreed to edit my book, but that was not to be.

Another was John B. (Jack) Massen, also a long-time friend, who was an atheist colleague. Jack's moral vision and ethical principles were inspiring to those of us seeking a peaceful world free of religious divisiveness. It's an honor to keep his memory alive here.

Finally, there was my son, William (Bill) Nagengast, the middle of my five children. He died in May of 2011 in a motorcycle accident on I-35 in Oklahoma on his way home from visiting his daughter and her family in California. Bill had a generous spirit, full of the joy of living. I saw him for the last time when he came over to trim my tree branches. He worked so enthusiastically that I told him he didn't have to do such a good job. He said, with his usual cheerful exuberance, "But that's the only kind of a job I know how to do!"

One more friend deserves special recognition—Jeri Rasmussen, lost to the memory death of Alzheimer's disease. We were colleagues in fending off the anti-abortion zealots when she was managing an abortion clinic in the face of constant death threats. A liberal Methodist, she loved being on our atheist public access TV shows where she could give her unvarnished opinion of misogynistic theocrats.

Still with us are many good people who kept me going. Special thanks to the members of Atheists For Human Rights, who contributed ideas, material, encouragement and help in many ways. The Introduction by Tim Gorski, M.D., is a tribute to his moral and rational insight. Randall Tigue, a constitutional lawyer, helped keep my discussions of legal issues understandable and accurate. Kirk Buchanan, in California, has been especially encouraging. As a former Catholic priest—now an atheist—he has assured me that my assessment of Catholic theology is appropriate. Bill Sierichs, a journalist and historian of Christianity, provided a look into the medieval mindset of Christianity that still exists today. The cover review came from Arvonne Fraser, a civic leader in Minnesota as well as in national and international human rights circles.

Those who provided me with their experiences to show the impact of religion-based laws have my sincere admiration and thanks, most notably Cecil Bothwell, Jacqueline (Jackie) Marquis, and Niles Ross. I am especially appreciative of Tama Matheson, a London playwright, who let me use an excerpt from her essay, "Childish Things," in Chapter 12. It is a visceral call to stop groveling before religion. An invaluable contributor was Stephen Mumford, whose book, *The Life and Death of NSSM 200*, deserves to be an all-time bestseller for its detailed exposure of how and why the U.S. Catholic bishops set off our culture war and political dysfunction. Read it!!

I have been fortunate in getting support, advice and help of all kinds from my children, Susan Jackson, Mike Nagengast, Julia Nagengast and Marianne Maves, along with their spouses and my eight grandchildren and four great-grandchildren. I love them all.

Lastly, my sincere thanks to the politicians who do their best to keep government religion-free. Some have left office for personal reasons; others lost an election to far-left identity politics or religious right fanaticism—the most notable at the national level being Hillary Clinton.

Those no longer in office include Asheville NC councilmember Cecil Bothwell and, in Minnesota, congressman and Minneapolis mayor Don

Fraser; state senator and congressman Bill Luther; state senator Jane Ranum; state representative Phil Carruthers; state representative Andy Dawkins and his wife, state senator Ellen Anderson; state senator Don Betzold. state representative and Minneapolis councilmember Don Samuels, Minneapolis councilmember Barb Johnson, and state representative Joe Mullery.

Those still in office include county commissioners Mary Jo McGuire and Linda Higgins, state senator Bobby Joe Champion, and state representative Ray Dehn. They are all heroes and I thank them.

BIBLIOGRAPHY

Barnstone, Willis, ed. & trans. *The Other Bible.* San Francisco: HarperSanFrancisco (*a division of* HarperCollins *Publishers*). 1984.

Boston, Robert. *Why the Religious Right is Wrong about Separation of Church and State.* Amherst, NY: Prometheus Books. 2003.

Bothwell, Cecil. *The Prince of War: Billy Graham's Crusade for a Wholly Christian Empire.* Asheville, NC: Brave Ulysses Books. 2007.

Bothwell, Cecil. *Whale Tales: An Exploration of Belief and its Consequences.* Asheville, NC: Brave Ulysses Books. 2010.

Brief Amicus Curiae of Atheists For Human Rights in Support of Respondent in the Supreme Court of the United States No. 02-1024: Elk Grove Unified School District and David W. Gordon, Superintencent, Petitioners, v. Michael A. Newdow, Respondent. 2004.

Castle, Marie Alena. *Running in Place* (a history of atheism in Minnesota, 1982-2010). Minneapolis, MN: Atheists For Human Rights (privately published; available by request at www.atheistsforhumanrights.org). 2010

Chase, Annie. *My Purpose Driven Death: How I Managed to Become One Lucky Stiff.* Minneapolis, MN: Atheists For Human Rights (privately published; available by request at www.atheistsforhumanrights.org). 2010

Fraser, Arvonne. *She's No Lady: Politics, Family and International Feminism.* Minneapolis, MN: Nodin Press (*a division of* Micawber's Inc.). 2007.

Holy Bible, Catholic Family Edition. New York: John J. Crawley & Co., Inc. 1953.

Holy Bible, King James Version. New York: American Bible Society. 1998.

Hughes, Philip. *A Popular History of the Catholic Church.* Garden City, NY: Image Books (*a division of* Doubleday & Company, Inc.) 1954.

Lader, Lawrence. *Politics, Power & the Church.* New York, NY: Macmillan Publishing Company. 1987.

Lynn, Rev. Barry W. *Piety & Politics.* New York, NY: Harmony Books. 2006.

Mumford, Stephen D. *The life and Death of NSSM 200: How the Destruction of Political Will Doomed a U.S. Population Policy.*

Research Triangle Park, NC: Center for Research on Population and Security. 1996.

O'Brien, Rev. John A., Ph.D. *The Faith of Millions.* Huntington, IN: Our Sunday Visitor. 1938.

Pinker, Steven. *The Better Angels of Our Nature.* New York, NY: Viking Penguin Group. 2011.

Pollitt, Katha. *Virginity or Death!* New York, NY: Random House Trade Paperbacks. 2006.

Ranke-Heinemann, Uta. *Eunuchs for the Kingdom of Heaven.* New York, NY: Doubleday. 1990.

Ranke-Heinemann, Uta. *Putting Away Childish Things.* San Francisco: HarperSanFrancisco (*a division of* HarperCollins *Publishers*). 1994.

Rumble, Rev. Dr. Leslie, and Carty, Rev. Charles Mortimer. *Radio Replies*, Second Volume. St. Paul, MN: Radio Replies Press. 1940.

Rumble, Rev. Dr. Leslie, and Carty, Rev. Charles Mortimer. *Radio Replies*, Third Volume. St. Paul, MN: Radio Replies Press. circa 1940s (binding destroyed; cover and publication pages missing).

Sloan, Richard P., Ph.D. *Blind Faith: The Unholy Alliance of Religion and Medicine.* New York, NY: St. Martin's Press. 2006.

Stewart, Katherine. *The Good News Club.* New York, NY: Public Affairs Books. 2012.

Swomley, John M. *Compulsory Pregnancy: The War Against American Women.* Amherst NY: Humanist Press. 1999.

The Constitution of the United States and Amendments. Minneapolis, MN: Minnesota Civil Liberties Union Foundation. 1992.

Toobin, Jeffrey. *The Oath: The Obama White House and the Supreme Court.* New York, NY: Doubleday. 2012.

Afterword

On Wednesday evening, February 28, 2018, around midnight I fainted, called 911 to come and pick me up off the floor, seemed OK but on Thursday morning got worse (hard to breathe, with an exciting near-death experience where I saw, not a white light but a giant blue-and-white whirligig lollipop, and called 911 again

Ended up in North Memorial Hospital's ICU with a pulse count of 23 (basic life-support low point allowed is 60), died briefly, got revived, and had a pacemaker implanted along with getting a prognosis of death by mid-summer from congestive heart failure.

Everyone dies, no exceptions. Nothing new here. I have enjoyed being one of the luckiest people on Earth. Fate gave me a 91-year break from an otherwise endless Oblivion and filled it with political and social activism—workers' rights, women's rights, anti-war, gay rights, political skullduggery, built a geodesic dome home as a hands-on contractor, raised five good kids, organized and helped build atheist and political organizations, worked as writer-editor-publisher of atheist, commercial and technical newsletters, magazines, booklets and one book, with this follow-up version now in production. I hope to live long enough to see and hold, if not to give book reviews for it. None of this uphill climbing has been especially pleasant, but all of it has been interesting.

A Great Opportunity to "Die with My Boots On"—and I Took It!

A lot of atheists worry about how to react when believers push religion on them. Why not get ahead of them with atheism? I did this at the hospital and rehab center. I made it pleasantly clear from the outset that I didn't want any god stuff around me. I said the one thing I liked about the re-hab center was that it was so secular. I was amiable and cheerful. I took dying as just the way the world works. When religious staff members said kindly that "God will decide when you die," I kindly replied, "I don't really understand this god stuff. We are in a hospital. You are taking care of sick and suffering people. How do you square the suffering with any god worth the title? You wouldn't allow it if you were God. You are worshipping a god who's not as nice as you are. Please don't do that. You deserve better."

I even got to work in some of my political activism. Part of my checkered past includes being a labor union activist. I noticed what shit work the lowest paid employees had to do and I thanked them. I got to talk with three of them on separate occasions. I said they deserved the highest pay, not some fat-cat CEO. They agreed. I said they should have a union to fight for better wages. They said they did have a union but it was weak. I said, "Well, at the next union election, all of you go down there and vote in some stronger leadership!"

I talked about standing up for one's rights and sticking together. I talked about strategic bargaining. I watched the light of potential opportunity begin to shine in their eyes. They saw an open door they hadn't realized was there! Would they go through it? I don't know but a seed was planted and it felt SO GOOD to still be in the real world, even briefly, fighting for what is right. THAT is life!! THAT is what it means to be fully human!

Love to you all.

ABOUT THE AUTHOR

MarieAlena Castle earned a degree in journalism at age forty-five while working as a full-time factory assembly worker.
A lifelong social/political activist and writer, she earned the Minnesota Democratic Party's "Woman of Distinction" award in 2008. An award-winning writer and editor (now retired) for business, human relations, entertainment, political, and technical publications, she is the communications director for Atheists for Human Rights, a nonprofit charity in Minneapolis, Minnesota.

NOTES